MW00396126

CLITSO DEDMAN, NAVAJO CARVER

His Art and His World

REBECCA M. VALETTE

UNIVERSITY OF NEBRASKA PRESS | LINCOLN

The University of Nebraska Press is part of a land-grant institution with campuses and programs on the past, present, and future homelands of the Pawnee, Ponca, Otoe-Missouria, Omaha, Dakota, Lakota, Kaw, Cheyenne, and Arapaho Peoples, as well as those of the relocated Ho-Chunk, Sac and Fox, and Iowa Peoples.

Publication of this volume was assisted by the Boston College Association of Retired Faculty.

Library of Congress Cataloging-in-Publication Data
Names: Valette, Rebecca M., author.
Title: Clitso Dedman, Navajo carver: his art and his world / Rebecca M. Valette.
Description: Lincoln : University of Nebraska Press, [2023] | Includes bibliographical references and index. | Summary: "This first biography of artist and carver Clitso Dedman presents the life and work of one of the most important but overlooked Navajo artists of his generation"—Provided by publisher.
Identifiers: LCCN 2023013597
ISBN 9781496235817 (hardcover)
ISBN 9781496237439 (epub)
ISBN 9781496237446 (pdf)
Subjects: LCSH: Dedman, Clitso, approximately 1879–1953. | Wood-carvers—United States—Biography. | Navajo wood-carvers—Biography. | Navajo wood-carving. | BISAC: SOCIAL SCIENCE / Ethnic Studies / American / Native American Studies | BIOGRAPHY & AUTOBIOGRAPHY / Artists, Architects, Photographers
Classification: LCC E99.N3 D358 2023 |
DDC 927.36/40899726
[B]—dc23/eng/20230718
LC record available at https://lccn.loc.gov/2023013597

Set and designed in Garamond Premier by N. Putens.

[frontispiece] Clitso Dedman, 1930s. Photo by Thomas Noble. Courtesy Laramie McSparron Jarvi.

CONTENTS

ILLUSTRATIONS

FIGURES

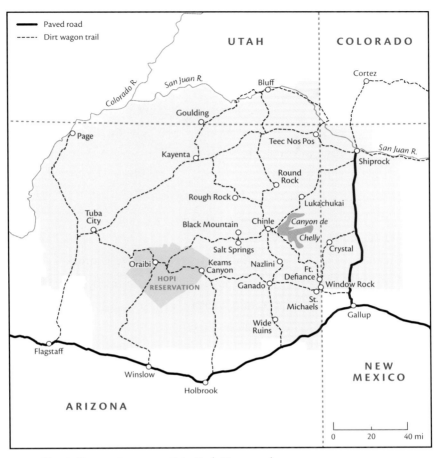

MAP 1. Navajo Reservation, 1930s. Erin Greb Cartography.

In the 1930s, only the east-west highway through Gallup (which paralleled the railroad) and the highway north from Gallup to Shiprock were graded and maintained. The other roads on the map were just dirt wagon trails.

In 1934 the Navajo Reservation occupied the area in light gray. In 1936, John Collier, Commissioner for the Bureau of Indian Affairs, established Window Rock as the seat of the Navajo Central Agency. It would subsequently become the capital of the Navajo Nation. The enclosed dark-gray triangular area on the map was the Hopi Reservation. Its boundaries would be significantly modified in 1974.

At the suggestion of a Santa Fe curator, I contacted Sallie Wagner, a former trader at Wide Ruins in the 1940s. She graciously invited us to her home and showed us the unique Clitso carvings that she and her husband, Bill Lippincott, had received as gifts from their friend and mentor Cozy McSparron. As we were leaving, Sallie encouraged us to contact McSparron's daughter Laramie McSparron Jarvi, who had spent her childhood in Chinle and would definitely have interesting memories of Dedman.

We fortunately were able to meet Laramie later that year at her home in Prescott, Arizona. She showed us a photograph of Dedman and several of his carvings, including that of a Navajo woman wearing a Yei mask and holding a ceremonial basket. After telling us about her frequent visits to Clitso Dedman's workshop near Chinle, Laramie casually mentioned that Dedman had once chiseled a ceremonial figure on the wall of a box canyon near their Thunderbird Ranch.

Intrigued by Laramie's stories, my husband and I decided to spend a couple of days in Chinle. We had no success in locating the box canyon, but we were, quite unexpectedly, invited one night to attend a Yeibichai dance that was being held on a barren nearby mesa. When we arrived at the site, we found the dance area illuminated with strings of light bulbs, rather than the large bonfires that would have welcomed us in Dedman's time. The surrounding meadow was crowded with pickup trucks, rather than horses and wagons. The ceremony itself, however, had not significantly changed. Each masked dance team would arrive from the distant brush shelter and parade up to the ceremonial hogan to be greeted by the medicine man and the patient. The dancers would then perform the ritual steps to a haunting chant and the rhythmic shaking of the rattles. A mesmerizing experience!

At lunch the following day, we happened to meet Rosetta LaFont, who had known the Dedman family and who explained how to find their former residence. We drove south of town and up a dirt road to the indicated location. As we were walking around, a young Navajo man approached to ask what we were doing. We showed him our *Arizona Highways* article and said we were looking for Clitso Dedman's old house. It turned out he was Dedman's great-grandson. What an unexpected encounter! He invited us in to meet his father and his visiting aunt who told us how as children they had helped their infirm grandfather paint and decorate his carvings. They confirmed the assertion that

Clitso Dedman had owned trading posts, namely at Nazlini and Salina, and generously gave us one of his old trade tokens as a souvenir.

The next summer, we returned to explore the splendid Canyon de Chelly in a more leisurely manner. One day, quite on the spur of the moment, we decided to go for a drive and see the places where Dedman had established his trading posts. At Salina (formerly Salt Springs), we found nothing. As we arrived in Nazlini, our search appeared to be equally disappointing. On the main road was an unimpressive modern convenience store with a large sign on the roof that read "Nazlini Trading Post." As I climbed a low fence to photograph the charred ruins behind the store, a Navajo man approached Jean-Paul to ask why we were interested in the burned timbers. Another fortuitous encounter! On learning of our interest in Clitso Dedman's former trading post, he identified himself as the artist's grandson and offered to take us to visit his eighty-year-old mother. Mary Dodge was moved by our color photos of her father's carvings. It had been almost fifty years since she had last seen his work. During the two hours we spent talking with her, she recalled her father's activities as a trader and spoke of her visits to his Chinle workshop.

Our Southwest trip then took us to Flagstaff, Arizona, where we stopped to see anthropologist and trader Bill Beaver at his Sacred Mountain Trading Post. When we spoke of our current interest in Clitso Dedman, Bill, to our great surprise, revealed that he had known Dedman in the early 1950s while he was distributing welfare checks to elderly indigent Navajos in the Chinle and Ganado area. He described Dedman's workshop in some detail and mentioned how impressed he had been by Dedman's command of English and his elegant Spencerian handwriting.

The following day, as we were passing through Farmington, New Mexico, on our way to Denver, we stopped quite by chance at the Fred Carson Trading Post, having been attracted by a Yeibichai weaving in the store window. In our conversation with owner Alan Carson, we happened to mention Clitso Dedman, and he told us that his father, Fred, had run the Nazlini Trading Post in the 1930s, and that Dedman's daughter, Mary, had once been his babysitter. To our great delight, he showed us a 1911 oil painting of Clitso Dedman on horseback in front of the original Nazlini building.

The results of these museum visits and conversations formed the basis of a piece that we wrote for the *American Indian Art Magazine* in 2000.[4] Because of space limitations, however, the editors abridged the manuscript and deleted much of the biographical background so that the focus of the article would be primarily on Clitso Dedman's carvings.

As we continued uncovering additional information about Clitso Dedman, the more we became convinced that he deserved a full-length biography. Not only a gifted artist, Dedman was truly an exceptional man who had led a remarkable life. As a child, he grew up near Chinle in a small mud hogan and spent his days herding sheep. At age eight, he was sent to the newly established Navajo boarding school at Fort Defiance where he was one of just thirty pupils. While many classmates were very unhappy and frequently tried to run away, Dedman prospered in this strange, demanding Anglo environment. Four years later, he volunteered to be transferred to the off-reservation vocational school in Grand Junction, Colorado, in order to learn carpentry and blacksmithing. By the time he returned home at age sixteen, he was one of a handful of Navajos out of a population of 20,000 who could speak English fluently and had also mastered the written language. Dedman subsequently found employment in the Gallup machine shops of the Santa Fe Railroad, the only Navajo blacksmith. (Many Navajos did work for the railroad, but only as unskilled, poorly paid laborers laying and maintaining tracks.)

At age twenty, with the encouragement of Ganado trader J. L. Hubbell, Dedman purchased a horse-drawn wagon and traveled two days on his own to the remote community of Rough Rock, northwest of Chinle, where he established a tent trading post. This pioneer endeavor entailed knowing not only how to buy wool but also how to sell merchandise and maintain accounts with both his Navajo clients and his Anglo wholesalers. Over the next two years, again on his own with no outside guidance and relying solely on skills acquired at Grand Junction, he taught himself how to quarry sandstone and constructed a permanent trading post, complete with bullpen and living quarters.

By 1915, Dedman had created new trading posts in Nazlini and Salt Springs, successfully selling Navajo blankets and jewelry to clients as far away as Phoenix, Santa Fe, and even Iowa. He was one of the first traders to have business stationery printed with his own letterhead and to write his correspondence by typewriter. He was also one of only five Navajos to own and drive a car, and, of these, the only one with the mechanical ability to handle his own repairs.

After circumstances forced him to close his trading posts, Clitso Dedman moved back to Chinle to establish himself as the community blacksmith. Here again, working alone, he built his own shop and forge, arranging to have the necessary anvil, bellows, and tools shipped to Gallup where he picked them up by wagon. When business was slow he offered his masonry services to Cozy McSparron, who was adding guest cottages to his Thunderbird Ranch. Dedman also designed and built a large eight-sided hogan-style house for author Laura Adams Armer at Black Mountain. It was not until age sixty, when arthritis obliged him to lead a less strenuous life, that Dedman found his true artistic vocation: the carving of Yeibichai figures.

Much like a quilt with its colorful patches, the present biography is a composite of information drawn from our various visits and stitched together with the help of numerous historical documents and studies of Southwest history and Navajo culture. The sources of these references are given in the endnotes, which also contain suggestions for additional reading. Note that for stylistic consistency I have maintained the historic Anglo spelling of Navajo terms and referenced in parentheses the corresponding spelling in the Navajo alphabet.

ACKNOWLEDGMENTS

I should like to express my appreciation to the many people who, in addition to those named in the preface, have assisted in bringing to life this portrait of Clitso Dedman and his world.

I was able to establish a family genealogy thanks to the friars of St. Michaels Mission, who allowed me to consult their census cards for Clitso Dedman, his mother, and his wife, Hadzizbaa. These files had been created in the 1920s and 1930s by Father Marcellus Troester, who interviewed thousands of Navajos residing in the eastern part of the reservation. Anglo genealogists Jim Dedman and Leroy Dedmon graciously shared with me the results of their ongoing family research.

Autobiographies of Clitso Dedman's Navajo contemporaries Left Handed, Tall Woman, and Frank Mitchell described the environment of Dedman's childhood in the Chinle area and what his early schooling must have been like. The annual reports of Navajo agents provided a detailed picture of the Fort Defiance and Grand Junction Schools during the years that Dedman was in attendance. David Wallace Adams generously answered my questions about Indian education in the nineteenth century. Bruce Gjeltema guided me to articles by Dedman's Navajo classmate Jacob Morgan. Adam Burns helped me follow the traces of the train trip that brought Dedman and Morgan from Gallup to Grand Junction. John Seebach provided details concerning the Grand Junction School.

For the description of Clitso Dedman's years as a trader, I am deeply indebted to Klara Kelley and her monumental encyclopedia of Navajo trading posts. Over many months she patiently responded to my seemingly endless queries. Robert McPherson answered my questions about trade tokens. Geologist Matthew Malkowski explained the challenges of sandstone masonry in the Rough Rock area. Navajo journalist Cindy Yurth furnished background on Salt Springs, now known as Salina. Martha Blue answered my queries about J. L. Hubbell and his relationship with Dedman. Kathy M'Closkey shared with me a photocopy of Dedman's Nazlini letterhead and provided precise references to documents in the Hubbell Archives at the University of Arizona. Dennis Aigner elucidated the appearance of swastikas in early twentieth-century Navajo weavings. Jonathan Batkin generously provided copies of Dedman's correspondence with Candelario's Curio Store in Santa Fe. To all of these individuals, I extend my sincere appreciation.

For photographs of Clitso Dedman I should like to thank Linda Wyatt, Laramie McSparron Jarvi, and the St. Michaels Archives. Mark Sadler provided biographical notes on E. A. Burbank, who hired Dedman, among others, to pose for his oil painting of the gambling scene at the Hubbell Trading Post. Richard Panofsky shared letters and background information concerning Frederick Melville DuMond's 1911 oil painting of Dedman in front of the Nazlini Trading Post.

The chapter on the turbulent year of 1915 grew out of references to two sad narratives in David Wallace Adams's book *Education for Extinction* (1995). The tragic story was confirmed by documents from the Arizona Bureau of Vital Statistics. I also want to thank University of Arizona archivist Erika Castaño, who provided me with copies of letters Dedman had written to Hubbell from El Paso later that summer.

The chapters describing Clitso Dedman's last forty years in Chinle grew primarily out of conversations with those who had known him, especially his two grandchildren, Robert Dedman and Susan Dedman Yazzie. I should also like to thank Carolyn O'Bagy Davis, for photographs of the Laura Adams Armer home; James Faris, for answering my queries regarding the Nightway; Charlotte Frisbie, for responding to my questions concerning the Franciscans in Chinle; George Goode, for input concerning Navajo horses and horseshoes; Ed Hobbs, for historical information on blacksmith shops; Joe Sabatini, for information on Willis postcards; Polly Schaafsma, for a picture of the White House Ruin duck petroglyph; and Barry Walsh, for background on early Hopi *katsina* dolls.

I should also like to express my appreciation to the many people who were of assistance in developing the inventory of Clitso Dedman's carvings. My appreciation goes to the following curators for allowing me to view their holdings and for sharing their files and related documentation: Jonathan Batkin, Wheelwright Museum, Santa Fe; Selena Capraro, Amon Carter Museum of American Art, Fort Worth; Erika Castaño, University of Arizona Libraries Special Collections, Tucson; Diane Dittemore, Arizona State Museum, Tucson; Kathleen Dull, New Mexico History Museum, Santa Fe; Kirstin Krause Gotway, Indianapolis Museum of Art at Newfields; Russell Hartman and Laura Eklund, California Academy of Sciences, San Francisco; Joyce Herold, Denver Museum of Natural History; Marian Rodee and Lea McChesney, Maxwell Museum of Anthropology at University of New Mexico, Albuquerque; Ellen Sieber, Indiana University Museum of Archaeology and Anthropology, Bloomington; Louise Stiver and Alison Colborne, Museum of Indian Arts and Culture at the Laboratory of Anthropology, Santa Fe; and Kim Walters, Southwest Museum (now the Autry Museum), Los Angeles.

Thank you also to the many collectors, dealers, and auctioneers who, over the past twenty-five years, have shown me their sets or provided photographs: Patrick Albrand, Al Anthony, James Aumell, Mark Bahti, Robert Bauver, Tom and Steve Begner, Mark Bradford, Rebecca Bradshaw, Jackson Clark, Rachel Daley, Danica Farnand, Jed Foutz, Robert Gallegos, Lars Garrison, Nello Guadagnoli, Russell Hartman, Robert Kapoun, Harriet and Seymour Koenig, Roland LaFont, John Malloy, John Moran, Nicholas Prior, Michael Schuelke, William A. Smith, James Solomon, Tobe Turpen, Mark and Linda Winter, Phil Woodard, Tom Woodard, and Linda Wyatt.

I especially would like to thank Boston College librarians Anne Kenny and Shannon McDowell, who managed to track down obscure references and obtained numerous articles and hard-to-find manuscripts for my research. The Boston College Association of Retired Faculty generously helped fund the book's publication.

Special appreciation is due to Al Anthony, Klara Kelley, and Russell Hartman, for their careful reading of the manuscript and their many suggestions for improvement. I should also like to express my thanks to David Adams, Charlotte Frisbie, Lars Garrison, and Mark Sadler, all of whom generously read and commented on specific chapters.

Special thanks to editors Matthew Bokovoy, Heather Stauffer, Ann Baker, and Natalie Jones at the University of Nebraska Press, who responded ever so promptly to my numerous queries as they shepherded the manuscript through to publication.

Finally, I would like to say *merci* to my husband, Jean-Paul, for his continued support and encouragement.

CLITSO DEDMAN, **NAVAJO CARVER**

Early Years in Chinle

About 150 years ago, on the Navajo Reservation south of Chinle, a baby boy was born who would later in life be known as Clitso Dedman.[1] Chinle, or Ch'ini'li (flowing out), is the place where the seasonal waters of the Canyon de Chelly and the Canyon del Muerto come together to form the Chinle Creek (Chinle Wash), which from there runs due north and empties into the San Juan River in Utah, west of Bluff. Today, Chinle, Arizona, is a town of 5,000 inhabitants and the tourist gateway to the Canyon de Chelly National Monument. At the time of Clitso Dedman's birth, however, the area was impoverished and very sparsely populated. The nearest settlement was Fort Defiance, fifty miles southeast on the other side of the Chuska Mountains.

During the Civil War, as part of the U.S. government campaign to control Navajo raiding, Gen. James Carleton ordered Col. Kit Carson to subdue the Navajos by force. In January 1864, Carson launched a devastating assault on the fertile Canyon de Chelly area, destroying crops, cutting down peach trees, and burning homes. Freezing winter temperatures, together with lack of food and shelter, soon obliged the Navajos of the area to surrender at Fort Canby (later renamed Fort Defiance). Over 8,000 men, women, and children from across Navajoland were sent from there to Fort Sumner in New Mexico on a four-hundred-mile forced march remembered today as the Long Walk. Conditions at the Bosque Redondo internment camp were so miserable that many Navajos died of illness or starvation. Finally, after four years of suffering, the survivors were permitted to return to a portion of their homeland within the boundaries of the newly created Navajo Reservation.[2] According to the Treaty of Bosque Redondo of June 1868, the U.S. government would establish a Navajo Agency at Fort Defiance that, every fall for the next ten years, would supply the returning Navajos with livestock, farming equipment, and seeds for planting.[3]

Clitso Dedman's Family

By tradition, Navajo society was matrilineal and matrilocal. The family group, sometimes referred to as a camp or outfit, consisted of a matriarch (the grandmother) plus her husband, her daughters, and their husbands and children. The younger generation would live in proximity to the matriarch with everyone sharing in child-rearing and the management of the combined flocks of sheep and goats. The hogans and the livestock were the property of the women, and horses were owned by the men.

When Clitso Dedman's grandmother and her family group returned from Bosque Redondo to their abandoned home in the Chinle area overlooking the Canyon de Chelly, they found that "war and neglect had rendered the land desolate. The old cornfields were overgrown with weeds, the ditches were filled with sand, and what had been orchards were now fields of tree stumps."[4] Their first priority was building new hogans, which they situated at a short distance from a natural spring bordered by cottonwood trees.

Their fork-stick hogan (or *hooghan*) would have been very similar to the one in Canyon de Chelly photographed by archaeologist Cosmos Mindeleff in the early 1890s (fig. 1).[5] In his official report to the Bureau of Ethnology, Mindeleff gave the following description of the Navajo winter hogans.[6]

> Notwithstanding [their] primitive appearance, resembling mere mounds of earth hollowed out, they are warm and comfortable, and, rude as they seem, their construction is a matter of rule, almost of ritual, while the

A HOGAN IN CANYON CHELLY

FIG. 1. Navajo hogan in Canyon de Chelly, 1880s. Photo by Cosmos Mindeleff.

dedicatory ceremonies which usually precede regular occupancy are elaborate and carefully performed.

Although no attempt at decoration is ever made, either of the inside or the outside of the houses, it is not uncommon to hear the term beautiful applied to them. Strong forked timbers of the proper length and bend, thrust together with their ends properly interlocking to form a cone-like frame, stout poles leaned against the apex to form the sides, the whole well covered with bark and heaped thickly with earth, forming a roomy warm interior with a level floor.

The interior of the hogan was an open, circular space with a central fire pit. Around the inside wall was often a low shelf on which household items could be stored. The door was always positioned to face east toward the rising sun. At night, the family would sleep on sheepskins placed directly on the dirt floor and cover themselves with blankets. As Mindeleff explained, for the Navajos, the hogan is a sacred place, a microcosm of the universe: the roof is the Father (the Sky) and the floor is the Mother (the Earth). The four pillars or corner posts represent the four Sacred Mountains. At dawn, the eastern sun enters the hogan doorway. The smoke hole above the hearth is a breathing hole, allowing prayers to rise to the heavens.

Every fall, beginning in September 1869, Clitso Dedman's grandparents and relatives would travel by foot to the newly established Navajo Agency in Fort Defiance to pick up their promised annuities consisting of two sheep or goats per adult, corn and squash seeds, as well as lengths of white muslin to sew into clothing. Even with this assistance, they were able only to eke out a bare living. Clitso's parents were probably married in a Navajo ceremony around 1875, seven years after the return from Bosque Redondo, and their first son was born a year later.[7]

According to the Navajo Creation Story, Changing Woman created four clans: Kinyaa'áanii (Towering House) clan, Honágháahnii (One Walks Around) clan, Tódích'ii'nii (Bitter Water) clan, and Hashtł'ishnii (Mud) clan. Over time, five additional major clans came into being: Tábąąhá (Water Edge) clan, Táchii'nii (Red Running into the Water) clan, Tsé níjíkiní (Cliff Dwellers) clan, Tó'aheedlíinii (Water Flows Together) clan, and Tsi'naajinii (Black Streak Wood) clan. These groups frequently contained many smaller clans. Over time, these clans multiplied and now number around seventy-five. Navajo society being matrilineal, clan affiliation is transmitted through the maternal, rather than paternal, side of the family. People thus identify themselves as being born into their mother's clan, and secondarily born "for" their father's clan. In introducing themselves, they will, in addition, name the clans of their maternal and paternal grandfathers. By tradition, members of the same clan are not permitted to intermarry.[8]

What we know about Clitso Dedman's family and his clan affiliation comes from his mother's interview in the 1920s with Father Marcellus Troester, the Franciscan friar who was creating a Navajo census file for St. Michaels Mission.[9] Well into her sixties at the time of her interview and simply identified by her nickname Clitso Bama (Clitso's mama), she was then living in her summer hogan at Fluted Rock near Nazlini. She explained to Father Marcellus that she was of the Táchii'nii clan, and born for the Honágháahnii clan. Clitso Dedman's deceased father, who was of the Tótsohnii (Big Water) clan, had been known in his later years as Tsinaghai (Who Goes Around Aimlessly), a nickname that he probably received once he began to show signs of senility.[10] Clitso, when meeting other Navajos, would introduce himself as a member of the Táchii'nii clan, born for the Tótsohnii clan. He would then name the Honágháahnii clan of his maternal grandfather. The clan of his paternal grandfather has not been recorded.[11]

Thanks to Father Marcellus's records, we also know that Clitso had two younger siblings: a sister who died in infancy, and a brother, Sam (b. 1883). In the late 1880s, Clitso's mother married Hastiin Tsoh (Big Man) of the Tábąąhá clan. Their son Robert Dine (b. 1890), Clitso's half brother, would be educated at the Albuquerque Indian School.[12] The couple also had a daughter, Zani (dzáni, meaning "young woman"), who would marry Dasa Biyazh of the Mą'ii deeshgiizhnii (Coyote Pass) clan. Zani and her husband had a son, Willie Dine, who would attend school in Fort Defiance. (By the time of Father Marcellus's interviews, both Zani and Willie had died.)

In nineteenth-century Navajo society, people were known by their nicknames, which reflected their kinship, a physical trait, or a personal attribute. As those characteristics changed over time, so would people's nicknames. Thus, during his first year, a little baby might simply be called aweé or aweé ashkii ("baby" or "baby boy"). Traditionally, each young Navajo child was ceremonially given a secret personal "war" name. However, a boy's war name was never spoken, since its power would dissipate were it to be used too often.[13] In Clitso Dedman's case, we have no record of his war name. As he grew a little older, he was given the nickname Łitsoi (yellow one) because of his distinctive light complexion and slightly auburn hair. Anglicized as "Clitso," this would be the name by which he would be known for the rest of his life.

Childhood on the Reservation

Clitso was born in Chinle around 1876. Immediately after his birth, his placenta and umbilical cord were buried in the traditional manner just north of his mother's hogan, so that they might become one with Mother Earth. In this way, his spirit would be bound to his ancestors and their land, ensuring that he would always return home, even if later in life he would live at different locales.[14] The newborn baby was ritually washed, then placed in a ceremonial position facing east on the new cradleboard that his father had fashioned out of two pieces of cottonwood (fig. 2). The right-hand board represents Mother Earth and the left-hand one Father Sky.[15]

For the first year, Clitso would have spent his waking hours propped up in his cradleboard observing the various family activities: his mother grinding corn or spinning wool, his father chopping wood and tending the winter fire. When Clitso was twelve months old, his mother would have begun taking him out of the cradleboard more frequently, teaching him how to stand and gradually how to walk. (Navajo children at that time were not encouraged to crawl.) Once he could get around easily on his own, he would no longer need his cradleboard.[16]

Life during Clitso's very early years was precarious and probably quite similar to that of Tall Woman, two years his elder, who also grew up in the Chinle area and shared her childhood memories with anthropologist Charlotte Frisbie.[17] Tall Woman recalled that when she was a little girl, food was scarce and she was often hungry. Her one set of clothes was made of plain white muslin. Most of the time she went barefoot, even in winter. Only when she was older did she get her first pair of moccasins.

Water throughout Navajoland was a precious commodity and usually had to be transported at some distance in goatskin water bags or piñon jugs. As Alwin Girdner, who grew up on the reservation north of Chinle near Teec Nos Pos, would later comment: "Navajos used water by the cupful. . . . There was seldom the luxury of washing either their persons or their clothing, and new items were often put on over the old garment and neither removed for months, as everyone slept clothed. In spite of this, Navajos were almost always neat in their appearance."[18]

When Clitso was four or five years old, he joined the daily routine of the cousins in his matriarchal family group. Every morning, he was woken up before dawn and told to run east shouting at the top of his lungs to greet the new day. Once the sun had risen above the horizon, he would turn around and race quickly back to the hogan. His initial experience might have been like that of Left Handed, who recounted how, as a young boy, he didn't want to run too far for fear of getting lost. His parents, however, explained to him why it was important to run every morning: "If you do that, you'll be lively all the time, even when you get to be old you'll be lively. That's what running a race early in the morning is for. It's good exercise for you and your lungs."[19]

FIG. 2. Navajo cradleboard. Photo by Simeon Schwemberger. Courtesy Arizona State University Library, SPC 331.50.41.

After a breakfast of goat's milk and corn mush, young Clitso would assist his family in their various activities. In spring, he helped his father with the planting of corn and beans in a nearby wash. In summer, when his extended family moved to pastureland at a higher elevation near Fluted Rock, he was sent out every morning with his older cousins to herd the sheep and goats.[20] During the long hours on the mesa, his cousins taught him about the plants and wildlife and how to track a lost lamb or catch a rabbit. He also learned how to find his way around the rugged landscape with its varying terrains and how to determine the time of day by observing the position of the sun in the sky and the direction of the shadows on the ground. In the late afternoon, having brought the herd back to the camp, Clitso helped with chores, such as gathering firewood and hauling water. After supper, as the family was sitting outdoors under the brilliant night sky, his parents would point out to him the various Navajo constellations, such as "Revolving Man" (Ursa Major) and "Revolving Woman" (Cassiopeia), and help him locate the "Central Fire" (North Star). All these orientation skills would serve him well in later life.[21]

In fall, Clitso would help load the packhorses for the long trek back to the family's winter hogan. There were no roads on the reservation at that time—only rough, unmarked trails. With the men and the horses leading the way, the women and children would bring up the rear, herding along the flocks. Once back in Chinle, Clitso and his cousins helped harvest the ripened crops.

Caring for the sheep and goats in winter was easier, since the flock's movement was restricted to nearby pastureland. At night, the family would gather in the hogan around the fire. During the long winter evenings, young Clitso would listen as his mother and grandmother recalled the traditional Navajo stories, especially the story of creation when the People emerged from the several levels of the underworld and fashioned the present land with its four Sacred Mountains. He learned that Coyote, the Trickster, had thrown a blanketful of mica into the heavens, thus disrupting the careful placement of the constellations and creating thousands of random stars. He heard the story of Changing Woman, the mother of the Navajos, and how her Twin Sons had freed the land from its destructive monsters.[22] Clitso also would learn about the spiritual deities known as Yeis (*Yé'ii*) and their leader Talking God or Yeibichai (*Yé'ii Bi'cheii*), the benevolent divinity who was said to live in the nearby Canyon de Chelly, among other sacred places.[23]

In the course of his childhood years on the reservation, Clitso was introduced to the ancestral Navajo way of life and came to appreciate the importance of maintaining *Hózhó* (peace, balance, beauty, and harmony).[24] He would have come to respect the local medicine man (*Hataalii*) who probably was also of his Táchii'nii clan, and would have learned about the essential role of healing ceremonies in restoring lost harmony.[25] Of the many Navajo chantways, he would have become familiar with the Blessingway, the Enemyway, the Mountainway, and most definitely would have often attended the Yeibichai dances, which are performed by masked Yei impersonators at the close of the Nightway ceremony.

Attending the Nightway

The Chinle region was an area of high ceremonial activity, especially during the cold months of the year when the Nightway could be performed. This powerful nine-day curative ceremony is directed by a medicine man with the aim of healing a patient by restoring lost harmony. Held at a remote site, the ceremony concludes with the spectacular Yeibichai dance.[26] On that final night, hundreds and occasionally thousands of Navajos gather to receive the blessings of the Yeis, as they watch the masked and ritually dressed impersonators perform the sacred dance steps.

Clitso was probably brought to his first Yeibichai dance as a young child. Early in the afternoon, the members of his family group would have set out on horseback for the designated location, where they would have joined the large crowd gathering near the newly constructed ceremonial hogan. As night fell, the people began to settle around the ceremonial ground, with the men usually standing on the left side and the women and children sitting on the right side. Eight large bonfires would be blazing, four on each side, to illuminate the dance area and provide some protection against the bitter cold. Young Clitso, wrapped in a warm blanket, would huddle against his mother and start to doze off.

A deep *hu-hu-hu-HU* call would suddenly wake him up. He would see the medicine man come out of the ceremonial hogan accompanied by the patient who was holding a basket of cornmeal.[27] Turning his head to the west in the direction of the calls, Clitso could make out Talking God, easily recognizable by his white mask crowned with tall feathers, as he approached through the

Talking God   Male Yei   Female Yei

FIG. 3. Ceremonial masks, from James Stevenson, "Ceremonial of Hasjelti Dailjis," Plate CXV, detail.

hazy smoke of the burning fires. He was followed by twelve masked Male and Female Yeis in kilts and white body paint. Bringing up the rear was Water Sprinkler, the clown, leaping about and shaking a ragged fox or squirrel pelt. The team crossed the performance area and stopped facing the ceremonial hogan, so that the medicine man and the patient could walk up and down the row of dancers, sprinkling each one on the right arm with the sacred cornmeal. The patient then sat down in front the hogan to watch, while the medicine man returned inside.

At a signal from Talking God, the dance began with the Male Yeis shaking their gourd rattles and the Female Yeis waving spruce or sumac twigs, all chanting and dancing in rhythmic unison. They executed their prescribed formations, first in a single row, then separating in two lines, one of Male Yeis and the other of Female Yeis, and finally promenading as couples. After repeating these formations four times, the dancers disappeared quietly into the night in the same way they had come.

After a long pause, a second team of dancers arrived in the same manner. Clitso would have noticed that, although this new team wore the same masks and had the same body paint as the first group, their kilts were of different colors and patterns. By the time the third team appeared at the ceremonial ground, young Clitso would probably have fallen asleep. His mother woke him up before sunrise to listen to the Bluebird Song that closed the ceremony. His father then left to get the horses for the trip back home.

When Clitso was somewhat older, he would have been initiated into the "secret of the Yeibichai."[28] It was customary on the fifth or eighth day of the Nightway to assemble all the young children living in the area of the ceremonial hogan for a special initiation rite conducted by Talking God and a Female Yei. Wearing only breech cloths, Clitso and the other boys would be called up one by one by the masked impersonators to be sprinkled with sacred cornmeal and then ritually struck by long pointed yucca wands. After the girls had received their cornmeal blessing (without yucca wands), the children were instructed to hide their heads under their blankets. Talking God and Female Yei then took off their masks and set them on the ground. When the children threw off their blankets, they saw how the "gods" had been impersonated and were sworn not to reveal this secret to younger siblings.

During his childhood, Clitso attended many Yeibichai dances. Sixty years later, he would create a new Navajo art form by carving figures of the Nightway participants as he had observed them in his youth, with young Navajo men impersonating the Female Yei dancers.

School Recruitment

In August 1884, Clitso's family received the unexpected visit of newly appointed Navajo agent John Bowman, who was traveling around the Chinle region on horseback with the aim of convincing parents to send their children to the new boarding school in Fort Defiance.[29] It was a difficult mission. Few were the parents who concurred with Navajo leader Henry Chee Dodge that an American education was a stepping stone to a brighter social and economic future. Most families wanted to keep their children at home to help with chores. Years later, an older Navajo man, speaking to missionary priest H. Baxter Liebler, expressed the concerns of his generation:

> They want us to send our children to school. We need our children to herd sheep, to carry water and firewood. They don't teach anything useful in school. They don't teach how to herd sheep, how to weave, how to track animals. They teach them how to talk American and to read and write. That is no good. Nobody understands American except only the traders and the teachers. The traders can talk Navajo, so we don't need to learn American to talk with them, and the teachers we can get along without. And nobody can read, so what is the use of writing?[30]

On his recruiting trip Bowman was accompanied by an interpreter who may have been one of the bilingual Damon boys from Fort Defiance whose father was Anglo and whose mother was Navajo. Eight-year-old Clitso, barefoot and in ragged clothes, would have been surprised to see this Navajo teenager in leather boots dressed in a well-fitted jacket and trousers.[31] Bowman explained to Clitso's parents that at the school their son would receive a basic education and acquire new vocational skills. Moreover, he would be well cared for with three meals a day and issued new clothes and shoes. As a closing inducement, Bowman promised Clitso's father that when he brought his son to school on opening day he would be given a new ax and new farming tools.

Bowman's arguments proved convincing. And so, in early October, Clitso and his father set out on horseback for the two-day trip from Chinle to Fort Defiance. As Clitso took leave of his mother and little brother in front of their hogan, she probably encouraged him to work hard and make the most of this educational opportunity, advice that he would take to heart.

The life of young Clitso, thus far shaped by family-centered pastoral Navajo culture, would soon be transformed. He would find himself in a completely new environment, surrounded by a new language . . . and even given a new name.

2

Boarding School

Many Navajos who were sent to Indian boarding schools remembered the experience as very traumatic.[1] Clitso Dedman was a notable exception, for he definitely blossomed in his new educational environment. His academic success was even more remarkable, given the complete disarray in which the schools he attended were floundering at the time. When he arrived at Fort Defiance in fall 1884, there were only twenty students in a new boarding school built to accommodate one hundred pupils. The situation did improve markedly, however, over the next four years. Then in 1889, when he and thirty fellow Navajos were transferred to Grand Junction, they found themselves in a totally dysfunctional off-reservation school where the only other students were seven Ute boys. There was just one teacher and no vocational program. Food was poor and the alkali in the water rendered it undrinkable. Eight of his older classmates ran away in November and miraculously managed to walk the 300 miles back to Fort Defiance. By spring, under new leadership, the educational environment was gradually ameliorated and new vocational workshops were built. Over his eight years in boarding school, Clitso learned not to be discouraged by difficult situations and to focus on optimizing the positive aspects of his experiences, attitudes that would contribute to the success of his future endeavors.

Fort Defiance Indian School

In signing the 1868 Treaty of Bosque Redondo, the Navajo people agreed to "give up the education of their children between the ages of six and sixteen to the white man" so as to "insure their civilization." According to Article 6, the Navajo signatories pledged "to compel their children, male and female, between the age of six and sixteen to attend school." The U.S. government, for its part, agreed that for every thirty students of school age, it would provide a "house" and hire a teacher "competent to teach the elementary branches of an English education." The duty of the agent would be to see that the above terms were carried out.[2]

Since one of the broader aims of Indian education throughout the United States was to "Christianize" the many diverse tribes, President Grant announced his "Peace Policy" in 1868, whereby the establishment of reservation schools would be the responsibility of the various religious denominations.[3] It originally fell to the Presbyterian Church to provide instruction for the Navajos.

In fall 1869, the Presbyterian Home Mission Board sent a young teacher, Charity Gaston, to Fort Defiance, headquarters of the newly created Navajo Indian Agency.[4] She was housed in an old adobe building with a small classroom for twenty-five students. Attendance, however, was often less than half that number, and on some days no students came at all. When she observed that her more regular attendees were either sickly or handicapped, it was explained to her that the Navajo families kept their healthy children at home to help with chores, but were happy to send to school those unable to work, knowing they would be fed and cared for.

Despite her dedication and prior training, Charity Gaston faced an immense challenge. She knew no Navajo and had to rely on an interpreter to translate Bible stories and introduce the students to totally unfamiliar Christian concepts, such as heaven and hell. Even more difficult were classes in what the Navajos called "writing paper": teaching the children how to say and spell English words, and how to write and add numbers. Spotty attendance continued to

FIG. 4. Fort Defiance School, 1884. Photo by Ben Wittick.

be an ongoing problem. By the second year, official enrollment had risen to thirty-five students, but the average daily attendance was only sixteen.[5] In fall 1871, Charity and her new husband, the Fort Defiance missionary-physician Dr. James Menaul, were transferred to the Laguna Pueblo.[6] Ten years and several poorly trained teachers later, average daily attendance at Fort Defiance School had fallen to seven. It was evident that the Navajo day school experiment was turning out to be a total failure.

In 1880, it was decided to build a boarding school under the assumption that on-campus housing would facilitate regular classroom instruction and greater immersion in English.[7] The new Fort Defiance School, an impressive three-story stone building, finally opened its doors in September 1883. It was thought that parents would be eager to enroll their children, since the school would be providing for their daily needs, but the reality was quite different. When parents did come to view the premises, they became concerned that their children's feet would not be in contact with Mother Earth. They were also loathe to let "outsiders" raise their children in a foreign culture. Less than twenty students at a time were ever in attendance. Superintendent Logan reported that during that first year, "he did not believe there was one single day when all of the school employees were on speaking terms with all of their co-laborers—that the children would come and stay a day or two, get some clothes, and then run away back to their hogans, but few of them attended regularly, consequently the school did but little real good."[8]

In summer 1884, as mentioned earlier, John Bowman, the newly arrived Indian agent at Fort Defiance, resolved to improve morale at the school and increase its effectiveness. In his annual report, he wrote that he had had tremendous difficulty in finding the "necessary number of students" for his new school, despite all his efforts at begging and cajoling, even bribing, parents to allow their children to be educated.[9] As a result of his recruiting efforts, twenty-two students were enrolled that October. By November the number had increased to thirty-three. It was a modest success, but a success nonetheless, for none of the pupils tried to run away.

In fall 1884, young Clitso would have been one of the new students brought on opening day to the Fort Defiance School. On arrival, he would have been puzzled when asked to give his first and last name. Since the incoming Navajo students, unless they had Anglo fathers, were known only by their nicknames, the teachers would freely assign new names and surnames.[10] One boy became Abe Lincoln, another Grover Cleveland, and still another Joe Tippecanoe. There was also a Rip Van Winkle. Clitso apparently was allowed to keep his nickname, probably because it was easy for the teachers to pronounce, and assigned the surname Dedman.[11] It is not known what or who inspired the name "Dedman." Was there a Dedman among the officers stationed at Fort Defiance? Or did one of the teachers have a relative named Dedman? The origin remains a mystery.[12] Moreover, in the absence of school records, it is impossible to know whether the name was originally spelled "Dedman" or "Deadman."[13]

On arrival at Fort Defiance, Clitso would have had his hair cut short to get rid of the ever-present lice. This procedure was still mandatory in the 1920s when another young Navajo, future Code Talker Chester Nez, was sent to Navajo boarding school at age eight. He recalled:

> On my first day at school, I lined up with the other boys. Tears streamed down many faces. The first order of business: a mandatory haircut.
>
> Hair fell in piles. I awaited my turn, hands squeezed into fists as I watched the shearing. I figured there must be some mistake. We Navajos believe in witchcraft. Cut hair and fingernail clippings should be gathered and hidden or burned. Such things could be used to invoke bad

Twelve-year-old Clitso Dedman was one of the thirty-one students who "volunteered" to transfer to Grand Junction. As the group set out on their long trip north, Agent Vandever said goodbye to his charges, confident that they would benefit from the acquisition of new vocational skills.[24] Unfortunately, this confidence was seriously misplaced. In addition, the change of schools had been decided so quickly that Vandever was unable contact the boys' families and ask their permission for the transfer, an omission that would bring unexpected negative consequences. And so, suddenly and without his parents' knowledge, Clitso found himself embarked on a totally new and unplanned educational experience.

Grand Junction Indian School

Clitso Dedman's destination, the town of Grand Junction, was located at the confluence of the Grand River (subsequently renamed the Colorado River) and the Gunnison River, about thirty miles east of the Utah state border and 300 miles due north of Fort Defiance.[25]

For centuries the Grand Valley, as well as most of Colorado, half of Utah, and even parts of New Mexico and Kansas, had been Ute territory. In 1821, the area was declared part of Mexico and in 1848, at the end of the Mexican-American War, it was ceded to the United States. In 1868, the same year the Navajo Reservation was created, the U.S. government entered into a treaty with the Colorado Utes granting them the western third of the state as a reservation, on condition that they withdraw from the Front Range, that is, the eastern side of the Rocky Mountains. This agreement, however, proved to be short-lived. The discovery of gold and silver in the San Juan Mountains and the expansion of the Denver & Rio Grande Railroad westward toward San Francisco meant that by 1878 the Colorado Utes found themselves restricted to a strip of land along the New Mexico border and a smaller reservation on the White River in the north. As a result of the deadly Meeker Massacre in 1879, where Indian Agent Nathan Meeker and ten of his employees were killed, Congress decreed that White River Utes be relocated to northeastern Utah.[26] In summer 1881, they were forcibly marched 150 miles westward to the desolate Uintah Reservation, thus opening western Colorado to Anglo homesteaders.

In 1886, under the sponsorship of Colorado senator Henry Moore Teller, the U.S. government authorized the establishment of an Indian school in the newly created town of Grand Junction. The mission of the school, which would later be named the Teller Institute, was to teach agricultural skills to the Ute Indians who had been displaced from their ancestral lands and relocated to smaller reservations.[27] At the time, there were roughly 1,000 Southern Utes in Colorado, 2,000 Uintahs and Ouray Utes in Utah, and 1,000 Paiutes farther west in Nevada.

The first such U.S. off-reservation Indian boarding school was the Carlisle Indian School, which had been established in Pennsylvania in 1879 by Capt. Richard Pratt. Its goal was to "Americanize" the Indian youths by insulating them from tribal influences. More specifically, the educational program would entail the abandonment of native languages, conversion to Christianity, and the introduction of strict military discipline. The school would seek out students from various different tribes, mixing them in dormitories and classes, so that English would become, de facto, the only language of communication. The dual mission of the school was to provide an eighth-grade education and to offer boys and girls broad and varied vocational training. Students would also be encouraged to participate in typical American extracurricular activities, such as team sports, marching band, and the publication of a student newspaper.[28]

A more subtle aim of the Carlisle Indian School was to break down the traditional Indian mentality that was based on communal property and sharing of wealth, and to instill in students the cardinal Anglo values of hard work, thrift, self-reliance, and self-support. To this effect, Pratt created summer "outing" programs whereby students were hosted by local families and offered jobs off campus. In return for their work, they would receive modest wages that would be deposited in a savings account and held for them until they left school.

The Bureau of Indian Affairs subsequently established five more such off-reservation boarding schools, locating them farther west and closer to the students' tribal homes, so as to minimize transportation costs. Whereas various religious denominations continued to create and maintain reservation schools like Fort Defiance, these new off-reservation schools, based on the Carlisle model, were funded by Washington and staffed by government employees. Their annual budgets were determined in large part by the total number of students enrolled and the average daily attendance.[29]

In 1886, the town of Grand Junction, then numbering about 2,000 inhabitants, received the news of Teller's proposed Indian boarding school with mixed emotions. Although its presence might possibly give the area a financial boost, the citizens were uneasy about bringing back the very Ute Indians who had recently been expelled from nearby White River to Utah. Under pressure from Washington, the local officials deeded the school a 160-acre building site, but selected an undesirable location next to the railroad tracks about two miles northwest of the town center. The land with its heavy clay soil, high alkali content, lack of water, and poor drainage would prove to be not only unhealthy for the students but far from ideal for an agricultural program.[30] This was unfortunate, and perhaps intentional, since much of the Grand Valley was very fertile and soon would be covered with orchards and vineyards.

The school's first superintendent, W. I. Davis, arrived in summer 1886, as the new classroom/dormitory building with a capacity of sixty students was under construction.[31] His first and most challenging task was to find students. The Utes, a nomadic tribe of hunters, saw no value in sending their children to reservation day schools and were even more negative about off-reservation boarding schools. The nearby Utes in Utah, having been recently expelled from Colorado, had absolutely no motivation to send their children back to the state that had forcibly ejected them. When the Grand Junction Indian School finally opened its doors in November, Davis and his clerk had brought in only seven students. By the end of the school year, after numerous recruitment trips as far afield as southern Colorado, Nevada, and Idaho, Davis had only managed to increase the enrollment to twenty-seven pupils. In his year-end report, dated September 1, 1887, Davis noted that he had overseen the building of a kitchen and laundry, and that the school had purchased four horses and three cows. Eighty acres of land had been plowed and irrigated, yielding crops of oats and vegetables. Six hundred forest trees, one hundred apple trees, and grapevines had been planted. The students, though few in number, had been introduced to basic farming skills. In his closing paragraph, he announced that he was officially retiring from the Indian service.

When the next superintendent, Thomas Breen, arrived on October 1, 1887, he immediately realized that, contrary to Davis's glowing report, the school was barely functioning.[32] Students were sullen and disobedient. Of the twenty-six pupils, only six were from the Utah reservations for which the Grand Junction School had been intended; nineteen were Paiutes from Nevada, and one was from southern Colorado. Of the total, four were under sixteen, and ten were between sixteen and twenty. Twelve were actually between twenty and thirty years old, and did not belong in the school at all. There were just five employees on hand: a clerk/physician, a matron, a seamstress, a laundress, and a cook. Breen's first task was to hire a principal, a teacher, a carpenter, and an industrial teacher. New construction projects included a carpentry shop, granary, horse sheds, a windmill and water tank. Sanitary conditions were significantly improved. Crops were planted in February, but in March the Ditch Company refused to provide irrigation water until the prior year's assessments were paid. By the time the dispute was settled, half the planned harvest and all the new trees had died. Breen's biggest problem, however, was the failure to recruit new pupils because of Ute trouble that fall. In April, half the school staff, upon hearing rumors that the school itself was about to cease operation, quit to find new jobs elsewhere.

The Grand Junction School did not close after all, and Breen remained in his position for the following academic year. Overall conditions and staff harmony, however, failed to improve. The agricultural program was again limited, due in large part to the poor quality of the soil and lack of tools. Among the students, general apathy prevailed. Recruitment remained difficult. Total attendance for the entire school year was twenty-seven, but the average monthly attendance ranged between only eight and fourteen.

When the new superintendent George Wheeler arrived in May 1889, he was met by only four employees and seven students.[33] His first action was to send the remaining pupils home on vacation. In his official report written at the end of summer, Wheeler concluded that the prior school year had been "near a complete failure" and expressed the hope that his next annual report would be "more creditable." His immediate aim that fall was to increase the enrollment, which he hoped to do by recruiting new pupils from non-Ute tribes.

As described earlier, it was Wheeler who, in late September, traveled to the Navajo Reservation where he successfully enlisted thirty-one pupils, among whom were twelve-year-old Clitso Dedman, a classmate who had been given the name Rip Van Winkle, and ten-year-old Jacob Morgan. Whereas a century later, one could drive the 350 miles north from Fort Defiance to Grand Junction in under six hours, the group's itinerary in 1889 covered over 800 miles and consisted of a sixty-hour train trip via the Atchison, Topeka and Santa Fe Railway (map 2). For the young Navajos, the expedition would be an unforgettable educational experience.

FIG. 5. Atchison, Topeka and Santa Fe train at a water stop in Thatcher, Colorado, 1889. Courtesy Kansas State Historical Society, #592.

In the early morning hours of September 28, Wheeler and his Navajo pupils assembled in front of the Fort Defiance School where several horse-drawn wagons were waiting to drive the group thirty miles southeast to Gallup, New Mexico. For many, if not most, of the students, it would be their first visit to this growing timber and coal mining town founded just eight years earlier. The group was deposited at the railroad depot. As Wheeler was purchasing their tickets with his government vouchers, the students outside were suddenly surprised by loud whistles and bells announcing the arrival of the eastbound AT&SF passenger train.

They were amazed at the size of the powerful steam engine with its coal tender and the nine large wagons: a mail car, a baggage car, a smoker, a day coach that would be their new "traveling home," a tourist sleeper, three luxury Pullman cars, and a caboose. The boys watched with fascination as the train took on more water. First, the boilerman went to the large, circular water tower and swung out a large spigot that he positioned over the tender. He then jerked a chain to initiate the flow. This was a sight they would see over

MAP 2. Atchison, Topeka and Santa Fe Railway network, ca. 1890. Erin Greb Cartography.

and over again on their train ride to Grand Junction, since the steam trains of the period needed to replenish their water supply every 100 miles. (Fig. 5 shows their train at a water stop in Thatcher, Colorado, northeast of Trinidad.)

At the "all aboard" signal, the students boarded the day coach and settled onto their wooden benches for the long trip ahead. They had been wondering why the well-dressed Anglo passengers were boarding wagons positioned at the back of the train rather than near the front, but as the train pulled out of the station and acrid engine smoke filtered into their wagon, they understood why the Pullman cars were coupled as far as possible from the locomotive.

The first leg of their journey took the students 125 miles eastward to the Rio Grande, which they crossed at Belen. Never had the students imagined so much water. From there, the train took them north to Albuquerque, and then continued 330 miles in a more northeasterly direction toward La Junta, Colorado. Before crossing the state line, the train stopped briefly at Raton to add a second locomotive for the steep passage over the Sangre de Cristo Mountains. As the train made its laborious uphill climb, the young Navajo passengers, who had been looking out the windows at the rugged scenery, suddenly found their sun-filled world turn to night. Fearful at first as to what might be happening, they were relieved several minutes later as the train exited the half-mile-long Raton tunnel and began its slow, winding descent into the lively mining town of Trinidad (population 5,500). From there it was an easier ride down across the plains to La Junta, where they would change trains.

The final and longest leg of the trip would take them 350 miles northwest from La Junta across the Continental Divide to Grand Junction. The most impressive stop by far was the city of Pueblo, Colorado, with its population of almost 30,000.[34] As the train approached the city, the young Navajos saw dozens of immense chimneys spewing forth dark black smoke from the five large coal-burning smelters that had been built to process gold and silver ore, as well as iron and zinc, from the mines located in the southeastern Rocky Mountains.

From Pueblo, the train continued north to Colorado Springs (population 11,000) before heading west into the mountains to Buena Vista and turning north again up the Arkansas River Valley to the booming mining center of Leadville (population 10,400). When the train later entered the Hagerman Tunnel to cross the Continental Divide, the Navajo boys had become seasoned travelers and were no longer surprised by the sudden momentary darkness. The train then descended to Glenwood Springs and followed the Colorado River Valley into Grand Junction.[35]

On October 1, 1889, after four days of travel on the uncomfortable benches of their railroad car, Clitso and his Navajo classmates were delighted, or perhaps simply relieved, to reach their destination.[36] Grand Junction, with its population of under 2,000, was small compared to the cities and towns they had crossed. They felt at ease as they took in the fresh air of the young orchards and newly harvested alfalfa fields, happy to forget the heavy smoke of the Pueblo smelters. The peaceful streets offered a welcome change after the bustle of the mining communities. However, disappointment lay ahead.

At the train station, the group boarded the horse-drawn wagons that would take them to their new school. As they traveled the two miles westward over a rough dirt road, the landscape grew more barren. On the horizon arose the silhouette of a lone two-story brick building with a few smaller structures. This would be their new home for the next several years. As Jacob Morgan later recalled: "I think what made the boys so anxious to go [to Grand Junction] was that we were told about all kinds of apples, peaches, and a great field of watermelons that was to be our food. But when we came there we were sorely disappointed in not finding what was promised us. . . . There was only one building in the midst of a great field of grease-wood. Maybe that man [in Fort Defiance] couldn't tell the difference between grease-wood and fruit trees he told us about."[37] Having arrived in front of the school, they stepped down onto hard-baked clay soil, which, after a rainstorm, they soon learned, would be transformed into slippery mud. On entering the building, they each were officially registered by the clerk. Clitso was apparently enrolled as "Deadman," rather than "Dedman."[38] His classmate Rip Van Winkle was listed under his recently assigned Anglo name, curious as it was.

All the while, the school seemed quiet, almost deserted. Indeed, as they would soon discover, the only other students were five Ute boys and two Ute girls. There was only one classroom teacher, plus one industrial/agricultural teacher who would quit two weeks later. There were no functioning workshops and no tools of any consequence. The eagerly anticipated vocational program simply did not exist. Compared to Fort Defiance, the Grand Junction School could hardly be called a school, much less a vocational school.

Living conditions were even more disappointing. The alkali content of the drinking water from the school well was so elevated that many of the young Navajos initially suffered stomach problems. Although fresh water for cooking and bathing was brought in from the Colorado River, this "ditch water," as it was called, arrived via an irrigation canal "in which dead animals and other decaying matter [were] often found."[39] During the first months, Jacob Morgan recalled he was "near starvation" most of the time, "even as food stuff was stacked high in the warehouse." He later remarked that Superintendent Wheeler was "the stingiest man that ever came out of Boston. I guess he never heard of how the Indians helped to keep the Puritans from starving." According to young Morgan, "the students at Teller lived on two slices of bread, half of a boiled potato a day and were given an occasional small piece of meat."[40] Many would wander off the grounds to nearby orchards to scavenge fallen fruit.

After only a few weeks at the school, some of the older Navajo students began planning how they might run away and return to Fort Defiance, where meals were copious and classes were well structured. From an early age, the boys had learned how to survive in the semiarid hills while herding sheep. They knew how to orient themselves by studying the positions of the sun by day and the stars at night. However, they were totally unfamiliar with the geography of the area south of Grand Junction down to Four Corners and the Navajo Reservation. These were former tribal lands of the Colorado Ute Indians who in recent years had been confined by the U.S. government to a small reservation near the New Mexico border. Obviously there were no maps.

In their limited conversational English, the Navajo students may well have discussed their proposed escape plans with an older student from the Southern Ute Reservation who was familiar with the terrain, having just traveled in the reverse direction to come to school. He described for them the route they would need to take. For the first 50 miles, they should follow the Gunnison River to Montrose and continue up the Uncompahgre Valley. Then they would need to cross 150 miles of forests and mountains, up over the snow-covered San Juan peaks, through the booming silver-mining towns of Rico and Ophir, and down to Dolores, finally reaching the small village of Cortez.[41] After Cortez, it would be another 100 miles of semiarid country south to Fort Defiance. It is quite likely that this unnamed Ute student, similarly dissatisfied with school conditions, offered to accompany the group as far as the San Juan River and the Arizona border.

One evening in early November 1889, a group of eight Navajo students, probably together with their Ute guide, packed what little food they had surreptitiously been hoarding, took the blankets from their beds, and quietly stole out of the dormitory. Clitso and the younger pupils were all asleep, and only became aware of their classmates' absence the next morning. The runaways crossed the town of Grand Junction and then followed the road to Montrose, traveling mainly at night and hiding during the day so as to avoid being caught by school personnel. When the group finally reached the protective forests of the San Juan Mountains, they were able relax their guard and travel by day. Their good spirits, however, would soon be severely tested.

As they were trekking up the wagon trail toward the San Juan peaks, they were suddenly engulfed in a raging blizzard. Although totally unprepared for such severe weather, they did manage somehow to make their way through the deep snow over the 10,000-foot mountain pass and down to the more welcoming lower elevations of Dolores and Cortez. Hungry and severely frostbitten, the eight Navajo students finally reached Fort Defiance, where they told of their harrowing experience in the mountains.[42] They also described the disastrous living conditions at the Grand Junction School and the lack of a vocational curriculum, both factors that had precipitated their decision to run away and return to the reservation.

Word of the students' unexpected return quickly circulated among the Navajo community. Most upset were the families who had not even been informed that their sons had been transferred to Grand Junction. Many parents subsequently grew increasingly hesitant about allowing their children to attend school in Fort Defiance, even when reassured that henceforth no students would be sent off the reservation without parental consent.[43] Finally it was agreed that Navajo students would only be sent to off-reservation schools in cities such as Albuquerque, Santa Fe, Phoenix, and Riverside, California, where visiting families would have direct railroad access.

Thus, for the next several years, Clitso and his twenty-three remaining Fort Defiance classmates would be the only Navajo students at the Grand Junction School. The students' accounts of the exceedingly poor conditions at the school were particularly disturbing to Navajo Agent Vandever who had naively accepted Superintendent Wheeler's glowing description of his vocational program and the opportunities it would provide for the Navajo students. Vandever must have immediately notified his superiors in Washington, for Wheeler was abruptly removed, and on December 6, 1889, a new superintendent, Sanford Record, arrived in Grand Junction as his replacement.

Superintendent Record's first priority was to strengthen the educational program while maintaining discipline and improving living conditions. As he wrote in his official report in fall 1890:

When I assumed control here, my immediate attention was given to the school itself. Previously the pupils had been allowed to commit nuisances in and around the buildings. This was at once stopped. They had wandered at will, trespassing upon neighboring ranches and helping themselves to any thing good to eat. This was checked, and work suited to the size and strength of the individual was provided for many of them.

Special attention was paid to school-room work. The pupils were graded according to ability, classes were formed, and recitations heard. Good order was required and prompt obedience expected. Both are now striking characteristics of my classroom.

While all have done better than might have been expected, I am pleased to see that the little fellows have led the big ones. Their advancement in the ordinary branches has been rapid, and I hope permanent; but they seem to take hold of drawing, penmanship, and music more readily.[44]

Clitso would have been among the "little fellows" to make rapid academic progress that first year. For artistically inclined Clitso, penmanship was a favorite class. Students learned to use a dip pen with a wooden holder and pointed nib. It required a steady hand to hold the nib in a horizontal position in order to create thin strokes across the page and broad strokes down. Clitso enjoyed writing in the flowing Spencerian script with its elegant capital letters.[45]

Superintendent Record immediately hired a replacement industrial teacher, although progress in the vocational domain was severely limited because of the "absence of everything pertaining to an industrial training school."[46] Little advancement was made in the farming program, due in part to the lack of agricultural implements. Record concluded his September 1890 report by stressing that the school could only make rapid improvement in its educational mission were it to receive substantial government subsidies. Without a major appropriation, he insisted that the school was doomed to fail.

Washington apparently provided the needed support, since over the following academic year, under Superintendent Record's continued and focused leadership, the school grounds were substantially expanded. Improvements included "the partial erection of a two-story brick house containing dormitories, dining room, kitchen, reception room, sewing room, sitting room, infirmary and bathrooms; a large and well constructed barn; a milk house; a two-story brick building containing carpenter shop, saddler and shoe shop, and tailor shop; as well as a small box blacksmith shop."[47] Although enrollment had increased to forty-eight students, this number was still well below the newly increased school capacity.

For the Navajo pupils, the promised vocational training slowly began to materialize. In the blacksmith shop, students learned how to stoke the small forge, using bellows to build the fire to the appropriate temperature to heat the iron bars. They would then take turns hammering the hot metal into shape on the anvil to create simple tools such as ax heads and chisels. Record had also hired a highly qualified carpenter and at the end of the year his young apprentices, Clitso certainly among them, were singled out for their excellent workmanship in helping build the barn, the milk house, and the walkways.

In September 1890, the U.S. Commissioner of Indian Affairs, Thomas J. Morgan, made an official visit to the Grand Junction School and was impressed by the school's progress.[48] He authorized Superintendent Record to hire an agricultural teacher for the farming program, to purchase much-needed equipment for the shops, and to hire four additional industrial teachers. Commissioner Morgan encouraged the townspeople to give their full support to the school and to cooperate in the establishment of an "outing system" whereby students would be placed in area homes during school vacation to strengthen their vocational and linguistic skills.[49] Clitso most likely spent the next summer living with a local family, speaking English and participating firsthand in daily farm activities.

It was during Clitso's third year at Grand Junction that the school, renamed the Teller Institute, finally began reaching the educational potential that its namesake, Senator Teller, had intended. In May 1891 the incoming superintendent Theodore Lemmon, knowing that a major stumbling block in the school's development had been the almost impossible challenge of finding willing Ute students, arrived in Grand Junction with fifty-three Apache, Mohave, and Yuma pupils from the overcrowded San Carlos Indian School where he had been teaching.[50] As Jacob Morgan recalled in his autobiographical writings, the Navajo students quickly found that their language was enough alike that of the Apache pupils that they "quickly learned to converse and got along on the best of terms."[51]

Energetic twenty-five-year-old Superintendent Lemmon, relying on his formal training as a teacher, spent the summer months restructuring the educational program. Students would be placed in "literary" classes according to level with a curriculum similar to the one he had developed the prior year in Arizona, using the McGuffey readers:[52]

First year.—First quarter: Learning English name; learning names of familiar objects; count to 24; committing sentences to memory. Second quarter: Learning names of surrounding objects; count to 50; making sentences; writing name; chart-work. Third quarter: Learning names of surrounding objects; count to 100; making sentences; chart and primer work; script alphabet.

Second year.—First quarter: Review: making sentences using personal pronouns; first half of first reader; combinations of numbers to 20; spelling; writing. Second quarter: Second half of first reader; making sentences; use of personal pronouns; singular and plural distinguished; addition; spelling; writing. Third quarter: Second reader; simple compositions; spelling; writing; addition and subtraction.

Third year.—First quarter: Second reader; simple compositions; spelling; writing; subtraction; oral geography. Second quarter: Third reader; simple compositions; spelling; writing; multiplication; geography and history combined in oral work.

Lemmon had observed in San Carlos that Apache pupils rapidly learned penmanship and mastered English words and counting. His conclusion, however, was that "the English sentence, calculations, and ideas of geography are apprehended so slowly one wearies with waiting."[53]

At the Grand Junction School, Lemmon created new lessons introducing vocabulary and phrases that pertained to the vocational trades, thus making reading and writing activities more meaningful to the students. In a similar vein, the industrial teachers were encouraged to incorporate arithmetic into their instruction by introducing measurements and calculations, be it in carpentry, tailoring, or leather work.

Beginning in fall 1891, the daily schedule at the newly named Teller Institute was modified so that in the mornings, half of the students would be engaged in "literary" work with two teachers in two classrooms, while the other half received instruction in various trades on a rotating basis. In the afternoons,

Teller Indian School, Grand Junction, Colo.

FIG. 6. *Teller Indian School, Grand Junction, Colorado.* Postcard, 1910.

the groups were reversed. This not only allowed greater flexibility in programming but also effectively reduced the class size by half. At the end of the year, Lemmon reported: "There is nothing in the school work more gratifying than the application and persistency of the children apprenticed to trades.... In all the industrial work, the apprentices work half a day, which I think accounts for the close application both in the schoolroom and in the industrial arts."[54]

That winter, Clitso received permission to visit his family in Chinle. Years later, he would recount to his children the details of his return trip. His father took him on horseback over the Chuska Mountains up to the Four Corners where they forded the icy San Juan River. In Cortez, he was placed on a carriage to Dolores, where he boarded a train on the newly completed spur of the Rio Grande Southern Railroad that brought him back to Grand Junction.[55]

By June 1892, it became evident to Lemmon that the school needed to expand its facilities. Word of the Teller Institute's successful vocational and educational program was spreading to the point that he had been obliged to turn down applicants from some Indian families. During the summer, Clitso and his fellow carpenter apprentices helped build a new two-story schoolhouse with three classrooms and an upstairs assembly hall. They learned how to plan out and prepare a stone foundation, how to raise the walls and lay the floors,

Route 66. Behind it, there was a second east–west road named Coal Street. The two were connected with short numbered streets. A photograph taken from the Cotton Company in 1905 (fig. 7) shows the intersection of Railroad Street and South Third Street.

The Santa Fe Railroad

In the mid-1890s, the Santa Fe designated Gallup as a division point or crew-change point. Union agreements at the time required that engine crews be relieved approximately every 100 miles and transported back to their town of origin. This new designation meant that the rail yard, as well as the facilities for the repair and maintenance of engines and rolling stock, would be significantly expanded.

From a railhead with twenty or thirty employees (not counting the crews that were laying and maintaining the distant tracks), the number of railroad employees in Gallup quickly climbed to 300. Conditions in the railroad repair shops could be very uncomfortable, especially in summer in the blacksmith shops. Accidents were frequent, often causing serious injury and even death.

Although the recruitment of unskilled track workers had not been difficult, the company found it a challenge to find skilled mechanics willing to work in the railroad shops of the desolate Southwest towns. Gradually, however, a cadre of machinists, boilermakers, and blacksmiths came to constitute about one-fourth of the local railroad staff.

Since these skilled workers were paid by the hour, the Santa Fe had inaugurated a system whereby each man would pick up a small numbered block when he arrived each day at the rail yard and surrender it when he went to lunch or quit in the evening. The payroll officer could thus keep active tallies of how many hours per week each employee had worked. Monthly wages were calculated at the end of the month and generally paid the third week of the following month.[4] In the 1890s, a blacksmith, for example, would earn on the average $2.60 a day, and a blacksmith helper would earn about $1.70.[5]

As the railroad continued pushing westward, it became necessary for the Santa Fe to provide housing for its employees at each division point. At first, workers were lodged in boxcars lined up in the rail yard. Quickly, however, the Santa Fe began building homes for families and dormitory-style housing for single men and for the visiting train crews. These latter developments were generally one-floor wooden structures with twenty rooms, two men to a room, plus nearby laundry and washroom facilities. The complex would also have a large reading room with books, periodicals, and newspapers, as well as tables for playing cards or checkers (no gambling!).[6]

Railroad Machinist

Upon arriving in Gallup in 1893, Clitso Dedman presented himself at the Santa Fe railroad shop with well-trimmed short hair (not the traditional Navajo bun) and wearing Western clothes. He interviewed easily in English with the foreman and had no trouble filling out the written application form. The blacksmith skills he had acquired at the Grand Junction School definitely qualified him for an apprenticeship. Given the expansion of the Gallup operations and the railroad's growing need for employees, he was immediately hired.

Dedman quickly fit in with his fellow employees. He was comfortable in an Anglo-American environment: eating with a knife and fork, sleeping in a bed, and using washroom facilities. With his solid command of spoken English and his acceptance of the Anglo work ethic, he quickly learned his job routine and assumed his share of responsibilities. He joined the local union and on one occasion went out on strike with his coworkers. As Theodore Roosevelt would observe, after conversing with him in 1913, Dedman had "in all ways precisely the experience of the average skilled mechanic."[7]

Railroad shop employees worked Monday through Friday, plus Saturday mornings. Shifts were generally ten hours long but were often reduced to eight or nine hours in winter when there was less daylight. Given that workers were paid by the hour, the majority of the shopmen preferred working longer days to bring in higher wages. During slack periods with less railway traffic, work-forces were reduced, often for a week or two. As a young apprentice, Dedman would thus have been one of the first to be briefly furloughed, allowing him to make occasional trips back to the reservation.

Deep down, Dedman was a Navajo at heart. He gradually realized that although he was well remunerated as a machinist, he did not wish to spend the rest of his life working in the confines of a hot and often dangerous railroad shop. After several months in Gallup, he began missing the family life and the open vistas of Navajoland. And so, over the next couple of years, he started carefully putting aside most of his earnings and began preparing for his next venture, that of a reservation trader.

4

Trading Post Years

During the four years from 1893 to 1897 that Clitso Dedman worked as a machinist for the Santa Fe Railroad in Gallup, he would have been able to arrange occasional visits to his home in Chinle as an assistant to one of the many freighters servicing the reservation trading posts. On these freighting trips, Clitso Dedman would have learned not only how to handle a wagon team along the rough and poorly indicated trails, but also how to care for the draft horses and how to make necessary repairs to the equipment in the event of minor accidents.

A primary destination for freighters from Gallup was the Hubbell Trading Post in Ganado. Owner J. L. Hubbell would certainly have noticed the arrival of a young Navajo freighter's assistant who spoke fluent English and was equally at ease conversing with Anglo visitors as well as Navajo trading post employees. It is quite probable that Hubbell asked the enterprising young Dedman to clerk occasionally in his store, assisting him in learning the essential elements of the Indian trading system.

Hubbell quickly developed warm personal ties with his protégé. In fact, in June 1902 he invited Dedman to accompany him on a train trip via Albuquerque and El Paso to attend the festive opening of the summer season at the Cloudcroft mountain lodge in New Mexico.[1] The weekend guests enjoyed horseback riding, golf, tennis, bowling, elegant meals, and evening bonfires. Apparently, twenty-five-year-old Dedman was an agreeable travel companion, easily fitting in with Anglo society and enjoying the various resort activities. These traits would later help him thrive as a businessman.

With Hubbell's support, Clitso Dedman would become one of the rare Navajos at the turn of the twentieth century to own a trading post. In fact, between 1897 and 1915, Dedman would own three trading posts, all in the general vicinity of Chinle: in Rough Rock to the northwest, in Salt Springs to the west, and the largest one in Nazlini to the south.

Early Navajo Trading Posts

Between 1864 and 1868, during the four years of their exile and confinement at Bosque Redondo near Fort Sumner, New Mexico, the once nomadic, sheepherding Navajos became dependent on Anglo goods for their daily existence. They were issued basic foodstuffs, such as flour, sugar, salt, coffee, canned goods, and also Pendleton trade blankets for warmth. Women's traditional woolen dresses were replaced by hand-sewn billowing skirts and long-sleeved blouses, necessitating needles and thread, as well as yard goods, such as calico and velveteen.

On their return from Bosque Redondo to their newly created reservation, the impoverished 8,000 Navajos who had survived the Long Walk, plus those who had hidden to avoid deportation, found themselves dependent on U.S. government agents for sheep to start reconstituting their herds and for tools and seeds to begin again growing corn, beans, and squash. Gradually, a new Navajo economy began to take shape. Families would sell their wool, hides, and weavings, and in return would purchase a variety of desired manufactured goods, including pots, water buckets, matches and tobacco, as well as processed food and yard goods. The center of this new way of life would be the trading post.[2]

Actually the term "trading post" is a bit of a misnomer in that the Navajo client did not really barter directly with the trader. The pricing of the store merchandise on a given day was fixed by the trader and expressed in American dollars. When a Navajo weaver, for example, brought in a blanket to sell, the trader would suggest a price and then she would generally ask for a better offer. Once the two had agreed on the value of the blanket, also in dollars, she would select the items she wanted to purchase one by one. The trader would indicate what each cost, subtracting the amount from the total due her. If she did not spend the entire sum on that day, the trader would give her credit for the remainder of the purchase price, usually in the form of "tin money," that is, in tokens imprinted with the name of his trading post. She could then redeem these trade tokens for merchandise at a future time, but they would be valid only at his store. This latter restriction was not a problem in the late nineteenth century, since there were few trading posts and travel was by horseback. Thus, Navajos would frequent the post closest to their home.[3]

The early traders were primarily Anglo-Americans who knew how to negotiate with suppliers, arrange for the transportation of their merchandise, and maintain business accounts. Since almost no Navajos at the time spoke any English, the traders learned "Navvy," a pidgin Navajo with the basic vocabulary needed for store transactions, plus a few polite phrases.[4] The most successful traders also learned to respect Navajo culture and to be responsive to the needs of their communities.

The Bureau of Indian Affairs required that any person planning to open a trading post on reservation land obtain an official license. However, the prospective trader could only operate if he were welcomed by local Navajo leaders, for they were the ones who would indicate on which parcel of land he would be permitted to construct his store. Generally the location would be near a spring, so that Navajos coming to trade would have access to water for themselves, their sheep, and their horses. The site of the trading post, as well as its structures, ultimately belonged to the tribe. Only the merchandise and the furnishings belonged to the trader.

Henry Chee Dodge (1860–1947) was the first reservation trader of Navajo ancestry. In the late 1880s, he partnered with Anglo trader and former cavalryman Stephen Aldrich to open a store in Round Rock. The two also were partners in a trading post at Manuelito, just off the reservation.[5] Actually, Chee Dodge was Navajo only on his mother's side. He had been raised by his Anglo-American uncle Perry Williams, a licensed trader at Fort Defiance, and had worked as a clerk in his store. Chee Dodge spoke fluent English and in the late 1870s had been hired as official interpreter by Indian Agent William F. M. Arny at Fort Defiance.

The first Navajo of traditional heritage to become an independent trader was Clitso Dedman, who, in 1897, set up a trading post in the remote settlement of Rough Rock. As a tribal member, he was not required to procure a trading license from the Bureau of Indian Affairs. However, in order to establish a store and manage its merchandise effectively, he needed to master the necessary business skills and obtain the financial backing of a wholesaler. This could present quite a challenge for a twenty-year-old with a modest education and no family trading history. Fortunately Dedman had found a mentor in J. L. Hubbell.

Hubbell Trading Post at Ganado

Juan Lorenzo Hubbell (1853–1930) was born in New Mexico Territory to an Anglo father and a Hispanic mother.[6] By age twenty-five, he had acquired a trading post in a settlement he named Ganado, halfway between the Navajo Agency at Fort Defiance and the Hopi Agency at Keams Canyon. He gradually built up a substantial trading clientele, due primarily to his respect for Navajo culture and his fairness in business dealings. Over the years, his enterprises at Ganado expanded to include ranches, farms, maintenance facilities, and a post office, as well as satellite trading posts in the surrounding area. After his death, his sons Lorenzo and Roman continued running the enterprise. The Hubbell Trading Post was declared a National Historic Site in 1960.

J. L. Hubbell was one of the earliest merchants to establish a trading post on the Navajo Reservation.[7] In 1875, Thomas V. Keam (1842–1904) had established his trading post near the Hopi mesas at what is now known as Keams Canyon.[8] When Hubbell opened his store in 1878, it was still necessary to freight supplies by heavily laden ox-drawn wagons over 250 miles from wholesalers in Santa Fe, an operation that could take almost a month. With the arrival of the railroad, newly created border towns, such as Gallup and Winslow, facilitated the distribution of merchandise, thus leading to a rapid expansion of Navajo trading posts in the southeastern part of the reservation. Traders would haul the goods in horse-drawn wagons over primitive dirt trails from the nearest railroad depots to their stores in the hinterland. Travel was not easy: in good weather, for example, the fifty-mile freight trip from Gallup to Ganado would still take two days.

In 1884, C. N. Cotton entered into a partnership with Hubbell at Ganado. In 1889, as mentioned earlier, Cotton opened a wholesale trading company in Gallup.[9] Hubbell subsequently expanded the Ganado trading post into a distribution hub, managing and servicing numerous smaller trading posts within a fifty-mile radius.[10] In 1901, Hubbell entered into an association with the Fred Harvey Company, which managed hotels and shops along the Santa Fe Railroad, selling the company textiles and providing Navajo and Hopi artists to demonstrate weaving, silversmithing, and carving to Anglo tourists.[11]

The original building on the Ganado site, known as the Leonard house, was a low wooden structure with a brush-covered roof. In 1883, Hubbell began the construction of a much larger trading post using sandstone quarried from the southern banks of the nearby Pueblo Colorado Wash. A 1906 photograph shows this trading post and two freight wagons loaded with gunny sacks of raw wool clip topped with piles of goat and sheep hides, ready to leave for Gallup (fig. 8).

Hubbell subsequently built a two-story sandstone barn with a roof supported by ponderosa pine beams hauled from forest land twelve miles to the east. Around 1902, he added a large family residence behind the trading post, decorating it with paintings and artifacts. Over the next twenty years, numerous additions were built, including housing for his managers and workers, a garage, a laundry, a woodshed, and a bread oven. By 1927, running water and baths had been installed.[12]

As more and more people began traveling to the Southwest, J. L. Hubbell invited artists, anthropologists, and tourists, as well as political figures, to stop at his trading post. Known for his hospitality, Hubbell always refused payment from his guests, but did encourage them to visit his store and purchase a Navajo blanket as a souvenir. One of his repeat guests was artist Eldridge Ayer Burbank (1858–1949) from whom he bought many paintings and drawings. E. A. Burbank was born in Illinois and attended the Chicago Academy of Design.[13] In 1897 his wealthy uncle Edward Ayer, president of the Field Museum of Natural History, engaged him to document American Indian life, thought at the time to be on the verge of extinction. His first portrait was of the Apache chief Geronimo, who was being held captive in Fort Sill, Oklahoma. Over the next thirteen years, Burbank visited over 125 tribes, painting and sketching twelve hundred portraits.[14]

Burbank had arrived in Gallup by train in late 1897 with a letter of introduction to C. N. Cotton, who suggested that he visit Hubbell in Ganado. The latter not only welcomed his guest for an extended stay but offered the artist his office as a studio for the Navajo portrait project. On November 21, Burbank wrote to his wife:

> I arrived here last night and am nicely fixed. This is the smallest place I have been to yet. Just two houses here. One big stone house where the Indian store is and living rooms. And another house where they cook & eat and a bedroom where I sleep. I have a nice old room to myself with an old-fashioned fire place in it. The Navajo Indians are here. This place is 60 miles from the railroad and the mail comes once a week on horseback.
>
> Mr. Hubbell who is a ranchman here is very kind to me. . . . He said he invited me here through my Uncle Ed and he said he had been here more than 30 years and had never yet taken a cent from any one for board and didn't intend to commence with me. He also gave me, made a present of, two elegant genuine old Navajo rugs, big ones.[15]

FIG. 9. E. A. Burbank, *Bull Pen*, 1908. Courtesy National Park Service, Hubbell Trading Post National Historic Site, HUTR 3457.

Four days later, Burbank wrote home again: "I finished the picture of a little Navajo papoose today. She had on a fine Navajo blanket. . . . Mr. Hubbell gave me today one of the finest old-fashioned rugs, Navajo, I ever saw. One that he could sell easy for $50.00.[16] . . . In my spare time, I am making copies of the old rugs for him in water colors, so hereafter the Indians can use them to make old ones by."[17]

Burbank stayed for a month in Ganado, using funds provided by his uncle Edward Ayer to pay Navajos to sit for portraits. Over the next fifteen years, Burbank returned regularly as Hubbell's guest, often helping out as a clerk in the trading post. In 1913 he wrote his host from Los Angeles: "Whenever I am away from Ganado I always feel as though I was away from home. I am happiest there than any place I have yet been to."[18]

During his visits to the Southwest, Burbank not only did individual Navajo portraits in red Conte crayon; he also made preparatory sketches for larger

FIG. 10. E. A. Burbank, *Navajo Gamblers*, 1911. Courtesy National Park Service, Hubbell Trading Post National Historic Site, HUTR 5277.

oil paintings he would later complete in his studio in California. One such painting (fig. 9) depicts the interior of the Hubbell Trading Post and offers a colorful depiction of the generic description provided by Frank McNitt in his book *The Indian Traders* (1962).

> The heavy front door opened onto a smallish area commonly known as the bull-pen. This for the Indians was a milling-about place, a place to stand, lean, squat, or sit while in the process of trade, sociability or reflection. . . . At some place in the bull-pen, at center or corner, there usually was an iron stove and woodbox. . . . Enclosing the bull-pen on three sides were wooden counters eight inches to one foot higher and wider than store counters found elsewhere in any part of the world. Quite simply, the counters were designed as barriers as much as they were loading platforms between customer and trader. . . . Space was a problem. Trading posts were small and Indians wanted to see what the trader had to sell. Shelves behind the high counters, therefore, were loaded to ceiling level:

groceries on this side, dry goods on that side. Still there was not enough room to display everything, and so the roof beams dripped merchandise as a cave roof collects stalactites.[19]

During his regular passages in Ganado to pick up supplies for his trading post ventures, Dedman was introduced to guest artist E. A. Burbank. Over the years, Burbank on his visits had observed how Navajo men would gather in the old Leonard building to play cards, often all night, and sometimes three nights in a row, wagering on the outcomes with trade tokens.[20] In 1910, Burbank began planning a major painting depicting such an evening, a project he later said "took months to complete and cost him several hundred dollars in model fees."[21] One of his models was Clitso Dedman. In the finished painting (fig. 10), the two seated Navajos in the center are playing Colonel, a two-person version of the Mexican card game Coon Can, which had become very popular in the Southwest in the late nineteenth century.[22] Clitso Dedman has been identified as the observer on the right wearing a blue headband and a large silver squash blossom necklace.[23]

Rough Rock Trading Post

In the late nineteenth century, Rough Rock was an isolated cluster of scattered Navajo camps located at the base of the Black Mesa in a remote area of the Navajo Reservation. For the few hundred Navajos living there, the nearest trading post was thirty miles to the southeast in Chinle, where Hubbell and Cotton had received a license to operate in 1886. It would require an excursion of several days on horseback or by wagon for them to bring their wool clip and hides to the store and then make the return trip laden with foodstuffs and other supplies.

It appears that in fall 1896, the two Rough Rock community leaders, Tsi'naajinii Bilii' Łikizhii (Painted Horse) and Biwóógizhii (Gaptooth), let it be known to Hubbell, either directly or indirectly, that they would like to see the establishment of a more convenient trading post in their community. To this end, they were ready to set aside a small plot of land near a local spring. When Dedman was told of this opportunity, he acted quickly and went by horseback to the Black Mesa area to learn more about the location and what types of merchandise would be most needed. As a Navajo, he had the distinct advantage of being able to communicate directly with the headmen, an advantage that they too appreciated. Thus it was in Rough Rock that Clitso Dedman set out on his first trading venture.[24]

In early spring 1897, Dedman purchased his own wagon and team of four horses, using the savings from his railroad wages. In Gallup, he purchased a large rectangular canvas officers' tent with four-foot-high walls and a peaked roof. He also bought wooden boards for the construction of a trading counter and display shelves, plus the required carpentry tools. Additional items would have included empty gunny sacks and a standing scale for weighing the wool clip. For his own use, he would need a barrel for hauling water from the spring and small cooking stove, plus pots, pans, buckets, dishes, and tableware. He loaded all these items onto his wagon, together with sheepskins and a blanket for sleeping, plus the ledgers, pen, and paper necessary for keeping records.

From Gallup, Dedman drove his wagon to Ganado, where he filled the remaining space with merchandise that Hubbell provided on consignment. On this first trading excursion, the merchandise probably consisted mainly of basic foodstuffs: wooden crates of Arbuckle Coffee, sacks of sugar and flour, matches, and a variety of canned goods, such as tomatoes and peaches. On subsequent trips, Dedman would also bring bolts of calico, flannel, and velveteen, together with needles and thread, plus hardware, buckets, harness equipment, and a variety of other items requested by the community.

And so, with a fully loaded wagon, Dedman set out from Ganado to Rough Rock. The seventy-mile trip could well have taken three or four days, given the rough condition of the rutted trails and the weight of his merchandise and equipment. Upon arrival, he was welcomed by the two headmen who provided him with local assistance in erecting his sturdy canvas wall tent. Using the carpentry skills he had perfected at Grand Junction, Dedman built a high trading counter that he set up near the door of the tent. To the side, he placed the scale for weighing the wool clip. Three feet behind the counter, he constructed a tall set of shelves on which to display his merchandise. The roomy interior of the tent, hidden from customers, served as a combination living area plus storage space.

As a Navajo, Dedman had a distinct advantage over other lone Anglo traders who, in the nineteenth century, would go into the reservation hinterland to set up a trading tent in some remote settlement. First and foremost, he spoke

Navajo and could communicate easily with community residents, understanding their clan backgrounds and the meanings of their nicknames. Second, he knew Navajo culture and how to establish and maintain relationships. Thus, he was quickly able to fit into his new environment. As ever, Dedman was a keen observer and a fast learner. Through his experience freighting and clerking for Hubbell, he had become familiar with the workings of a trading post, the pricing of wool and merchandise, and the corresponding bookkeeping requirements.

When a Navajo customer rode up to his tent store with her bag of wool, she would stay on her horse a while and survey the scene before dismounting. She would then slowly approach the counter, and finally she and Dedman would recognize one another. He would weigh the wool and write down the negotiated purchase price in dollars, but no money would change hands. She would lean on the high counter and select her desired merchandise, one item at a time. Dedman would deduct the cost of each purchase from the price of the wool. This item-by-item exchange would proceed at a leisurely pace until the total value of the desired merchandise equaled the price of the wool. Most women brought in weavings of thick hand-spun yarn that would be weighed and priced by pound, hence the term "pound blankets." Since Dedman's Rough Rock customers were illiterate, they relied on his honesty and the consistency of his pricing. They were not disappointed.

At the end of the day, Dedman would pack all the wool clip he had received into large gunny sacks, storing them in the back of the tent. The pound blankets would also be placed in gunny sacks. As the weeks went by, the number of gunny sacks increased while the amount of foodstuffs decreased. When it came time to replenish his stock, Dedman would load the collected bags of wool clip and blankets onto his wagon and set out on the long trip to Ganado. Hubbell would pay him for the wool and the weavings, deducting the cost of the prior consignment of merchandise. Based on the demands of his Rough Rock clientele, Dedman would select new merchandise for his return trip, adding requested items, such as Pendleton trade blankets, buckets, and tools. During his weeklong absences, the tent store probably remained closed under the protective surveillance of the headmen.

This cycle continued into late September 1897, when the Black Mesa residents would bring in a copious harvest of piñon nuts, as well as hides and wool from the fall shearing. As the days grew colder and nights grew longer, Dedman sold the last of his merchandise and returned to Ganado. His initial foray into the trading business must have been quite rewarding, because he decided to return the following year, leaving his tent with his personal effects in Rough Rock over the winter.

In preparation for the 1898 trading season, Dedman would have gone to Gallup to have "tin money" made up for his new post. These trade tokens, usually in denominations of five cents, ten cents, twenty-five cents, fifty cents, and one dollar, would be given as change to Navajo clients, who could then redeem them at the trading post at a later time.[25]

In choosing a template for his tokens, Dedman opted for a design with scalloped edges rather than the more common circular coin format. The front of the tokens was embossed with the words "C. D. Deadman Indian Trader." The spelling "Deadman" is curious. Navajos would never want anything to do with a "dead man." Perhaps that was the way his name had been spelled at the Teller Institute. In any case, he would subsequently sign his name as "Dedman." The back of the tokens carried the standard wording: "Good for Merchandise" plus a numerical value. The coin in figure 11 was worth twenty-five cents. Since Dedman's tokens did not indicate the location of his Rough Rock store, he was subsequently able to use the same tokens at his trading posts in Salt Springs and Nazlini.

Although tin money was widely used across Navajoland, traders and their suppliers dealt with one another in actual U.S. currency. Consequently, traders needed to master the rudiments of bookkeeping in order to maintain two sets of accounts. Moreover, they were faced with the linguistic and cultural challenge of interacting appropriately with both Navajo clients and Anglo suppliers. Dedman, with his knowledge of bookkeeping, his working command of English, and his innate business acumen, was one of the very few Navajos who succeeded in building and independently managing his own trading post.

The 1898 trading season was even more successful, in large part because Clitso Dedman had earned the respect of the headmen and was better able to provide merchandise that responded to the needs of the community. He also encouraged the local Navajos to increase their production of weavings and handcrafted silver jewelry.

FIG. 11. Clitso Dedman trade token, 25 cents.

It was probably in 1899 or 1900 that young Dedman began making plans for the construction of a more permanent trading post from which to operate, no simple project in the remote Rough Rock area. Dedman would be working alone, with no professional guidance and only the assistance of willing local Navajo men whom he would have to train. He would need to call on the carpentry skills he had developed years earlier at Grand Junction, and his practical experience there in the construction of school buildings.

The easiest option would have been to use local timber, but the juniper trees in the vicinity did not grow large enough to serve as building material. His tent store, however, was situated next to a broad bluff from which he could quarry sandstone for his building without any need for transportation. Rough Rock (Tséch'izhi in Navajo) had been named for the exposed granular sandstone forming the sides of the mesa. Although Dedman had received no formal instruction in masonry, he would have closely observed how the masons in Grand Junction laid stone foundations.

Using chisels, mallets, and points that he purchased in Gallup, Dedman began experimenting with the local sandstone. He would first need to break off a larger section of sandstone from the low rocky bluff behind his trading tent, and then learn how to chisel it down into several rectangular blocks. Once he had mastered the technique, he would teach a few willing Navajos how to produce the required cut stones, paying them for their labor in merchandise from his store. As the project progressed, the workers would quarry deeper into the bluff, creating a rather large "dugout."

In conceiving the plans for his trading post, Dedman optimistically envisaged a forty-foot-long cut-stone structure with a slightly sloping roof. At the same time, however, he realized that the biggest challenge would be to assemble the building materials. In addition to the sandstone building blocks, Dedman would need twenty roof beams each about twenty feet in length. The nearest stand of tall timber was located at the upper Oraibi Wash, about ten miles distant.[26] It would take several trips via the horse trail up to the top of Black Mesa and across to the wash to where Navajo workers would saw down the twenty tall trees, remove their bark, and trim them to the appropriate length, before dragging them back to Rough Rock. Fortunately the last six miles of the return trip would be downhill, facilitating the cumbersome transportation of the roof timbers.

To complete the assembly of building materials, Dedman would bring in from Gallup a sufficient supply of boards and tar paper for covering the roof beams. He would also need milled lumber for the door and glass for the windows.

The actual construction of the trading post probably did not take place until summer 1901. The first step was to lay out and level a site that measured forty feet in length and fifteen feet in width. At the center of the front wall, facing east, would be a door about six and a half feet high and three feet wide. There would be two windows on either side, each about two and a half feet wide and three feet high. Openings were not planned for the back wall or the two side walls.[27]

A rough stone foundation was laid along the perimeter. The walls were then built up with rectangular cut stones and chinked with a mortar made from the local mud that was high in lime content. Wooden lintels were positioned over the door and window openings. The roof beams, which were slightly slanted toward the back of the building, extended over the front elevation by several feet. Once the building was completed, the bare earth floor was tamped down and the inside walls were whitewashed. Since Dedman's trading post was quite narrow, the bullpen probably took up two-thirds of the area, with the trader's counter against one of the side walls. An interior wall would have set off the other third, which would function as a both a storage space and a modest

FIG. 12. Original Rough Rock Trading Post, 2022. Photo by Klara Kelley.

living area. Although the trading post was closed decades ago, Dedman's solid masonry has withstood the ravages of time (fig. 12).

During the summer of 1902, Dedman began transforming the quarry that had been hollowed out from the sandstone bluff behind the trading post into a dugout/residence. First, he enlarged the opening so that it measured fifteen feet in width and eight feet in height. He excavated additional sandstone from the interior so that the resulting "cave" was fifteen feet deep. The eight-foot ceiling at the entrance gradually sloped down until the back wall was only three and a half feet high. The newly quarried stone, which had been piled outside the entrance, was then shaped into rectangular blocks. Using these sandstone blocks, he built two five-foot-wide side walls extending out from the cave opening and a front facade with a door and one window facing east (like the trading post). He also added a window on the short southern wall. The roof of the cut-stone extension was supported by log beams that extended several feet over the facade, forming a protected entryway. Southwest historian Michael Anderson, who surveyed the site in 2000, observed, "The fact that the interior was once whitewashed, the existence of windows, and the aged roof beams suggest that it may have been the residence of one of the earlier traders."[28]

Once Dedman had moved to his newly constructed trading post in Rough Rock, he must have felt his situation was stable enough for him to think about establishing a family. According to the Navajo Census Archives at St. Michaels, we know that his first wife was a young woman named Susie of the Bit'ahnii (Within His Cover) clan.[29] According to Navajo tradition, Dedman would have first approached her father with the offer of a "dowry." The actual ceremony would have taken place just before sundown at the bride's home. Her father would have brought a wedding vase of water and a gourd dipper. Behind him, the bride would have carried a wedding basket of corn mush, with its opening aligned with the hogan door, facing east. First, the bride would have ladled water over the groom's hands, and then he would similarly have cleansed his bride's hands. Second, the bride's father would have blessed the cornmeal mush with a ritual sprinkling of corn pollen. Finally, as a bonding ceremony, the groom and bride would have taken turns eating the mush, scooping it out with their fingers.[30]

Almost nothing is known about Clitso Dedman's Rough Rock family. According to Father Marcellus's census cards, a son, Julius Dedman, was born in 1903.[31] With his father's encouragement, Julius would attend the Navajo boarding school in Rehoboth, six miles east of Gallup, which had been founded by missionaries from the Christian Reformed Church, a Dutch Protestant denomination. He would subsequently continue his education at the Sherman Indian School in Riverside, California.

According to Father Marcellus, Clitso Dedman soon married a second time. The new wife is identified only as Hastiin Ałts'sigi Bitsi' (Squinty's daughter) of the Kinyaa'áanii (Towering House) clan. There is no mention of any children and the marriage may not have lasted long.

In Navajo culture of the time, polygamy was both an accepted and expected practice. For instance, Navajo leader Chee Dodge had eight wives and six children. While a man might have several wives simultaneously, a woman would have only one husband at a time. In the matrilocal society of the time, the couple would generally reside on the wife's property. When she wished to divorce, she would let her husband know by placing his belongings, such as his blanket and saddle, outside the door of the hogan. He had no recourse but to pick up his things and move elsewhere.

Clitso Dedman, like most Indian traders of the period, would have trained one or more local Navajo managers to take care of trading post business during his necessary trips to Ganado to settle accounts with Hubbell and obtain fresh supplies for the store. Such absences could easily stretch out from one to two weeks, and, in bad weather, the travel time could be much longer. One serious obstacle on his route was the steep hill in Nazlini, about twenty miles north of Ganado. In rainy weather, the muddy slope would become impassable, often forcing freighters to spend one or more nights in that community while waiting for the wagon trail to dry out.

It was perhaps in 1905, during such a forced stopover in Nazlini, that Clitso Dedman met Hadzizbaa, who would become his third wife.[32] Hadzizbaa, who went by the nickname "Sonnie" (from the Navajo *dzání*, meaning "young woman"), was born around 1893 into the Tsi'naajinii (Black Streak Wood People) clan and for the Tsénjíkini (Cliff Dwellers) clan.[33] The fact that the young bride was only thirteen was not unusual. Most young Navajo girls at the time were married not long after their *Kinaaldá* or coming-of-age (first menstruation) ceremony. It was also quite common that men would be ten to twenty years older than their wives.

Hadzizbaa apparently insisted that their wedding be performed by one of the Franciscan Friars from St. Michaels and wanted their children to be raised Catholic. At the time, missionary priests were permitted to perform a religious wedding only after the couple could show them an official marriage license issued by the Navajo Agency in Fort Defiance.[34] Clitso Dedman and Hadzizbaa obtained their license on June 10, 1906, and their formal wedding most likely took place at St. Michaels a few days later.[35] At the time, Hadzizbaa was already pregnant with their first child, Jimmy Dedman, who was born on June 28 and baptized soon thereafter. The young boy unfortunately was crippled and died before reaching age nine.[36]

Until new information comes to light, it is impossible to determine how long Dedman continued to trade at Rough Rock. Around 1907, he acquired part ownership of a trading post in Salt Springs, twenty miles west of Chinle and over fifty miles from Rough Rock, a distance representing two days' travel by horse-drawn wagon. Then, in 1908, he opened his own trading post in Nazlini, twenty miles south of Chinle, again almost fifty miles from Rough Rock.

Dedman, with his business acumen, would not simply have abandoned an enterprise that he had carefully built up over ten years. Moreover, he had a wife and young son in Rough Rock. Perhaps he delegated the day-to-day running of the Rough Rock trading post to a local Navajo manager returning, as needed, to review accounts. Since Dedman evidently maintained close business contacts with Hubbell, it would not have been too difficult for him to schedule regular freighting runs between Rough Rock and Ganado.

When Dedman finally did quit the Rough Rock trading post, he would have removed all of his merchandise and furnishings. The next trader, whose identity we do not know, installed his store in the beautiful stone buildings that Dedman had constructed with such care. By 1915 and perhaps as early as 1913, the post was under the management of William Staggs, a former industrial arts teacher at the Tuba City Boarding School. Henceforth, the local Navajos would refer to the Rough Rock trading post as "Staggs' Store."[37]

Salt Springs Trading Post

In 1907, or perhaps earlier, Clitso Dedman joined with a Navajo partner, identified only by his very common Navajo nickname "Yashe" (*yázhí*, meaning "little" or "short"), to open a small trading post twenty miles west of Chinle in the remote Tselani/Cottonwood area. According to Clitso Dedman's daughter Mary Dodge, the store was situated about three miles south of what would be the larger Cottonwood Trading Post.[38] Since both Dedman and Yashe were Navajo, and therefore did not need trading licenses, there is no government record of precisely when their store was created. The actual building, probably constructed of wood rather than stone masonry, no longer exists.

It was most likely the enterprising young Dedman who convinced Yashe that they should move beyond doing business only with Hubbell. By selling blankets directly to off-reservation retailers, the trading post would be able to increase its prices and profits. With this aim in mind, Dedman had official invoice forms printed with the heading: "C. Dedman & Yashe, Navajo Tribe. Indian Traders. Wholesale Dealers in Navajo Blankets" (see fig. 15). In smaller print, the form indicated that the trading post also dealt in wool, pelts, and goat skins. The post office was given as Chin Lee (the old spelling of Chinle), and the location of the trading post as Salt Springs (today known as Salina). Merchandise would be shipped from the Gallup railroad station.

In setting up his new trading post, Dedman would occasionally need to travel to Gallup to pick up his new invoice forms and to purchase additional trade tokens engraved with his name. Since the trip by wagon from Salt Springs via the poor reservation trails would take two days, even under favorable weather conditions, he would likely stop each way overnight at St. Michaels. There he made the acquaintance of Brother Simeon Schwemberger, who, when he was not occupied with cooking for his Franciscan brothers and mission workers, was learning photography and taking pictures of Navajo life.[39] On one such occasion, Dedman agreed to pose for his portrait, first wearing glasses and then without (figs. 13 and 14). He was dressed in his customary Anglo attire with a white shirt and striped tie. Since shirt sleeves at that time were loose and had no buttons, Dedman wore sleeve garters to pull them up so as to make it easier to work. Overalls provided pockets and were both comfortable and convenient.

By 1910, Dedman had bought out his early partner Yashe and substantially expanded his trading business to include not only blankets but also silver jewelry and other handcrafted items. Always in search of new clients, he would buy magazines and newspapers in Gallup, scouring them for advertisements of retailers or wholesalers whom he might attract as potential customers. One ad that captured his attention featured Candelario's Curio Store in Santa Fe.

Jesus Sito Candelario (1864–1938), a successful Santa Fe pawnbroker, had entered the curio business in 1901, in partnership with his friend Jake Gold.[40] Two years later, the two separated amicably and Candelario established his own shop, the Curio Store, which he subsequently renamed The Original Old Curio Store. Over the next decade, Candelario developed an extensive wholesale network in addition to his retail store. He was constantly on the lookout for new markets as well as new suppliers. At the same time, he was also a very cautious businessman, checking out the quality of products before placing larger orders, and hiring R. G. Dun & Company of New York to run credit checks on clients before shipping merchandise on consignment.[41]

In the spring of 1910, Dedman wrote Candelario, inquiring if he might be in the market for new Navajo material (see fig. 15, p. 64). Candelario responded

FIG. 13. Clitso Dedman with glasses, ca. 1907. Photo by Simeon Schwemberger. Courtesy Arizona State University Library, SPC 331.50.85.3.

FIG. 14. Clitso Dedman without glasses, ca. 1907. Photo by Simeon Schwemberger. Courtesy Arizona State University Library, SPC 331.50.101.

immediately asking Dedman to send him a descriptive price list. In his letter of April 16 (fig. 15), Dedman offered Candelario the following items:[42]

Silver concha for ladies' belt buckles, per ounce . . . .$1.10 to $1.50

Silver bracelets without setting, per ounce . . . .$1.10 to $1.50

Silver bracelets with matrix turquois according to
   color and size of stones. . . . . $2.00 to $9.50

Silver finger rings with turquoise . . . . $1.25 to $5.00

Blankets according to the weaves and patterns and
   color, per pound. . . . . $0.75 to $2.50

Old style blankets, per pound . . . . $1.25 to $2.50

Buckskin rope, braided lariat about 30 feet long. . . . . . . $4.00 to $5.00

Dedman indicated that his terms were "all cash" and invited Candelario to send him a "trial order."

Subsequent correspondence indicates that Dedman did indeed gain Candelario as a client. In fact, in fall 1913, Dedman drove to Santa Fe, most probably to deliver merchandise.[43]

Dedman maintained his Salt Springs Trading Post until spring 1915. It seems likely that already in 1913, he had begun to suffer from the competition of Anglo traders George and Mary Jeanette Kennedy, who had arrived that spring with "wagonloads of building materials" to construct a much larger trading post.[44] Finding it increasingly difficult to manage two trading stores that lay twenty-five miles apart on very rough roads, he began limiting operations at the Salt Springs store and freighted most of his merchandise to Nazlini. In the 1915 Navajo census conducted by Indian Agent Peter Paquette, Clitso Dedman is listed as owning only the Nazlini store.[45]

Nazlini Trading Post

The community of Nazlini, as its name (Flows in Crescent Shape) indicates, is located at a bend in Nazlini Creek. In 1900, the valley, with its broad pastures, was home to many clusters of Navajo families. It was on a bluff at Wood Springs, about eight miles south of Nazlini on land belonging to the maternal family of his wife, Hadzizbaa, that Clitso Dedman, in 1908, decided to open a small store.[46] Obtaining supplies on credit from Hubbell in Ganado was a rather simple matter. The big problem he faced, however, was how to bring

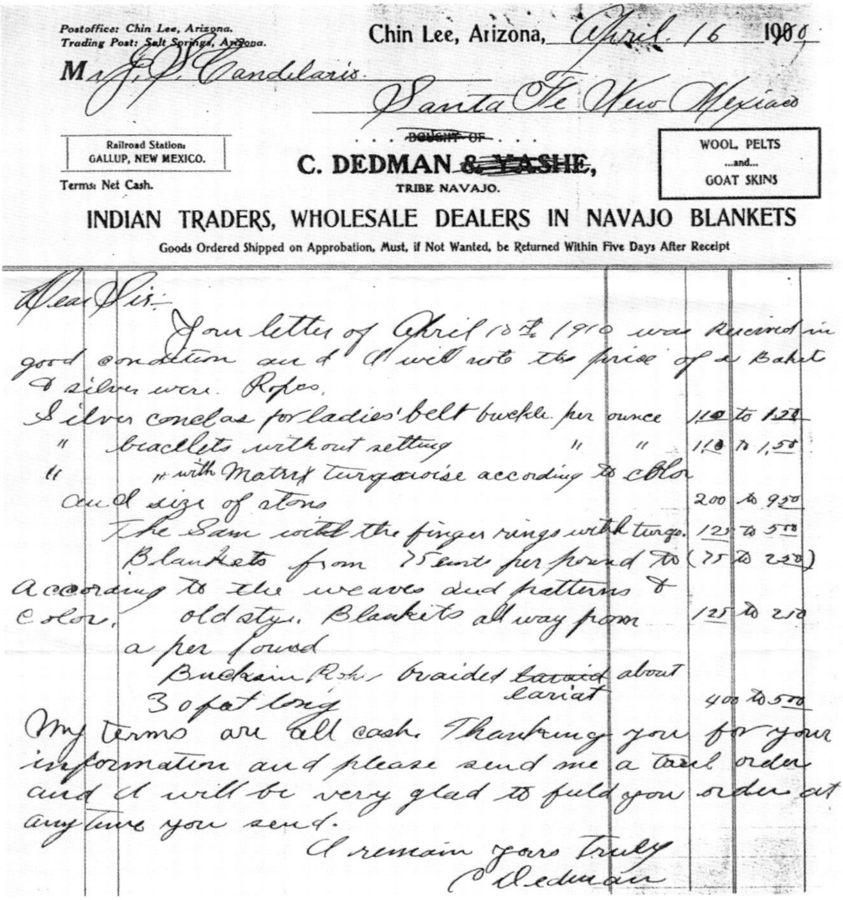

Postoffice: Chin Lee, Arizona.
Trading Post: Salt Springs, Arizona.

Chin Lee, Arizona, April 16 1910

Mr J. S. Candelaris
Santa Fe New Mexico

Railroad Station: GALLUP, NEW MEXICO.
Terms: Net Cash.

~~BOUGHT OF~~
C. DEDMAN ~~& YASHE~~,
TRIBE NAVAJO.

WOOL, PELTS ...and... GOAT SKINS

INDIAN TRADERS, WHOLESALE DEALERS IN NAVAJO BLANKETS

Goods Ordered Shipped on Approbation, Must, if Not Wanted, be Returned Within Five Days After Receipt

Dear Sir:
Your letter of April 10th 1910 was Received in good condition and I will note the prise of a Basket & silver ware. Ropes,
Silver conchas for ladies' belt buckle per ounce 1.10 to 1.25
" bracelets without setting " " 1.10 to 1.50
" " with Matrix turquoise according to color and size of stone 200 to 950
The Same with the finger rings with turqo. 125 to 500
Blankets from 75 cents per pound to (75 to 250) according to the weaves and patterns & color. old style Blankets all way from 125 to 250 a per pound
Buckskin Ropes braided ~~lariat~~ lariat about 30 feet long 400 to 500
My terms are all cash. Thanking you for your information and please send me a trail order and I will be very glad to fill your order at any time you send.
I remain yours truly
C Dedman

FIG. 15. Clitso Dedman letter to J. S. Candelario, April 1910. Courtesy Fray Angélico Chávez History Library, New Mexico History Museum, Candelario Collection, Box 12, Folder 2.

those supplies from the Nazlini-Ganado road up the steep horse trail to his new store. Clearly a broader graded access way was required.

Here again, Dedman was up to the challenge. First, he laid out a more gradual, curving route about a mile and a half in length. Then, drawing on his knowledge of black powder coal-mining explosives, he "made his own dynamite" with which to break up any large obstructions.[47] Local Navajos were hired to help with the actual construction. Taking advantage of his familiarity with the Bureau of Indian Affairs (and his command of English), Dedman wrote the commissioner in Washington and obtained reimbursement for the building of his road, since it was on reservation land.[48]

In 1909, the Nazlini headmen invited Dedman to establish a larger, more central trading post in the valley, just off the wagon trail leading north to Chinle.[49] His initial Nazlini Trading Post, which measured about fifteen feet by twenty-five feet, was built of logs from the nearby forests. Unlike Rough Rock, the Nazlini valley had no easily accessible sandstone quarries.

Dedman soon decided to enlarge the trading post building with a two-room adobe extension to house his growing family: Billy (b. 1910), Lily (b. 1912), and Miller (b. 1914). Whereas the Navajos in the region were still living in hogans, Clitso Dedman and his family enjoyed the lifestyle of successful Anglo traders. Their house was furnished with tables and chairs, beds, and a washstand. On the walls were oil paintings. In the kitchen were a stove, cooking utensils, and dishes. Clitso had a clock on his desk and Hadzizbaa had a treadle sewing machine. In the evenings, the family would listen to records on their new phonograph.[50]

Clitso Dedman was probably the first Navajo to own a typewriter. Very few Navajos at the time were able to hold a simple conversation in English, and even fewer knew how to read and write. The fact that Dedman could type his own business letters, as evidenced in his regular correspondence with Hubbell, was quite remarkable. The little typos, though immediately noticeable to a reader today, were not considered a problem in the early twentieth century where most Americans had only a grade-school education and were quite creative with spelling when it came to writing letters.

Dedman also designed his own stationery (fig. 16) with images of his trading post in Nazlini (then spelled Nozlini), a Navajo blanket, and a weaving on a loom featuring a large swastika.[51] It should be noted that in the early decades of the twentieth century, Americans across the country considered the swastika to be a symbol of good luck. Swastikas could be found on highway signs, logos, tiles, and even building facades. Native American artists were encouraged by traders to incorporate swastikas in their pottery, beadwork, silver, and weavings. Dedman would have seen the swastika rug paintings that E. A. Burbank had made for J. L. Hubbell and he would have had his own weavers include the design in their blankets. It was only in the late 1930s with the rise of Nazi Germany that the swastika acquired an extremely negative connotation.[52]

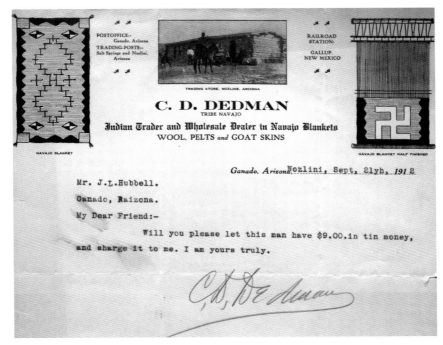

FIG. 16. Clitso Dedman letter to J. L. Hubbell, September 21, 1912. Courtesy University of Arizona Libraries, Special Collections, Hubbell Archives, AZ375, Box 23.

Dedman gradually expanded his trading post operations, adding a corral for livestock. By 1911, he had brought his brother Sam into the business operations, often sending him to Hubbell's in Ganado to deliver cattle, pick up merchandise, or make payments. Occasionally, he would also delegate his sister Zani Dine or his mother, Clitso Bama.[53]

Since trading posts were easily the target of robberies, traders barred their windows and generally had a shotgun handy in their store. Dedman was no exception.[54] Moreover, in 1910, he also ordered from J. L. Hubbell "a revolver, pearl stock, plain not fancy, and a good pistol holster and belt and box of Colt's cartridges."[55] These precautions seem to have sufficed, for we have no record of any attempted theft at any of his stores.

Clitso Dedman promoted his trading post business by advertising in the first three annual issues of the magazine *Franciscan Missions of the Southwest*, which began publication at St. Michaels in 1913. In his 1914 ad (fig. 17), he

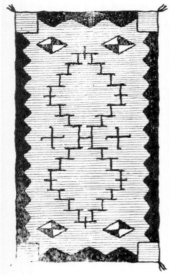
FIG. 17. Clitso Dedman ad, *Franciscan Missions of the Southwest*, vol. 2, 1914.

announced: "I am in a position to fill large and small orders at all times. Term: Cash Net. Prices range from 85 cents to $1.40 per pound and weights from six to twenty pounds.[56] Get my Prices and compare with others. All my Blankets are genuine Hand Made."

One urban retailer who responded to Dedman's advertisements was the Graves Indian Shop located in downtown Phoenix, Arizona. In a publicity article that appeared in the *Arizona Republic*, Mr. Graves pictured a recently acquired weaving that had been inspired by the wording on an Arbuckle Coffee crate. The accompanying text explained: "I have had so many questions asked me about the 'Roasted Coffee' blanket that I want to publish a few more facts about it. . . . Someone asked about Clitso Dedman, from whom I bought the blanket. Clitso is a well-known Navajo, and does a nice little business in Indian wares. . . . Clitso gets the best blankets from a number of good weavers, and also picks up some exceptionally pieces of silver, and when Mr. Graves is on the reservation he takes his pick from Clitso's selected stock."[57]

Clitso Dedman was definitely broadening his clientele of satisfied customers and gaining wider recognition as a trader. In spring 1913, for example, he sent two packages of blankets to a customer in Iowa City.[58] Also directly benefiting from his business success were the weavers and silversmiths in his area who, with his encouragement, were increasing their production of quality rugs and jewelry. The future of Dedman's Nazlini Trading Post was looking bright. By spring 1915, however, it would be in jeopardy.

5

From Wagon to Automobile

In the nineteenth century, all Navajo travel was by horseback or on foot. There were some wagons on the reservation during that period, but these were owned by Anglo traders, though they often were driven by Navajos or Mexicans. It was not until 1900 that Navajo families began acquiring wagons for their own transportation. Clitso Dedman, when he started trading at Rough Rock in 1897, was probably one of the only Navajos in the region to own a wagon and team of horses. Ever in the forefront of innovation and efficiency, he would be one of the first Navajos to purchase and drive an automobile.

Clitso Dedman and His Ford Model T

In his 1915 Navajo census, Superintendent Peter Paquette reported that only five Navajos in his Fort Defiance jurisdiction owned automobiles: Chee Dodge (a Dodge), and Tom Damon, Willie Damon, Hosteen Yazza, and Clitso Dedman (Fords).[1] The first two owners were sons of Navajo mothers and Anglo fathers and had been raised bilingually and biculturally. The only two traditional

Navajos were Clitso Dedman and Hosteen Yazza. The latter might well be the same person as the Hosteen Yashe who had been co-owner with Dedman of the Salt Springs Trading Post, but this remains to be verified.[2]

Dedman's Ford was probably a Model T Touring Car, with a back seat for transporting people or merchandise. His ownership of a car at that time is remarkable for several reasons. First of all, it meant that Dedman was earning enough money as a trader to allow him even to purchase an automobile. In 1910, the Model T Touring Car was priced at $900.[3] By late 1912, when Dedman bought his car from Gallup dealer C. C. Manning, the price had dropped to $690. This still represented a substantial cash outlay. As a result of his schooling and early work experience, Dedman had learned about American money and the importance of saving for larger purchases. With the assistance of J. L. Hubbell's son Roman, he was able to make the required down payment and obtain credit for the remainder. That winter, with trading post business moving slowly, Dedman was unable to make his monthly payments. As he explained in a letter to Roman on February 8, 1913: "I got a letter from C. C. Manning from Gallup, saying that he wants the car that I bought from you. He wants me to return it to him on my account I owe. I told him or wrote him saying that if he wants the car he can buy it from you because I owe you some on it."[4]

As an alternative, Dedman added that he had let Manning know that if the latter were to drive to Nazlini, Dedman could make the equivalent payment in wool or blankets. Two weeks later, the situation was apparently resolved. In a follow-up letter to Roman Hubbell on February 27, Dedman explained: "Mr. C. C. Manning said that he can let my account stand and [I can] pay him when I get the money, and did not want the car. I saw him at Fort Defiance. . . . The auto works fine, have no trouble yet."[5]

Second, Dedman would have had to learn how to drive, mastering the Model T's complex system of three foot pedals (gear shift, reverse, and brake) plus two levers on the steering wheel (throttle and "spark advance" for the ignition). Father Berard Haile recounts how, in 1911, he accidentally caused the Franciscans' new car (a gift from Hubbell) to overturn in a ditch, because his first reaction on seeing an impediment in the road ahead was to shout "Whoa" rather than apply the foot brake.[6]

Third, there were no paved highways. The National Old Trails Road, which would later be realigned as Route 66, did have a graded gravel surface. The

FIG. 18. *Navajo Men Gathered around Car*. Photo by Leo Crane. Courtesy Northern Arizona University, Cline Library, Special Collections and Archives, NAU.PH.658.674.

"roads" on the Navajo Reservation, however, were rutted dirt trails used by horse-drawn wagons (fig. 18). If a car got stuck in the sand or in a ditch, it would require a team of horses to pull it out. In 1916, George Kennedy, who had left Salt Springs and was running the former Sam Day Trading Post in Chinle, also bought a Model T. In reflecting on driving conditions at that time, his wife, Mary Kennedy, recalled: "Since the roads were still bad, it was necessary to always remember to take along a jack, hammer, spade, and plenty of baling wire in case of a broken spring. It was several years before I knew that one could go to Gallup and back without car trouble of some kind."[7]

Weather was also a problem. When it rained, the washes would flood, making certain stretches of road impassible, often for days at a time. In 1912, the Hubbells had contracted to carry U.S. mail by automobile from Ganado to Keams Canyon and also to St. Michaels. During a severe winter storm in February 1913, with Lorenzo at the wheel, the Hubbell car stripped a gear and the mail delivery was delayed by several days. When the officials at the postal service complained that J. L. Hubbell was not delivering mail on schedule, as had been contracted, he wrote, "The conditions of the roads . . . are not well understood in your office or the proposition made that we run automobiles at a specified time would be utterly impossible. For you cannot tell when a road would be impassable."[8]

Driving conditions were still just as bad in the 1940s when Bill and Sallie Wagner Lippincott were running their trading post at Wide Ruins, south of Ganado. In her memoirs, Sallie devotes an entire chapter to driving mishaps, writing that "the roads were often impassable, due to mud in the fall, snow in the winter, and drifted sand in the spring."[9]

Fourth, and most importantly, driving a car meant being your own mechanic when a part broke or when a tire popped. Obviously, Dedman's training in the railroad machine shop was a definite asset when it came to managing the inevitable problems. He would make the repairs himself, asking Hubbell to order the needed parts, such as wheel chains, rear axle bushings, a new headlight, a storage battery, cylinder head bolts, gaskets, a new wheel and hub cap, or an ignition master vibrator.[10] In December 1913, Dedman must have had a rather severe mishap with his car, since he purchased from Hubbell two front tires, a radiator, and a clutch for a total of $85.[11]

It is interesting to note that in 1912, according to Gertrude Golden, then principal of the Fort Defiance School, wealthy Navajo leader Chee Dodge insisted that he "had no use for automobiles." She went on to explain: "He said he would never be bothered with one of the contraptions, for when you started out in one, you never knew whether you would get there or not. He took keen delight in riding his horse alongside our auto, racing with us and usually being able to keep up on the rough mountain roads. It was a great triumph when he passed us by with a proud wave of the hand, leaving our stalled car and the driver to 'get out and under.'"[12] However, by 1915, Chee Dodge, too, had purchased his first car. He never drove it himself, though, and relied totally on the navigation and mechanical skills of his hired chauffeur.[13]

Last, for Dedman, there was the challenge of obtaining fuel. The Model T, according to the Ford Company, could travel thirteen to twenty-one miles per gallon. The fuel tank, which held ten gallons, was mounted to the frame under the driver's seat and relied on gravity to fuel the carburetor since there was no fuel pump. This meant that if the fuel level fell below two or three gallons, the car could not climb a steep hill—and there were definitely steep hills around

Nazlini. Gasoline would have been available in Gallup, but that town was seventy miles away. Fortunately, by 1911, Hubbell had built a fuel storage tank at his trading post in Ganado. Dedman could thus drive to Ganado, which was only twenty miles distant, rather than to Gallup, to fill up his car. In fact, he probably arranged with Hubbell to have freighters bring gasoline in large drums to his Nazlini trading post. He would also buy Polarine motor oil from Hubbell.[14]

In 1916, George Kennedy arranged to have fuel available in his trading post in Chinle, not only for his own car but also for the cars of archaeologists and tourists visiting Canyon de Chelly. Hubbell probably also sold fuel at his "Big House" in Chinle, which he had established as both a trading post and a hotel. It would not be until 1936 that Cozy McSparron would install gas pumps in Chinle at his Thunderbird Ranch.[15]

With his new Model T, Dedman enjoyed much greater mobility and was frequently on the road. Not only did his new mode of transportation make it much easier for him to get back and forth between his trading posts in Nazlini and Salt Springs, but it also significantly reduced his travel time to other places, such as Chinle, Ganado, St. Michaels, Fort Defiance, and Gallup.

Guide and Chauffeur

Given his fluency in English and his outgoing personality, Clitso Dedman would occasionally be asked by J. L. Hubbell to drive Anglo visitors around the reservation. The Franciscan Fathers at St. Michaels also would avail themselves of Dedman's services. Before he acquired his first car, Dedman would drive guests to their destinations by horse-drawn wagon. After 1912, he could chauffeur clients much more rapidly and more comfortably in his Ford Model T Touring Car.

Clitso Dedman and Frederick Melville DuMond

Frederick Melville DuMond (1867–1927) was born in Rochester, New York.[16] As a young man, he left for Paris to study painting and established himself in France as a painter of portraits and large historical scenes. In 1909, he moved back to the United States, establishing a studio in New York City. His first view of the Southwest came that summer, as he brought his nine-year-old daughter Camille to live with his parents who had moved to Monrovia, California. According to a family anecdote, he vowed, "Soon I will come back to paint this."

FIG. 19. Spider Rock Overlook, Canyon de Chelly. Photo by Vit Ducken. Courtesy Pixabay.

Clitso Dedman met DuMond in July 1910, during the latter's two-week stay in Ganado as part of his first "Wild West discovery" trip. DuMond had been intrigued with the cliff dwellings that he had visited at Mesa Verde and Puye (near Espanola, New Mexico) and was eager to explore the ancient sites in Canyon de Chelly. He arrived by train in Gallup, and from there traveled by stagecoach to Ganado. Trading post owner J. L. Hubbell generously outfitted him for a several-day excursion to Chinle and offered the services of Jay Alkire, a clerk at his Oraibi Trading Post.

Upon returning to Ganado from his visit to the Canyon de Chelly cliff dwellings, DuMond was eager to make a second trip to the area in order to view and sketch from above the impressive sandstone spires he had glimpsed from the canyon riverbed. Hubbell arranged that Dedman would drive him by wagon, first to Nazlini Canyon and then across the mesas to an overlook on the southern rim of Canyon de Chelly where DuMond would be able to take photographs, paint sample oil sketches, and make descriptive notes. Once back in his New York studio, DuMond painted the actual oil canvases. Three of the landscapes that grew out of his Arizona visit became part of the March

1912 exhibit of his Southwest paintings at the American Museum of Natural History in New York.[17]

This trip to Canyon de Chelly with Clitso Dedman also provided DuMond with fodder for a dramatic story that he told his daughter Camille and which was recounted sixty years later by her friend Eleanor Bradley:

> There were many times during DuMond's trip when living conditions were not easy, and at least twice DuMond came near to losing his life.
>
> Once when his Indian guide had gone back to the trading post for supplies, DuMond was overcome by food poisoning while painting on the edge of a canyon. Losing consciousness, he fell over the edge. A large cactus plant kept him from going down into the canyon, a fall that, no doubt, would have killed him. Gaining consciousness from time to time, he sent up prayers to heaven as he lay in the hot sun during the day and in the cold at night. His condition was poor when the guide found him four or five days later.[18]

Well aware of DuMond's propensity for grandiose exaggeration in recounting his Southwest exploits, biographer and great-grandson Richard Panofsky believes that what most probably happened is the following: Clitso Dedman (the "Indian guide") had left DuMond alone one morning to paint at the Spider Rock Overlook (fig. 19) and had gone by wagon to Chinle for supplies. When he returned in the evening, the easel was standing there, but the artist was nowhere to be seen. Dedman discovered DuMond dangling several feet below the edge of the canyon wedged in a bush (not a cactus!) and was able to bring him back up to the rim. What is accurate in the account is that Dedman definitely did save DuMond's life.

In appreciation, DuMond, once back in his studio, painted a portrait of Clitso Dedman astride his horse in front of the Nazlini Trading Post (fig. 20). The dedication in the lower left corner reads: "To my good and patient friend, Clitzo / F. Melville DuMond–1911."[19] DuMond based his painting on a photograph that he had taken with his "Kodak" at the end of his Canyon de Chelly excursion. In his letter dated March 11, 1911, to J. L. Hubbell announcing a shipment of several paintings, including the one for Clitso Dedman, he wrote, "The photo [is] not very clear. I could get no more in the way of portrait. Still it looks like him."[20]

FIG. 20. Frederick Melville DuMond, Clitso Dedman in Nazlini, 1911. Courtesy Alan Carson. Photo by author.

Hubbell apparently gave DuMond's photograph of the Nazlini Trading Post to Dedman, who subsequently reproduced it on his trading post stationery (fig. 21).

The March 1911 shipment to J. L. Hubbell also contained a painting for Jay Alkire, who had taken DuMond to see the Canyon de Chelly cliff dwellings. Richard Panofsky is of the opinion that these paintings were DuMond's way of reimbursing his Ganado guides for their services, since at the time of his visit he had been unable to pay them in cash.

Clitso Dedman and Theodore Roosevelt

In late summer 1913, Clitso Dedman's chauffeuring services were again requested by J. L. Hubbell, this time to drive him by automobile to Keams Canyon to pick up an important guest, former president Theodore Roosevelt. Colonel Roosevelt, as he was known at the time, had just spent four weeks exploring northern Arizona with his two teenage sons, Quentin and Archibald, and their cousin, Harvard student Nicholas Roosevelt.[21] On horseback, the four had visited the Grand Canyon and northern Navajoland and were on their way to the Hopi mesas by wagon from Kayenta to witness the annual Snake Dance at Walpi.[22]

Already by 1912, the Hopi Snake Dance had been so frequently written up

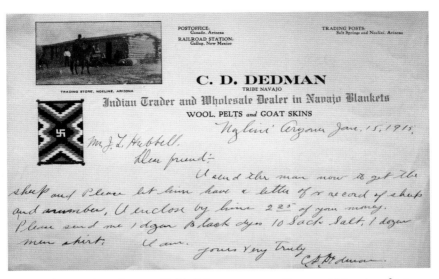

Noeline Arizona June. 15, 1915,

Mr. J. L. Hubbell.

Dear friend:—

I send the man now to get the sheep and Please let him have a letter of r record of sheep and number, I enclose by him 2 25 of your money. Please send me 1 dozen Black dye 10 Sack Salt, 1 dozen men shirt; I am. yours Very truly C. D. Dedman.

FIG. 21. Clitso Dedman letter to Hubbell, January 15, 1915. Courtesy University of Arizona Libraries, Special Collections, Hubbell Archives, AZ375, Box 23.

in the press that it had become a major tourist attraction and was even actively promoted by the Santa Fe Railroad.[23] Probably realizing that Roosevelt would be attending the 1913 ceremony, an enterprising filmmaker arranged to record the event, inserting a short cameo sequence of the former president seated next to music ethnologist Natalie Curtis.[24] Word of Theodore Roosevelt's visit must have received wide publicity in the Southwest. In an advertisement in the *Arizona Republic* that December, Mr. Graves of the Graves Indian Shop confirmed the event: "Clitso . . . is the only Navajo that owns and drives an automobile, which is a Ford, by the way. Clitso had the honor last September of having Col. Roosevelt for a passenger, conveying the Big Chief and his two sons and Senator Hubbell from Keams Canyon to Ganado, the night of the Hopi snake dance."[25]

In describing his visit to the Hopi Snake Dance in his memoirs, Roosevelt wrote admiringly of his chauffeur:

> No white visitor to Walpi was quite as interesting as an Indian visitor, a Navajo who was the owner and chauffeur of the motor in which Mr. Hubbell had driven to Walpi. He was an excellent example of the Indian

who ought to be given the chance to go to a non-reservation school. . . .
He is now a prosperous merchant [on the reservation], running two
stores; and he purchased his automobile as a matter of convenience and
of economy in time, so as to get quickly from one store to the other, as
they are far apart.[26]

Clitso Dedman and St. Michaels Mission

St. Michaels Mission, located six miles south of Fort Defiance, was established
in 1898 on land purchased by Mother Katharine Drexel (now Saint Katharine
Drexel) of the moneyed Philadelphia family, and staffed by Franciscans from
the Cincinnati Province in Ohio. Unlike most other religious groups working
to convert Native Americans to Christianity and teaching them English, the
Franciscans were committed to learning the Navajo language and understanding Navajo culture. Father Berard Haile developed his own Navajo spelling
system and would devote his life to documenting Navajo ceremonies.[27] Father
Anselm Weber, a superior of the Navajo Mission from 1900 to 1921, built a
school for Navajo children in 1902. It is quite likely that Clitso Dedman and
Hadzizbaa were married in the St. Michaels chapel in 1906. What is certain
is that they later enrolled their children at the St. Michaels Indian School.

Once Dedman had acquired his Model T, he regularly offered his services
to the St. Michaels community. Father Egbert Fischer, one of the Franciscan
missionaries, relates a revealing anecdote about Dedman's navigation skills.[28]
In June 1913, the priest was called to give the last rites to a dying woman whom
he had baptized the previous week. He rode his horse the ten miles from St.
Michaels to Fort Defiance, where he learned that the Navajo agent and the
doctor had already left by car for the woman's hogan thirty miles to the north,
near Crystal. Rather than his continuing by horseback, the doctor's wife suggested he ask Dedman, who happened to be in Fort Defiance, to drive him.
Dedman agreed, although he was unfamiliar with the Crystal area. He found
his way by following the agent's car tracks on the wagon trail. At one point, the
car's radiator ran dry, but Dedman managed to find a small brook and added
the needed water. As the two approached Crystal, a herd of sheep obscured
the agent's car tracks. Dedman, however, was able to scout on foot until he
found the correct narrow turnoff. The pair arrived at the hogan in time, to

FIG. 22. St. Michaels School, ca. 1904. Photo by Simeon Schwemberger. Courtesy National Park Service, Hubbell Trading Post National Historic Site. HUTR 5327.

the great surprise of the doctor who had requested the priest's presence but had not expected him to make it.

Father Anselm Weber, too, appreciated Clitso Dedman's driving skills. Weber was deeply committed to improving the conditions of the Navajos and would regularly petition the U.S. government to grant the people greater land rights and expand their reservation. When he learned in May 1920 that a delegation of ten U.S. congressmen was traveling to Gallup to visit the Navajo Reservation, he invited the Washington dignitaries to stop at his school. The group's crowded schedule began with a morning program followed by a banquet at Fort Defiance. Father Weber recorded the subsequent events as follows:

> I and Father Fridolin had accompanied [the Washington guests] from Gallup. After the banquet, they [were to drive] to Ganado and Keams Canyon, 85 miles, by way of St. Michaels. They had no time to visit our school, but I was determined that at least our own Congressman, Carl Hayden, should see our school. Consequently, I invited him to leave with

me in our car, immediately after the banquet, and drive ahead of the others. Our Buick was in good condition and I had the best chauffeur in the crowd, the Indian, Clitso Dedman—we flew. Carl Hayden had time to inspect our whole school before the others arrived. In the meantime I had marched our pupils in "dress parade" and our renowned school band in front of the school. As soon as the automobiles appeared, our band began to play patriotic airs with vim and vigor. Of course, all the Congressmen stopped. Thus I forced them to take notice of our school.[29]

Over the years, more and more Navajos began to acquire cars. By 1930, it is estimated that one in fifty families owned a vehicle. After World War II, as roads were improved, vehicle ownership increased dramatically. By the mid-1960s, almost all Navajo camps would have at least one vehicle, generally a pickup truck. The days of the horse-drawn wagon had come to an end.[30]

6

An Unanticipated Career Shift

The year 1915 began quietly. Navajo Superintendent Peter Paquette had, as instructed by the Bureau of Indian Affairs, just completed a census of his southeastern Navajo jurisdiction, which then included the districts of Fort Defiance, St. Michaels, Ganado, and Chinle.[1] (This area covered almost half of the total reservation land.) From April to September 1914, four "enumerators" had traveled throughout their respective districts recording every person's name, clan affiliation, age, and "address," plus any other relevant details. The final report listed 11,915 people as living in Paquette's jurisdiction, representing about 40 percent of the total Navajo population.

In the Paquette census, Clitso Dedman was assigned the number 562. He and his wife, Hadzizbaa, and their three children were given roll numbers 562–3111 to 562–3115. The entries for Clitso Dedman indicate that he lived in a house (not a hogan), that he had attended school, and that he owned 160 acres of land together with two sheep, seven goats, one cow, and ten horses. As mentioned earlier, he was also listed as one of five Navajos who owned an automobile. The Paquette report enumerated thirty-seven trading posts, of which only four were "run by Navajos." One of these was Clitso Dedman's store in Nazlini. Since the Nazlini Trading Post and its corrals would have been located on community property, the acres ascribed to Dedman probably referred to the land that his family had occupied for years near Chinle and which had been passed on to him by his mother. The report makes it evident that Dedman was one of the most prosperous Navajos in Paquette's jurisdiction.

Not mentioned in the census report was the fact that in summer 1914 Clitso Dedman had taken a new teenage wife, Ada (not her real name). In accordance with the matrilocal tradition of Navajo culture, Ada was living in her mother's camp at some distance from Nazlini. In fact, it was probably the young bride's mother who had arranged her daughter's traditional marriage with an older, well-established husband. Although multiple households were discouraged by the U.S. government, Navajo men at the time, as noted earlier, often had more than one wife, each living with her maternal relatives.

In fall 1914, Ada was eager to return to boarding school at Fort Defiance in order to complete her last year of study and earn her diploma. This decision was apparently encouraged by her mother and probably also by Dedman. Nobody could have imagined that within a year Dedman's career as a successful Indian trader would come to an abrupt end.

Tragedy at Fort Defiance

The Fort Defiance School in 1915 was very different from the one young Clitso had attended thirty years earlier. When Gertrude Golden, the new principal, had arrived in spring 1912, she immediately noted that the buildings were nearly all new and that the employees had their own club in a roomy, comfortable home (fig. 23). The pupils at the time numbered three hundred, almost a tenfold increase since 1884. Some things, however, had not changed very much. She wrote: "They were among the most likable and appreciative children I have ever taught. They were eager to learn, but their chief handicap was their ignorance of the English language. The Navajo nation was about the last to be given schools, and many [of the children] had never seen a town or ever heard of such a thing as English."[2]

Every June, there was a year-end "graduation" where pupils would perform

FIG. 23. Gertrude Golden at Fort Defiance School. Photo by Simeon Schwemberger. Courtesy Arizona State University Library, SPC 331.15.22.

for their parents before leaving for summer vacation. In 1915, this was to be a real graduation with official diplomas. Three girls and ten boys, seventeen and eighteen years of age, would be the first pupils in the history of the school to complete eighth grade, which was the highest grade in the reservation schools at that time. Also different that spring was the fact that the school would be closing in late April, rather than June, since the young Navajo man in charge of the commissary had too generously been giving away food to family and friends on the reservation. As a result, there was not enough food on hand to feed the students for the remainder of the academic year.[3]

Sadly, the oldest girl in the graduating class, Ada, would not be there to receive her diploma.[4] As the school year had progressed, she noticed that she was gaining weight, but managed to hide the fact under her loose-fitting school uniform (fig. 24). Had school officials realized that she was pregnant, Ada would quietly have been asked to leave the school. However, she was determined to receive her well-deserved recognition.

FIG. 24. Navajo schoolgirls at Fort Defiance. General Photograph Collections, Northern Arizona University. Cline Library, Special Collections and Archives, NAU.PH.2001.5.

On the morning of March 22, Ada looked very weak and pale as she was standing in line for breakfast. The school matron helped her back to bed and called the Fort Defiance physician, Dr. Wigglesworth, who immediately diagnosed the origin of the girl's distressed state.[5] Ada vigorously refuted his interpretation, but when the body of a dead newborn was discovered in the box at the foot of her bed, she tearfully confessed to the doctor what had happened. Late that night, sensing premature labor pains yet suffering in silence, she had locked herself in the girls' bathroom and given birth to a baby girl, whom she suffocated with a towel for fear it would cry out. Her three roommates knew what had happened but had kept quiet. According to the supplementary birth certificate, officially filed by Dr. Wigglesworth, "the child described herein was never named, as the mother murdered it soon after birth."[6]

The Fort Defiance School superintendent, Paul Picard, fearing that the tragic incident would be harmful to student morale and reflect badly on his administration, immediately sent Ada to the school hospital, allowing no visitors. Several days later, when Ada was able to travel, he quietly had her transferred to the larger off-reservation Phoenix Indian School for the remainder of the term.

Estelle Aubrey Brown, an administration officer of the Phoenix school, received the new student and gradually gained her confidence. Writing in her oft-scathing memoirs of the many years she had worked for the Bureau of Indian Affairs, Brown dramatically narrates the events of that fateful Fort Defiance morning, changing the student's name to "Lucy":

> When the physician lifted a startled face from his brief examination, he asked: "Where's the baby?"
>
> In company with the horrified matron he searched the room and the carton gave up its secret.
>
> "Lucy! You wicked, wicked girl! This must have begun on the reservation last summer. Why didn't you tell me?"
>
> Only the girl's dark, unfathomable eyes replied, in denial and dread. Her eyes reflected fear of what this matron had taught her.
>
> "Why didn't you pray to God to keep you from temptation as I have taught you to do? Why didn't you tell me? Now we shall have to send you home."
>
> Lucy muttered one word—"Married."

"Married! Who to?" Lucy did not answer. The physician intervened.

"Were you married at home, Lucy? By your own ceremony?"

"Yes, sir. Like my mother. She wanted it."

"But I've told you and told you that is not the right way, Lucy," said the matron. "You should have been married in church."

The physician again intervened. "That was all right, Lucy, being married your way. But it was very wrong to kill your baby. If you are married, why did you kill it?"

There was no answer.

"We shall have to send you home, and tell your parents. Will they punish you for killing your baby?"

"Yes, sir. Bad. But not like the matron."

"Lucy! I shouldn't have punished you. I should have prayed with you that God might forgive you."

The physician was insistent. "Tell me why you killed the baby, Lucy."

Lucy's eyes lifted to the matron. "So she wouldn't know. She say it is a sin, to marry so. Her God will burn me forever if He finds out. Now she will tattle to her God and He will burn me."[7]

At the Phoenix school, without friends and in shock and shame, Ada/Lucy failed to regain her health. Before the year was out, she died of tuberculosis.

Decades later, Gertrude Golden, the Fort Defiance School principal, under whose watch the tragic event had occurred, still was feeling pangs of guilt.

> The more I pondered her case, the more I began to blame myself. When the missionary padre could not come, as he usually did once a week to teach catechism and instruct the pupils of his denomination, I, as principle teacher, had to take over in instructing the girls.[8] I had been very, very emphatic in stressing the wickedness of doing anything that would bring illegitimate children into the world—children who would be without father, home or name and who would suffer the disgrace all through their lives.
>
> Poor Ada had taken my admonitions to heart and, paradoxically enough, what I had intended for good turned out to be evil. I felt that, had I not driven the point home so forcefully, she might have confided in someone who would have arranged to send her home where she at least would have been spared from committing the worst of crimes.[9]

Also suffering pangs of guilt would have been Clitso Dedman, the father of the child, whose name Dr. Wigglesworth obtained so that he could file the official birth and death certificates. Dedman probably had not been aware of the pregnancy, for Ada had kept her condition hidden from everyone, even her family. It must have come as a shocking revelation to Dedman, when Navajo Agent Peter Paquette requested that he come to Fort Defiance to answer questions about the violent death of his newborn daughter. (It is not known whether Dedman was able to visit his young wife in the hospital or whether she had already been transferred to Phoenix.)

Clitso Dedman was informed that the decision had been made to hush up the case and not to prosecute Ada for murder, in large part to protect the school matron who "had plainly neglected her duty, or she would have been alert to Ada's condition and at least saved her from the crime she committed."[10] It must have been a relief for Dedman to know that there would be no official investigation, and that he would not, therefore, be called upon as a public witness. Paquette, true to his word, made no mention of Ada's death in his annual report to the Bureau of Indian Affairs.

Nonetheless, the tragic event had devastating consequences for Dedman's career, for he immediately took measures, most probably at the insistence of Paquette, to shut down his Nazlini trading post, as well as his smaller Salt Springs store, and to leave the area. Trading post historian Klara Kelley speculates: "Paquette was in a position to make the tragedy public, and when Dedman's involvement became known in the communities where he lived and operated, he would have been humiliated and feuds would have arisen among the families involved."[11]

Immediately after his visit with Paquette in Fort Defiance, Dedman arranged with J. L. Hubbell that the latter would take over the two stores with all their merchandise and their Navajo accounts. The actual buildings, as noted earlier, could not be sold, since all trading posts on the reservation belonged to the Navajo people, and not to the traders who had erected them.

Clitso Dedman and his wife, Hadzizbaa, with their three young children, Billy (age five), Lily (age three), and Miller (age one), found themselves obliged, with very little notice, to move back to her mother's property, taking with them only their clothing and their livestock. Given the matrilocal nature of Navajo society at the time, this move back to Wood Springs was not surprising.

(The precipitous nature of their departure would explain why the painting of Clitso Dedman by Frederick Melville DuMond was left behind and ultimately came into the possession of Fred Carson, when he took over the trading post in the 1930s.)

Within three weeks, by April 15, 1915, Hubbell's managers had completed a full inventory and evaluation of Clitso Dedman's abandoned properties in both Nazlini and Salt Springs.[12] The total cash value came to $1,322. Hubbell probably returned many of Dedman's possessions, such as his typewriter, estimated as worth $50, and his wife's sewing machine, worth $25, as well as furniture and kitchen utensils.[13] After deducting the value of the remaining items, plus Dedman's outstanding debts from his two trading posts, Hubbell paid Dedman the balance in cash.

Failure in El Paso

Faced with the realization that he could no longer operate a trading post on the Navajo Reservation, Clitso Dedman decided to explore the possibility of opening an Indian curio shop in a more distant location. His one concern, apparently, was that Superintendent Paquette might not be pleased with his departure, but he decided to leave anyway.

In late April, Dedman traveled by train to El Paso, Texas, a city he had visited in 1902 with J. L. Hubbell, and where, in recent years, he had had dealings with the W. G. Walz Company, purveyors of Mexican art and curios. In 1915, the population of the city was rapidly expanding and had already reached 50,000. Sensing a business opportunity, Dedman wrote Hubbell on May 4:

Dear friend,

. . . I am thinking of renting a store here on the main street of El Paso and put in a stock of Navajo blankets, baskets, Moki [Hopi] pottery and silverware of Navajos. The rent will cost $146.00 a month; the store is 12 ft by 25, right across from the banks and hotels and moving picture shows. I think it is a very nice location for Navajo blankets. This place is now a tack shop and the man is going to leave or move to some other place. So if you think this will be all right, send me about $175.00 in cash and blankets and some other goods and tell me what Mr. Paquette says

FIG. 25. *First National Bank Building, El Paso, Texas.* Postcard, 1915.

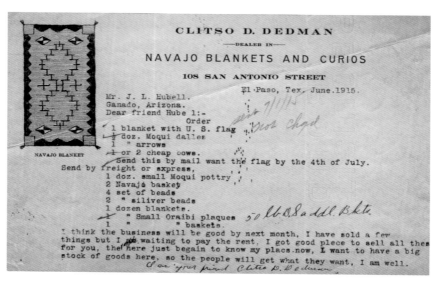

FIG. 26. Clitso Dedman letter to Hubbell, June 1915. Courtesy University of Arizona Libraries, Special Collections, Hubbell Archives, AZ375, box 23.

about me. If he don't care that I am down here, send me goods in my own name....

I am going to try this business for a while to see if I can do any good here. My opinion to this matter, I think I can do good business here, if not I will just send things back to you and go home to Nozlini but I'm hoping that I will do well here.

Let me hear as soon as you can, as I am your friend,
C. D. Dedman[14]

We do not have Hubbell's responses to Dedman's El Paso letters. More specifically, we do not know why the latter was worried about Agent Paquette's reaction to his move to Texas. In any event, Paquette apparently did not mind that Dedman was in El Paso, because Hubbell sent the requested merchandise. Two days later, on May 6, Dedman wrote a follow-up letter to Hubbell, describing the location of his proposed store and enclosing some postcards.

My dear friend,

... I will send you some post cards of the place. This place is right next to Wigwam Moving Picture shows and ... across from the First National Bank and the main street. Lot of people go past this place day and night. Therefore, I think I can make some money at this stand. I am going to try it anyway. If I cannot make money there, I will quit and do something else.

So in opening this place, I need a little of everything: Moki Indian dolls and baskets, ... lots of rings and bracelets, not too large. ...

When you send me the statement of the account and see if I got any money balance due from Nozlini store, I would like to have some ready cash, and have you send it to the Bank. I hope to hear from you soon.

I remain your friend.
C. D. Dedman[15]

By late May, Dedman had stationery printed for his El Paso store (fig. 26). In an undated letter of early June 1915, he wrote Hubbell requesting merchandise. He began on an optimistic note, writing, "I think the business will be good by next month."[16] On June 7, Dedman officially opened his new store. In a letter to Hubbell written on June 17, he indicated his need for extra cash to tide him over until sales would pick up.

My dear friend:

The blankets and the basket got here this morning. I opened up my store on Monday and sold only one Blanket at $16.00 your price to me. And I am putting on display the basket today and quite a few people are looking at it and some are coming and they said will buy them soon. I have bought a good location in town.

According to my figures, I owe you now $915.90 [for merchandise received].

When I bought this place I paid out all the money I had and need about $200.00 more. So I wanted to get a loan from this bank. So I told them that I will write to you and tell you to send me or them a letter stating of my good standing with you when I do my trading. Will you do this for me? This is the bank: Texas Bank and Trust Company.

I think I will go over right away and tell them to write to you too.

Let me hear as soon as you can, as I am your friend,
C. D. Dedman[17]

Four weeks later, however, Dedman was forced to admit to Hubbell that his El Paso experiment was not the success he had anticipated. The United States was slowly coming out of the 1913–1914 depression, and there was a widespread lull in the Indian art market. Summer 1915 proved to be a hard time to start a new business. On July 17, he wrote:

Dear Mr. Hubbell,

I am thinking of going home again on the 20 or 22 of this month, I like to know how [my brother] Sam is getting along with the cattle, and debits that Indians owe me....

Let me know by return mail and tell me, will Mr. Paquette say anything to me if he knows that I am at home again. You have not sent me my statement of any kind, so I don't know where I am at. I know I am not doing much business here just now. I got to see you about this business again, better than I can write you about the business.

I am well and hope to hear from you.

I am your friend, Clitso D. Dedman[18]

Once back in Nazlini, Dedman met with Hubbell and concluded that the wisest decision would be to close the El Paso operation. Hubbell arranged to have a Texas colleague ship the store's unsold merchandise back to Ganado.[19]

Clitso Dedman's career as a Navajo trader in Nazlini had come to a sudden end. His subsequent attempt to open an Indian store in El Paso had proven a failure. Moreover, there were no business opportunities in the isolated community of Wood Springs. Never one to surrender to adversity, Dedman decided to have Hadzizbaa and the children remain in Wood Springs while he would move to his mother's property in Chinle where he hoped to create a new life for himself and his family.[20]

7

Back to Chinle

In fall 1915, Clitso Dedman traveled twenty miles north of Nazlini to his family property in Chinle, determined to use what resources he had left after his failed El Paso experiment to establish himself as the local blacksmith. Actually, this career shift was not as radical as it might appear. Clitso, as he would again be called, was familiar with the region and able to build on skills he had acquired twenty years earlier. His initial vocational training at the Grand Junction School had been significantly enhanced during the four years he spent in the machine shops of the Santa Fe railroad in Gallup. Furthermore, at Rough Rock and later at Nazlini, he had designed and built trading posts, skills he could apply in the construction of a blacksmith shop.

Located at the edge of the Canyon de Chelly (in Navajo, Tséyi', or Deep in the Rock), the Chinle community had grown in importance since Clitso's childhood years.[1] In 1886, C. N. Cotton and J. L. Hubbell had established a trading post there, which by 1923 would become Camillo Garcia's Canyon de Chelly Trading Post.[2] In 1902, Sam Day's family built a second trading post just southeast of Chinle, which in 1919, after several intermediate owners, would be purchased by Cozy McSparron and renamed the Thunderbird Ranch (fig. 27).

In 1910, Navajo Nelson Gorman and his wife Alice Peshlakai opened a third Chinle trading post, which they were forced to abandon in 1919 for financial reasons.[3] In 1915, J. L. Hubbell built a two-story trading post with upstairs accommodations for visitors to Canyon de Chelly, naming it the "Big House."[4] The founding of the Franciscan mission in 1902, and the subsequent arrival of a government Indian boarding school in 1910, had further accelerated Chinle's expansion into a "central place" for Navajo families to settle.

In spite of its growth, Chinle in 1915 was still a remote settlement without running water or electricity. Father Leopold Ostermann described the situation quite graphically in a 1918 letter to his superior, in which he was requesting a new Franciscan volunteer for the mission: "However, before he comes out here, tell him what he is running up against. When he comes to Chin Lee it is like arriving on another planet. There are no electric cars passing the door; no hot and cold water in every room; no toilet room in the house; no heating system nor electric buttons to push. . . . There is no use out here for sissies, mama-pets, and softshellers."[5]

For Anglo-American visitors, Chinle had become a gateway to the Canyon de Chelly—first for archaeologists, ethnologists, and geologists, and subsequently for tourists eager to explore and visit the prehistoric cliff dwellings dating back to the Basket Maker culture of Ancestral Puebloans. In 1873 journalist J. H. Beadle's illustrated account of his visit to the area had encouraged a first influx of sightseers, most of whom carried back home small artifacts as souvenirs.[6] By 1903, the looting of the ruins by private collectors and for sale to museums had reached such a point that the U.S. government appointed Sam Day's son Charlie as official custodian of the historic site. However, it would not be until 1931 that Canyon de Chelly was designated a national monument.

In spring 1904, when Edward S. Curtis, the pioneer photographer from Seattle, arrived in Chinle with his bulky camera equipment, it was with the intention of photographing the life of the local Navajos and in particular the healing ceremony that Washington Matthews had described in his 1902 book *The Night Chant*. To that end, he hired Charlie Day as his guide and interpreter. Curtis was quickly informed, however, that the ceremonial season

FIG. 27. Sam Day Trading Post in Chinle, ca. 1902. Photo by Ben Wittick. Courtesy Palace of the Governors Photo Archives (NMHM/DCA), HP.2011.54.1.

was over. More importantly, Navajo traditions strictly prohibited the permanent reproduction of sacred imagery. Undaunted by these restrictions, Curtis asked Charlie's younger brother Sammie to convince local Navajos to pose in ceremonial attire as Nightway performers and to execute a few steps of the sacred Yeibichai dance for his movie camera.[7] The resulting images, along with numerous imposing views of the Canyon de Chelly, appeared in 1907 in the first volume of his masterwork *The North American Indian*.[8] This publication would inspire even more tourists to visit the area.

Local Blacksmith

Clitso Dedman's move back to Chinle was also a return to his roots, since his blacksmith shop would be situated near the hogan where he was born.[9] Located a mile and a half south of town, "Dedman Acres," as the property would later be named, provided a promising location for his proposed enterprise. More and more Navajos in the region were beginning to own horse-drawn wagons, which, given the poor condition of the rutted roads and trails, necessitated frequent repairs. The carriages and automobiles bringing tourists to the Canyon de Chelly also would often require bodywork by a blacksmith.

Since iron forging requires a reliable source of water, Clitso decided to build his new blacksmith shop near a spring by the cottonwood grove on the edge of the property. Determining the placement of the site was the easy part. It had been almost twenty years since he had last worked as a blacksmith, and back then he had been employed at a large railroad machine shop. Now he would need to design and build his own more modest smithy, with an adjoining shed where he could store the basic supplies, such as coal and various sizes of iron bars.

Constructing a blacksmith shop was much more complex than constructing a trading post. Before drawing up the plans for his new building, Clitso probably spent some time in Fort Defiance speaking with the blacksmiths there, carefully observing the shop layout. Realizing that he was at ease reading English, they may have recommended that he order the Sears Roebuck blacksmith manual by John Holmström and Henry Holford with its detailed instructions and guidelines. Most useful would be chapters 2–4 on setting up the shop, making tools, and repairing wagons, and also chapters 9 and 10 on shoeing horses.[10]

The central feature of the blacksmith shop would have been the coke-burning forge, similar to the one shown in figure 28.[11] There Clitso would heat each piece of iron before shaping it with a hammer at his anvil. The flat stone hearth with its depressed firepot needed to be built at his waist level for comfortable access. A tube, known as a tuyere, would be installed at the back of the forge, linking the firepot to a large bellows. In order to operate the forge, the coke in the firepot would be ignited and the bellows would be activated with a long wooden handle to blow air into the fire, thus raising its temperature.[12] Additional coal would be placed around the fire in a horseshoe shape so that the heat would transform it into coke. Smoke from the fire would be funneled up through the chimney.[13]

The other essential piece of equipment in the shop was the heavy wrought iron anvil. Clitso would saw a large section of tree trunk, which he would partially bury in the dirt floor for stability. The anvil would be placed on the top of the trunk, close to the forge, so that with a single arm movement, Clitso could easily move the piece he was working on from the forge to the anvil and back. Since iron cooled quickly, it would have to be reheated several times during a single operation. Most importantly, Clitso needed to calculate the height of the anvil so that it was level with the bottom of his hammer stroke.

FIG. 28. *Inside the Blacksmith Shop*. Photo by Brian J. McMorrow.

Next to the anvil, a large metal water bucket would serve as the slack tub in which he would cool the hot metal during forging.

For the purchase of his anvil and other tools, such as hammers, chisels, and tongs, Clitso most likely again turned to Sears Roebuck.[14] The popular mail-order company published a specialized catalog entitled *Tools Machinery Blacksmiths Supplies* from which he could order the desired equipment, either as individual items or as a preselected set (figs. 29 and 30).[15] Sears would ship his order to the Gallup railway depot for pickup.

As a starter, Dedman may have ordered the Masterworkman Blacksmith's Outfit for $58.25.[16] Since the shipping weight of that outfit came to 540 pounds, he would have needed to haul it by horse-drawn wagon to his property in Chinle. This could explain why he purchased a new wagon from J. L. Hubbell in August for $85.[17]

All large anvil work requires an assistant, often referred to as a striker. While the blacksmith holds a piece of hot iron in his tongs with one hand and guides a shaping tool with the other, the assistant wields a heavy sledgehammer, striking

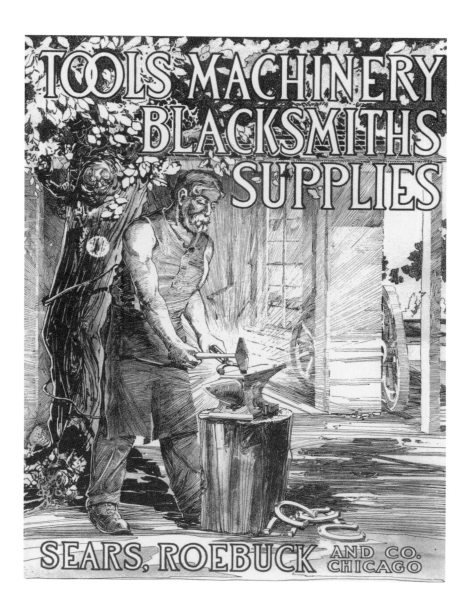

FIG. 29. *Tools Machinery Blacksmiths Supplies*, Sears Roebuck catalog, 1915.

Big Masterworkman Blacksmiths' Outfit

Contains ALL the Necessary Tools

This outfit will take care of the heaviest work, and contains all the tools needed by the blacksmith and horseshoer. We selected it especially for high class ironworkers, men who demand the best.

$58^{\underline{25}}$ $58^{\underline{25}}$

No. 9B51004

FIG. 30. Blacksmith supplies, Sears Roebuck catalog, 1915, p. 72.

the metal at just the right point and angle. Both men wear leather aprons as protection against flying sparks. Clitso Dedman probably trained local Navajos as his assistants. As his sons grew older, he taught them the blacksmith trade.[18]

Clitso also became the local farrier, shoeing horses. In the nineteenth century, Navajo and Apache warriors used to create "horse boots" out of buffalo or deer hide to protect their horses' feet when they were riding long distances over difficult terrain.[19] By the early twentieth century, metal horseshoes had replaced the boots for horses pulling heavy wagonloads. (Free-range horses in the Navajo herds went unshod.) At first, Clitso may have forged individual shoes for each horse, but more likely, as his business expanded, he would have bought kegs of mail-order horseshoes, fitting them as needed.[20]

Blacksmithing was a very hazardous craft, and older blacksmiths generally bore scars from their frequent burns and suffered various work-related joint injuries. According to his grandson Robert Dedman, Clitso "used certain herbs and plants to make a burn heal real fast. He was a medicine man in this way. When it healed there was no scar left." He also built a sweat lodge "to help himself in his sickness from arthritis and back pain."[21]

The blacksmith business, especially at the outset, was somewhat sporadic, giving Clitso the opportunity to drive regularly from Chinle to Nazlini to be with his wife, Hadzizbaa, and their three young children, Billie, Lilly, and Miller. In spring 1916, a second daughter, Pearl, was born. The following year, as Clitso's blacksmith work increased, his long-distance marital relationship became strained. He had built a house in Chinle, but his wife preferred staying with her extended maternal family in Nazlini.

On January 4, 1918, Clitso Dedman filed for an official U.S. divorce at the Apache County Courthouse in St. Johns, Arizona, stating that for over a year his wife had "willfully deserted" him and had "without just cause and against his will . . . lived separate and apart" from him.[22] The threatened divorce, however, was never finalized and Clitso evidently accepted that fact that he would have to travel regularly to Nazlini in order to spend time with his wife and children. Over the next several years, four more children were born: Mary (b. 1918), John (b. 1920), Aweé (b. 1922, who died as a baby), and Francis (b. 1923). At some point, the couple also adopted a young boy, Claude (b. 1916).[23] The children would all attend the Franciscan Indian School at St. Michaels, where they would receive instruction in the Catholic faith and be baptized. Clitso Dedman himself, however, would not be baptized until 1947.[24]

In March 1923, upon learning that little John was very sick, Clitso drove to the Franciscan mission in Chinle to have a priest come baptize his dying son. Father Leopold Ostermann instructed Clitso how to administer a private baptism in case John's condition got worse before he and a Franciscan brother could get there by buggy. When the Franciscans did finally arrive in Nazlini, they learned that the boy had died two hours earlier, but not before Clitso had baptized him. As Father Leopold wrote: "The Brother and myself selected a suitable place for internment on a hill under a tree, dug a grave, and gave the child Christian burial. The father made a neat cross of wood, which was placed at the head of the grave. Returning to Clitso's home, another one of his children [Francis], about two months old, was found to be very sick, which I baptized before leaving for home."[25]

Sometime after 1924, Clitso Dedman and his wife separated permanently. By 1929, Hadzizbaa Dedman had remarried and was living in Nazlini with her second husband, Richard Bia of the Ma'ii Deeshgiizhnii (Coyote Pass) clan. This was also the clan of Navajo leader Chee Dodge. The couple had a son, Joseph (b. 1930), to whom she passed on the surname Dedman.[26] Three years later, Hadzizbaa was married again, this time to Nezini Biye of the Tódích'ii'nii (Bitter Water) clan. With her third husband, she had son who was named Jimmy Dedman (b. 1934), and also a boy known as Tsosi (Slender one) (b. 1936) who would die in early childhood.[27]

In Chinle, meanwhile, Clitso had enlarged his blacksmith shop to include space for carpentry and wheelwright work. He quickly became expert in repairing heavy iron wagon wheel rims required for travel over the rough terrain of the reservation. When the wagons broke down, as they often did, he rebuilt their frames, forged new springs, and replaced broken axles.[28] According to his daughter Mary, he may also have built wagons.[29]

Although Clitso was the only blacksmith in Chinle, there was never enough work to keep him occupied full time. During his trading post years, he had done some construction work in the community, and would continue, after his return in 1915, to undertake various building projects.

Stonemason and Carpenter

Already in the early 1900s, awareness of Clitso Dedman's fine masonry work in Rough Rock had spread to Chinle, which was on his regular freighting route down to Ganado and Gallup to pick up new trading post merchandise. After Clitso opened a second store in Salt Springs with partner Hasteen Yashe around 1907, he used the recently established Chinle post office for his mail-order business, necessitating even more frequent trips to that community. During slack periods, with Yashe or a Navajo assistant managing the store, Clitso would find local employment as a stonemason or carpenter.

One of his early employers was John Kirk, an Anglo trader who in 1910 bought the former Cotton-Hubbell trading post. As his son Tom would later relate: "At Chinle, John hired a Navajo stone mason, carpenter, and jack-of-all-trades to make the home and store livable. Clitso was a well known Navajo artisan."[30] John Kirk brought his young wife and child from Gallup to their newly refurbished Chinle home by wagon, a trip that took three days. However, after two years in that remote area, Kirk sold the post and moved back to Gallup.

Another part-time employer was the new Franciscan mission in Chinle. Once the friars had established their boarding school at St. Michaels in 1902, they began making plans for a second Navajo mission. As Father Leopold Ostermann would later explain, Chinle was selected for several reasons.

1) There were at that time already rumors abroad that the government intended to erect a boarding school for Navajo children at that place. A branch mission at Chinle, therefore, would bring the fathers in contact not only with the children but also with their parents and other adult Indians.

2) Chinle is situated near the center of the Navajo reservation. Consequently, various parts or regions of the reservation could easily be reached or visited from there.

3) Indians living in the Black Mountain district came to Chinle or passed through there on their way to Fort Defiance, St. Michaels, Gallup, and other points.

4) The large peach orchards in Canyon de Chelly brought many Navajo from all parts of the reservation to Chinle in the fall, when the peaches were ripe. It was therefore an advantageous or strategic point, where one could easily meet a large number of Navajo, become acquainted with them, make known to them our intentions, and gain their confidence and goodwill.[31]

In 1903, Father Anselm Weber, with the support of local trader Sam Day, received official authorization from Indian Agent G. W. Hayzlett in Fort Defiance to open their new mission in Chinle.[32] Father Leopold Ostermann was named to head the effort. At the time, the locality consisted of two trading posts and some widely scattered hogans. The Franciscans originally hoped to build their own school in Chinle, but ran into difficulty obtaining the necessary funding. Finally, it was the Bureau of Indian Affairs, in 1909, that undertook the construction of a Navajo boarding school on a site a mile from the mission homestead. In 1910, Father Ostermann obtained the written permission of almost all the parents of the first contingent of eighty pupils to transport them to Mass every Sunday and provide religious instruction. As enrollment at the new boarding school reached its capacity of 200 pupils, the attendance at mission services also increased.

the vegetation. On approach it was truly one of the bleakest spectacles I ever had laid eyes on. Low gravelly mesas on the left and a sea of sand on the right provided a backdrop of unparalleled monotony in texture and color."[45]

Over the years, the McSparrons added new amenities to their property. A sandstone shed was erected near the guest cabins in 1925. The following year, Clitso and his workers built the bathhouse, which also housed a laundry facility and a maid's room.[46] Other new structures included a barn, a freight garage, a stone shed, and a corral. Numerous trees and bushes were planted so that over time the Thunderbird Ranch would become a welcoming oasis in the semiarid landscape.

In 1931, the U.S. government designated Canyon de Chelly as a national monument, with the Thunderbird Ranch falling within the park boundaries. Cozy McSparron was named official park custodian. Several years later, when the park service undertook the construction of a small pumphouse in 1936, Clitso Dedman was again designated construction foreman, overseeing a team of Navajo masons. For this last building that he erected on the Thunderbird Ranch property, he insisted on using stones quarried from a single site, resulting in a much more harmonious facade than that of his earlier cabins.[47]

By the mid-1920s, with the resurgence of the national economy, the Thunderbird Ranch had become a haven of hospitality for visiting archaeologists and occasional travelers, as well as for the many regular guests who would come each summer to enjoy the striking surroundings. Cozy McSparron would organize daytime tours of the Canyon de Chelly, either on horseback or by wagon. In the evening, dinner would be served at a long table in the large living room of the ranch house, with McSparron entertaining the group with stories of trading post life. On Saturday nights, he would sponsor playful boxing matches.[48]

Around 1928, after ten years of marriage, Stella McSparron filed for divorce. She claimed that given her work over the prior decade, she had a right to half of the Thunderbird operation. According to oral history, the situation was informally resolved: "Following the advice of his lawyer, Cozy provided her with $2,000 in cash in small bills, with a few large bills at the top of the pile.[49] He said that his former wife was so overwhelmed at the sight of the cash that she was about to receive that she settled on the spot, much to Cozy's delight."[50] After Stella's departure, Cozy McSparron's aunts came from Gallup to help their nephew run the guest operations and to maintain a "formal" home for him.[51]

FIG. 33. Meredith Guillet, *Clitso Dedman*, 1944. Photo by John Jacobsen. Lars Garrison Collection.

Four years later, in summer 1932, while visiting his sister in Gallup, Cozy McSparron was introduced to a young woman from Kansas, Inja Constant, who happened to stop over on her way home from a trip to the Grand Canyon. It was love at first sight. The next August, after a twelve-month daily exchange of letters, the couple married.[52] Inja quickly adapted to her new environment, taking over the management of the dude ranch, thus allowing her husband to focus on his trading post operations and relations with his Navajo customers.

FIG. 34. Canyon de Chelly, White House ruins. Photo by Deborah Trotter.

Visitors included photographers Ansel Adams, Imogen Cunningham, and Laura Gilpin, as well as Cozy McSparron's friend and physician Dr. Thomas Noble from Indianapolis, who took photo portraits of local Navajos.[53] Dinners were formal, with linen tablecloths and elegant place settings. Those who arrived late would not be served.

A frequent visitor to the Thunderbird Ranch in the 1940s was Meredith Guillet, who served as manager of the Canyon de Chelly National Monument from 1942 to 1950.[54] Inspired by the framed photograph of Clitso Dedman that Dr. Noble had taken (see frontispiece), Guillet rendered it in oil as a gift to the McSparrons in appreciation of their hospitality (fig. 33).

Upon her arrival in Chinle, Inja McSparron was fascinated by the Canyon de Chelly and particularly intrigued by a curious petroglyph on the cliff wall below the White House Ruins (fig. 34). Just below a large human etching, she had spotted a small animal figure. To please his new wife, Cozy McSparron commissioned Clitso Dedman to decorate their fireplace mantel with a replica of the two-legged animal that had attracted her attention. Later, their daughters Laramie (b. 1934) and Marion (b. 1935) would name the animal their "duck-dog" because it seemed to have the tail and legs of a duck and the head of a

FIG. 35. "Duck-Dog" petroglyph. Photo by Polly Schaafsma.

dog or fox (fig. 35).[55] Clitso subsequently created a stencil of the "duck-dog" to decorate the back door of the trading post.[56] When Inja purchased a piano for the ranch house around 1940, she asked Clitso to carve the "duck-dog" motif on the sides of her piano bench.[57]

Clitso Dedman's first sculptures had been created in stone. For his early trading posts, he had chiseled sandstone bowls to hold the tobacco that he offered his Navajo clients. In the 1920s, he made a similar tobacco bowl for Cozy McSparron (fig. 36). A few years later, for Christmas, Clitso created a unique replacement for the stone bowl: a seated dog protecting the tobacco box between his front paws (fig. 37). In the opinion of daughter Laramie, Clitso's sculpture had been inspired by the RCA Victor logo, which he had seen on his phonograph records and which featured the little mongrel dog Nipper sitting in front of a gramophone with head cocked listening to "His Master's Voice." The resulting stone sculpture was unfortunately too large for the trading post counter, so Cozy McSparron placed it outside next to the store entrance.[58] There it caught the eye of artist Laura Armer. In her book *Southwest* (1935), while writing about the enthusiasm of Hopi children in her art classes at Oraibi, she reflected, "Their eagerness was proof to me of the need in all people to express the inner sense of beauty which is man's heritage as surely as is his need to feed his body." She concluded, "I saw the results of the inner impulse in the work of Clitso when he sculptured a dog out of white stone."[59]

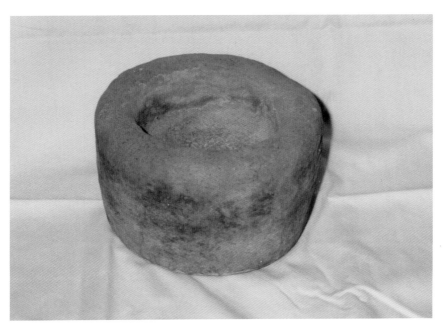

FIG. 36. Clitso Dedman, stone tobacco bowl. Laramie McSparron Collection. Photo by author.

FIG. 37. Clitso Dedman, white dog tobacco bowl. Laramie McSparron Collection. Photo by author.

Clitso Dedman and Laura Armer

Laura Adams Armer (1874–1963) was born in Sacramento, California, in 1874. Upon graduation from the San Francisco School of Art, she opened her own successful photo salon. After a summer trip in 1923 spent exploring northern Arizona with her family, she became totally enamored with Southwest cultures. She returned the next year to paint the colorful rock formations in the remote Blue Canyon and teach art at the Hopi school in Oraibi.[60]

When Laura Armer indicated to Lorenzo Hubbell in 1925 that she wanted to spend time in an isolated Navajo community, he suggested that she visit Black Mountain about fifty miles northeast of Oraibi. She was so captivated by the beauty of the location and encouraged by the welcome she received from many of the local Navajos that she decided to create her own studio there. Hubbell offered her a small site on a knoll behind his Black Mountain Trading Post and, as a builder, suggested that she hire Clitso Dedman. Although Clitso lived twenty-five miles to the east in Chinle, he was familiar with the Black Mountain area since his former trading post had been located just four miles distant in Salt Springs.

Over the next decade, with Lorenzo Hubbell's support, Laura Armer spent extended periods of time among the Navajos studying their ceremonies. In 1928, she filmed and produced *The Mountainway Chant*. Her book *Waterless Mountain*, featuring a young Navajo boy, won the Newbery Medal for the best children's book of 1932.[61]

In her 1935 book *Southwest*, Laura Armer describes the construction of her novel eight-sided hogan-style home (fig. 38). First the site had to be made even. Then Clitso, without the aid of a compass, needed to determine the exact placement of the foundation. "When the ground was leveled, we went out at night with a string. We wanted our house to face the east as all Navajo houses do. We tied the string to a juniper tree under the North Star and walked south to plant a stake in line with the tree. . . . In the morning, after the string episode, we used a square and established the east to the satisfaction of our Navajo friends."[62]

The house would measure twenty-four feet across from east to west, with eight walls built of logs. Clitso had determined the approximate length of the needed logs and cut corresponding lengths of string, adding an extra foot or so for good measure. Armer continues, "We gave pieces of string to four Navajos

FIG. 38. Armer hogan. Photo by Edythe Klopping. Courtesy Carolyn O'Bagy Davis.

and sent them to the mountains, 20 miles away, to fell spruce trees, bark them, and deliver them to our building site, cut the length of the strings."[63]

In the construction of the roof, Armer again relied entirely on Clitso, marveling at his precision in positioning the ceiling beams, then fitting slabs of milled wood, bark side down, and sawed side up, and finishing the outside with water-tight shingles. Armer made a painting of the interior of her home as an illustration for her book, entitling it "The nezhoni [beautiful] hogan" (fig. 39).

In 1962, shortly before her death, Laura Armer published a collection of essays, entitled *In Navajoland*, recalling her years on the reservation. She provided the following description of Clitso Dedman's building skills.

> Clitso still observed an eight-hour day. He carried no watch, but measured time by the sun. He constructed a simple sun dial. When a shadow fell in a certain place, he told his helpers it was time to eat the noonday meal. As foreman, Clitso received five dollars a day for his excellent craftsmanship. His helpers were paid two dollars.
>
> He designed a front door made of mill slabs. It was accomplished entirely by hand, perfect in design. When it came to making a chimney, Clitso told me he had taken a correspondence course in chimney building. He could understand the construction details, but please would I be so kind

as to do the arithmetic for him. I must find the square of the opening of the hearth, divide it by ten, then he would know what the area for the opening at the top of the chimney should be. I did the arithmetic and was awestruck as Clitso proceeded to build. The result was a perfectly good draught with no smoke in the room. A deluxe mantelshelf evolved out of one long sandstone slab. Clitso was in his element as a craftsman.[64]

Once the main house was finished, Clitso would often drive to Black Mountain from Chinle, bringing Armer fresh eggs and green vegetables and helping her create a cactus garden.[65] At her request, he also constructed a log summer shelter, lining it with brown and white cow hides.[66]

When Lorenzo Hubbell sold the Black Mountain Trading Post to Mormon trader Albert Hugh Lee in 1937, Laura Armer was unable to prove independent ownership of the site and thus was forced to abandon her beloved Navajo home. The hogan subsequently served as the residence of a series of trading post managers, including Myles Headrick who lived there with his family from 1938 to 1940. The 1939 photograph (fig. 40) is unfortunately not in focus, but it is the only extant photo of the interior of the hogan with its stone fireplace (on the right). The Black Mountain Trading Post closed in 1974. Armer's home burned down a year later, leaving no traces of Clitso Dedman's architectural gem.[67]

Family Life at Dedman Acres

After his separation from Hadzizbaa in the mid-1920s, Clitso Dedman married once more. His new wife, Mary Stewart Brown (b. 1894), was a talented Navajo weaver from Canyon de Chelly.[68] Originally her name had been Edith, but several years earlier, she had fallen seriously ill and credited her recovery to a blessing she had received from a Franciscan priest. Shortly thereafter, she converted to Catholicism and assumed the baptismal name Mary.[69] When Clitso met Mary, she was raising her deceased sister's three children: Joe (b. 1919), Thomas (b. 1920), and Agnes (b. 1922?). He subsequently adopted his wife's nephews and niece, giving them all the Dedman surname.

After his wedding to Mary, Clitso Dedman began the construction of a large home for his new family. It was a two-story structure with downstairs living areas and an indoor staircase leading to the upstairs bedrooms. Mary had her own weaving area with space for a large loom. According to Laramie McSparron Jarvi, "It was quite a house for a Navajo in those days!"[70]

FIG. 39. Laura Armer, *The Nezhoni Hogan*, *Southwest*, 113.

FIG. 40. Myles Headrick family in the Armer hogan, ca. 1939. Photo by Edythe Klopping. Courtesy Carolyn O'Bagy Davis, *Arizona's Historic Trading Posts*, 61.

FIG. 41. Tacab Tasap Hopi carving, ca. 1910. Courtesy John Moran Auctioneers.

Even more serious for Clitso was the Navajo prohibition against creating any permanent image of the Holy People. Ceremonial sandpaintings, in which Yeis were often depicted, were always to be destroyed by nightfall and the sands ritually deposited north of the hogan.[8] Early twentieth-century weavers, at the request of traders, had begun representing stylized Yei figures in their blankets, but they often felt menaced by the "Yeibichai curse," which traditional Navajos believed would bring blindness and paralysis to anyone who dealt improperly with ceremonial imagery. These women would, therefore, weave their Yei blankets in secret and only show them to the trader in a private back room of the trading post in order to avoid condemnation from tribal members. They also insisted on receiving much higher prices for their weavings in order to pay a medicine man to perform a protective Blessingway ceremony for them. Some Navajo women felt that weaving blankets with images of dancers impersonating the Yeis, rather than representations of the Yeis themselves, was less dangerous, although certain Navajos considered even the Yeibichai weavings to be inappropriate.[9]

Clitso Dedman took great care to protect himself against these traditional restrictions. He tried to mitigate the danger of accidental breakage by carving most of his figures with their arms attached to their torsos. Moreover, he never made carvings of the Holy People or Yeis, but only of their Navajo impersonators. In his early carvings, he limited himself to depicting the "secular" Begging Gods who went out during the Sixth Day to solicit donations and with whom he had had frequent contact during his trading post years.[10] Later, as he began carving the Yeibichai dancers of the closing Nightway ceremony, he portrayed them with the unconsecrated masks of the Begging Gods, respectfully indicating the eyes with simple holes, rather than revealing the triangular markings that would be painted on the actual masks before they were blessed with pollen on the morning of the Ninth Day.[11] He also protected his identity by signing the carvings simply as "Clitso" and not as "Dedman" or "Clitso Dedman."

Some traders would later use the story of the Yeibichai curse to promote the Clitso carvings to potential buyers, exaggerating the dangers to which the carver had exposed himself and the opposition of the Navajo community. Certain Navajos would point to the crippling illness that Dedman suffered at the end of his life as retribution from the Holy People, without realizing that he was crippled before he began carving.

The Nightway and the Yeibichai Dance

The Nightway was familiar to the Anglo public through Washington Matthews's widely read 1902 illustrated account.[12] As mentioned earlier, this curing ceremony extends over a period of nine days and can be held only during the cold months of the year. It is performed under the direction of a singer/medicine man (in Navajo, *Hataalii*) for a suffering patient whose harmony with the physical and spiritual universe has been disrupted by some willful or unintentional transgression against the established order. In the course of the nine days, four sandpaintings are created on the floor of the ceremonial hogan with pictures of the Holy People. Three of these latter are depicted in figure 42: Yeibichai or Talking God with his round white face and feathered headdress holding his Abert's squirrel bag, red-and-black Fringe Mouth with his pointed hat, and Female Yei with her square blue face with feathers in her hands.

On the Ninth Night, the Yeibichai dance, known as *na'akai* to the Navajos, provides a spectacular conclusion to the Nightway. As described in chapter 1, the dance is a public spectacle open to all Navajos. The carefully rehearsed choreography is typically performed by several teams of fourteen masked Yei (*Ye'ii*) impersonators that alternate throughout the night until just before daybreak. The purpose of the dance is to bring the blessings of the Yeis not only to the patient but also to the hundreds and occasionally thousands of people in attendance and, more generally, to the Navajo community at large.

The ceremony begins after nightfall, when the medicine man and the patient come out from the ceremonial hogan to greet the opening team of Yeibichai dancers as they arrive at the dance ground from the nearby brush enclosure where they have donned their masks. The first figure to appear is Talking God (Yeibichai or *Ye'ii Bi'cheii*, the maternal grandfather of the Yeis), followed by six Male Yeis alternating with six Female Yeis. Traditionally, the impersonators of the Female Yeis were younger men or boys in their late teens, although in some areas of the reservation the Female Yeis were impersonated by women. Bringing up the rear of the dance line is the mischievous Water Sprinkler (Tonenili or *Tó Neinilii*, the bringer of rain).[13]

Clitso depicted the fourteen participants in the Nightway dance in a very realistic manner (fig. 43).

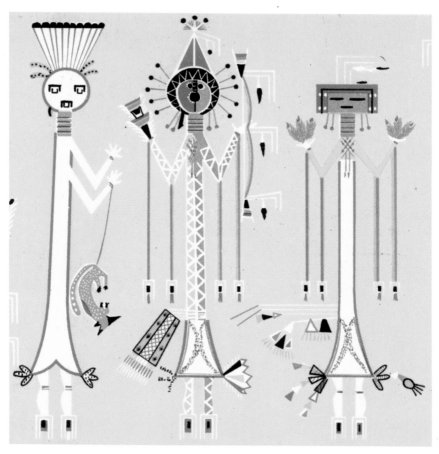

FIG. 42. Sandpainting drawings of Talking God, Fringe Mouth, and Female Yei. Washington Matthews, *Navaho Legends*, Plate 1, detail.

Talking God. Talking God is a powerful and benevolent Navajo deity. The impersonator of Talking God leads the dancers but does not himself participate in the dance. He is readily recognizable by his white headmask decorated with a black corn stalk and his fan-shaped headdress with twelve eagle feathers tipped by tufts of white down. Attached around the neck of his mask is a spruce twig ruff. He is dressed in shirt and pants, with a white sacred deerskin knotted over his left shoulder. In one hand, he holds a fox pelt that he shakes up and down to signal changes in the dance formations.

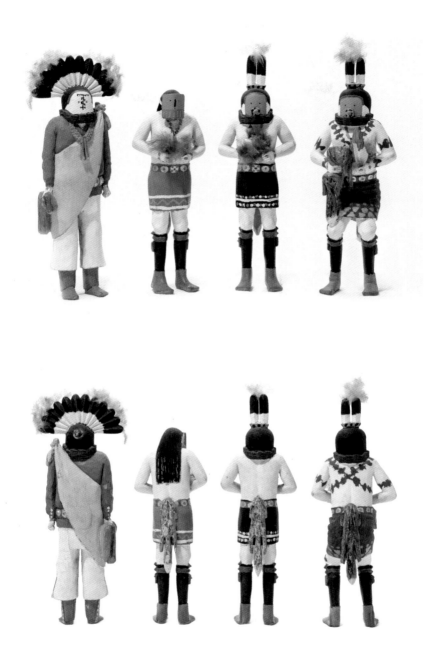

FIG. 43. Clitso Dedman figures: Talking God, Female Yei, Male Yei, and Water Sprinkler. Valette Collection. Photo by Chris Soldt.

Six Male Yei Dancers. The impersonator of the Male Yei is minimally dressed, despite the usual cold winter weather. He wears a headmask made of two sections of soft deerskin sewn together. The front half is colored blue with mineral pigments and is topped by a fringe of red woolen tresses, which, in the Clitso carvings, are represented by a brownish-red line painted above the forehead. A breathing tube is inserted in the mouth of the mask and decorated with fur or owl down. Green spruce ruffs hold the mask in place around the neck. Two eagle feathers tipped with down are affixed to the top of the mask, with smaller owl feathers at the base. The dancer covers his bare torso, arms, and legs with white clay body paint, which protects him against the evil spirits of the night. He wears a turquoise and coral necklace, silver bracelets and rings, silver concha belts and colorful kilt, plus blue woolen leggings held up below the knee by red woven garters and brown moccasins. Attached to the back of the concha belt is the pelt of a kit fox. He carries a gourd rattle in the right hand and a sprig of juniper or spruce in the left.

Six Female Yei Dancers. In accordance with the ceremonial practices prevailing at the end of the nineteenth century, Clitso typically represented the Female Yeis as impersonated by men wearing kilts and fox pelts similar to those of their Male Yei partners. (When Clitso did depict a woman impersonating the Female Yei, she is dressed in a long-sleeved velveteen shirt, a calico skirt and white deerskin leggings.) Instead of a full headmask, the Female Yei impersonator wears a rectangular blue face mask made of stiff buckskin, and no feathers. Attached to the bottom of each mask is a cloth flap decorated with silver and gold-colored ornaments. The Female Yei impersonators, whether men or women, untie their traditional buns and let their long hair hang freely down their backs. Female Yeis do not carry gourd rattles; rather, in both hands they hold juniper or sumac twigs.

Water Sprinkler. The last person to enter the dance arena is the impersonator of Water Sprinkler who provides comic relief by clumsily imitating Talking God and performing other antics with his tattered fox pelt. Clitso carvings generally depicted him with bent knees. His basic attire is that of a Male Yei, including a blue-faced headmask with two eagle feathers. In addition, he wears bracelets of juniper twigs on his arms and wrists, and longer juniper garlands as bandoliers across his torso.

FIG. 44. Clitso Dedman figures: Female Patient, Male Patient, and Medicine Man. Valette Collection. Photo by Chris Soldt.

When Clitso Dedman began carving sixteen-piece Yeibichai dance scenes, he would also include the Medicine Man responsible for conducting the ceremony and the Patient for whom the ceremony was being performed (fig. 44).

Medicine Man. Clitso depicted the Medicine Man or Singer in the traditional attire of Navajo men in the late nineteenth century: colored calico shirt, striped trade blanket draped over one shoulder, white cotton pants slit at mid-calf, high-top moccasins adorned with a vertical row of silver buttons, and an abundance of jewelry, including turquoise and coral necklaces, ear pendants, silver bracelets, and rings. The Medicine Man's hair, held by a red bandana, is pulled back and twisted into a long bun tied in the middle with a white wool band. In his right hand, he carries his medicine pouch.

Patient. The Patient, who stands next to the Medicine Man, holds a ceremonial basket with the sacred cornmeal that will be sprinkled on the dancers as a blessing. The Patient may be either a man or a woman, with women appearing twice as frequently as men in the Clitso carvings. Patients are portrayed in traditional attire, with trade blankets over their left shoulders. Both men and women have their hair pulled back in a bun tied in white wool bands. Men are depicted wearing a colored headband. Women are portrayed with turquoise earrings.

Beginning of an Artistic Career

According to Cozy McSparron, it was in late 1939 that Clitso Dedman began carving Nightway figures. In a letter written in 1954 to the Museum of New Mexico, Cozy McSparron explains: "[These Yeibichai] figures are carved by Clitso Dedman, Navajo. When 63 years old, he made the first sets. He was the only Navajo who did this work. The figures are carved so accurately that the medicine men were quite concerned. It is supposed that they wished a curse on him. Clitso was a cripple before he started the carvings, and later became confined to bed. He defied the Navajo—and did not believe in Navajo religion—and continued to carve until his death in 1953."[14]

There was a cottonwood grove near the blacksmith shop where Clitso could easily obtain his basic material. Since for the Hopi a prime function of the Kachinas was to bring rainfall, a Kachina doll could only be carved "from the root of the water-seeking cottonwood tree, and it [had to be] thoroughly dried and seasoned."[15] Whereas the cottonwood roots were quite malleable and easy to carve with a simple knife, Clitso preferred using the trunks and branches of the cottonwood for his figures. This harder wood with its straight grain proved to be surprisingly strong and easy to handle with his commercial woodworking tools. It did not split easily, nor did it chip when shaped with a chisel.

Initially, Clitso did not carve the participants in the Yeibichai dances of the Ninth Night of the sacred healing ceremony who, in their consecrated masks, embodied the Holy People. Rather, he began by carving the four men who as Begging Gods would go out into the surrounding area on the Sixth Day to collect donations of food and tobacco, and occasionally money.[16] When Talking God and Water Sprinkler, accompanied by two Female Yeis with yucca wands, would arrive at a hogan or the local trading post, they would stand outside uttering the *hu-hu-hu-HU* call and would hold out their large fawnskin bags. Even though they were wearing masks that had not yet been painted with eyes and blessed with pollen for the final dance, they were not allowed to talk and communicated only by gesture. At the end of the day, the four would return to the ceremonial hogan.

Clitso Dedman's earliest carvings, signed "Clitso 1940" on the bottom of each foot, depict two Female Yeis as Begging Gods holding wire yucca wands (fig. 45). Their small square buckskin masks were relatively simple to carve, avoiding the necessity of chiseling delicate facial features. Similarly, the smooth black hair flowing down their backs was much easier to carve than the traditional bun with its white sheep's wool ribbon. Their turquoise jacla necklaces are delicately painted in blue and red. The straight kilts in earth-tone colors are fastened with concha belts, as suggested by a row of white circles with black dots representing turquoise stones. Attached to the back of each belt is a carved kit fox pelt. Both wear blue stockings with red painted garters and brown moccasins.

Over the next several months, Clitso began carving a complete Begging God quartet with the addition of Talking God and an upright Water Sprinkler, both carrying light tan spotted fawnskin bags. These figures wear round headmasks, hiding their difficult-to-carve hair buns. Water Sprinkler's mask has two carved feathers, while Talking God is represented with a panoply of wooden feathers topped with chicken down. Their spruce ruff collars are suggested by the green rings around their necks. Talking God is represented

FIG. 45. Clitso Dedman, two Female Yei Begging Gods, 1940. Courtesy Adobe Gallery.

wearing a colored shirt and long pants, with a sacred deerskin fastened over his left shoulder. In his right hand he has a small medicine pouch. Water Sprinkler is depicted in white body paint wearing a kilt similar to that of the Female Yei impersonators. The spruce garlands on his arms and across his torso are suggested by lines of splotchy green paint.

Since Clitso's infirmities made it difficult for him to get around, he asked his Chinle neighbor Reed Winnie, an interpreter for the Franciscan friars, to explore whether any off-reservation traders would be interested in buying his new four-piece Begging God set (fig. 46). The unsigned carvings were purchased by Al Frick for his Route 66 trading post in Lupton. In 1962, the

FIG. 46. Clitso Dedman, Crane set of four Begging Gods, ca. 1940. Courtesy Denver Museum of Nature & Science, 6203 to 6206.

set, erroneously attributed to Reed Winnie, was acquired by Francis and Mary Crane for their Southeast Museum in the town of Marathon on the Florida Keys. Since this relatively remote location attracted very few visitors, the Cranes closed their museum in 1968 and donated their Native American collections to the Denver Museum of Natural History.[17]

On Christmas Day 1941, Clitso Dedman arrived at the Thunderbird Ranch bringing a box with four "dolls" for the McSparron family. Older daughter Laramie, age seven, was excited when she saw the present with her name on it. She had been dreaming of a Sonja Henie doll, having seen one pictured in an old issue of *Life* magazine, and the wrapping paper seemed to conceal a gift of just the right size.[18] The name Sonja Henie has now been almost forgotten. However, in 1936, the Norwegian figure skater had gained worldwide fame by winning an unprecedented third Olympic gold medal. By 1939, her popularity was such that the Madame Alexander Company had begun marketing a line of Sonja Henie dolls.[19]

FIG. 47. Left: Clitso Dedman, Female Yei with Basket, 1941. Laramie McSparron Collection. Photo by author.

FIG. 48. Right: Clitso Dedman, Fringe Mouth, 1941. Courtesy California Academy of Sciences, 2007-0004-0002.

Sixty years later, Laramie could still vividly recall her great disappointment upon unwrapping her present. Instead of a thin, long-legged girl doll with wavy blond hair and wearing a white silk skating outfit trimmed with white fluffy down, she discovered a wooden masked lady with long black hair holding a large round basket. Her sister Marion's gift was a figure "painted black and brown, with a full mask and hands up in a prayer stance."[20] Her father received a Medicine Man, which may well have been Talking God with his medicine pouch.[21] Laramie did not remember which figure Clitso gave to her mother, Inja, but it could have been one of his early representations of Water Sprinkler.[22]

FIG. 49. Left: Clitso Dedman, Talking God, 1941. Courtesy Toh-Atin Gallery.

FIG. 50. Right: Clitso Dedman, Water Sprinkler, 1941. Courtesy Linda Wyatt.

Cozy McSparron whispered to his sad-faced girls to smile and thank Clitso for his beautiful Christmas presents. He then placed the four wooden sculptures on a high mantel, so they would not get broken.

The masked woman with a basket and a silver concha belt (fig. 47) represents the Female Yei impersonator who appears on the Eighth Day of the Nightway. The figure that Laramie remembered as "black and brown" is actually the black and dark red impersonator of Fringe Mouth (fig. 48) who also appears on the Eighth Day.[23] The top of his headmask has a crown made of three sumac twigs with downy feathers. He carries a string of lightning, which he uses as a rope; in the carving this is represented by a curved pipe cleaner. Talking God (fig. 49), with his light-green spotted ring-shaped ruff, is holding a fawnskin

FIG. 51. Clitso Dedman, Wagner set of four Begging Gods, 1941. Courtesy Toh-Atin Gallery.

bag and also his traditional Abert's squirrel pollen pouch, which may have led Laramie to remember him as a medicine man. Water Sprinkler (fig. 50) is depicted carrying a spotted pelt bag and wearing an oversized headmask with a large green ring ruff. On his arms and torso are delicately painted green juniper sprigs and turquoise jewelry. Cozy McSparron was so impressed by the detailed rendering of the four figures that he enthusiastically encouraged his friend Clitso to continue carving, offering to provide needed paints and brushes.[24]

The following August, Inja McSparron brought a four-piece Clitso set of Begging Gods (similar to fig. 46) to the Gallup Intertribal Ceremonial as a decoration in her Thunderbird booth. In a 1967 letter to the director of the Amon Carter Museum, Inja recalled: "It was depression times and Clitso who had been a wonderful stone mason had been stricken with some malady that had caused him to lose use of his legs. I took [a] set of four dolls in with me, together with my Navajo blankets for display and sale at the Gallup ceremonial. I took many orders that year, enough that Clitso whittled all winter. At that time he only made sets of four dancers."[25]

FIG. 52. Clitso Dedman in his workshop. *Arizona Highways*, April 1944.

In 1941, Cozy McSparron gave one of the early sets of four Begging Gods (fig. 51) to Sallie Wagner, who, with her husband, Bill Lippincott, had been encouraging women to create Chinle-style striped weavings with natural dyes at their recently acquired Wide Ruins Trading Post.[26] An almost identical set of four figures (fig. 88) was later acquired by Harriet and Seymour Koenig.[27] In the Koenig set, the Female Yei impersonators have slightly longer masks than in earlier Clitso carvings. Both sets are signed "Clitso 1941" on the bottom of the feet.

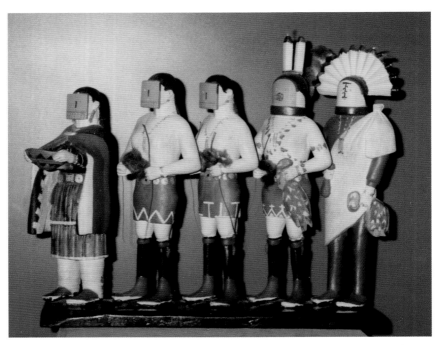

FIG. 53. Clitso Dedman, Stockton set of four Begging Gods and Female Yei with Basket, ca. 1942. Courtesy Museum of Indian Arts and Culture, 46170/12.

With requests for his carvings growing and with his mobility declining, Clitso Dedman recognized the necessity of building an easily accessible workshop next to his family's two-story home (fig. 52). The new small one-room building was a simple construction of upright logs and mud joints.[28] High windows on two sides brought in the necessary light. A wood-burning stove provided heat in the winter. The basic furnishings consisted of shelves for supplies and carvings, a wooden armchair, and a workbench about two feet wide and six feet long.

Around 1942, Cozy McSparron sold a group of five carvings (fig. 53) to Colorado artist Pansy Stockton, who had recently moved to Santa Fe. By that time, Clitso had begun using shinier commercial paints, including silver aluminum paint for the concha belts. The four Begging Gods were accompanied by a figure similar to the one he had carved for Laramie, that is, a Female Yei in a skirt holding a ceremonial basket. In 1972, Stockton bequeathed her

figures to the Museum of Indian Arts and Culture. For several years, they were on exhibit at the Bosque Redondo Memorial in Fort Sumner, New Mexico.[29]

In summer 1943, probably with Cozy McSparron's encouragement, Clitso decided to try his hand at carving the entire Yeibichai dance group as they would appear on the last night of the Nightway. This endeavor meant that he would need to learn how to chisel the delicate facial features of the Patient and the Medicine Man, for until that time he had only carved masked participants. Clitso also had to determine how to present the Male Yei dancers holding their gourd rattles. Talking God, the Medicine Man, and the Male Patient in this ambitious set were depicted in nineteenth-century flared white muslin pants, which were much more difficult to carve than straight dark pants. Clitso indicated the concha belts with white circles outlined in black, as he did in his very early carvings. In this first sixteen-piece Yeibichai set (fig. 54), Talking God is holding a fawnskin bag, rather than the fox pelt he would have carried in an actual Nightway performance.[30]

Cozy McSparron was so delighted that he asked Clitso to carve him a similar large set for his private Thunderbird Ranch collection (fig. 55).[31] Respectful

FIG. 55. Inja McSparron at the Thunderbird Ranch, ca. 1945. Courtesy Laramie McSparron Jarvi.

of the sensitivities of local Navajos who might disapprove of the Yeibichai scene, McSparron did not display the set in his trading post, but rather had a special vitrine built for it in his family dining room. In this set, Talking God is accurately depicted holding a fox pelt. The conchas of the participants are indicated in silver paint and resemble those of the belt suspended on the wall to the left of the vitrine.

One of the McSparron's regular guests at the time was Charles Wyatt, who served as park ranger at the Canyon de Chelly National Monument from 1940 to 1943. Wyatt was so fascinated by the Yeibichai carvings of "Hosteen Klitso Dedman" that he wrote an illustrated article featuring the artist for the April 1944 issue of *Arizona Highways*, heralding the arrival of "A New Navajo Art." At the time the article appeared, the United States was still engaged in World War II. Restrictions on gasoline and rubber tires were such that few travelers were able to come to the Thunderbird Ranch to admire the carvings. Readers of the article, however, began ordering carvings directly from the artist.

One such long-distance collector was Corporal Edward Pagel, then stationed in Camp Polk, Louisiana, who ordered a set of four Nightway figures by mail (fig. 56). In a letter of June 12, 1944, Clitso Dedman informs Pagel that his set

FIG. 56. Clitso Dedman, Pagel set of four Begging Gods, 1944. Courtesy Skinner Auction, Inc.

has been carved and is being painted. He writes, "The price will be $15 plus 30 cents postage."[32] He ends his letter by saying, "I cannot keep these figures after 18 of June because I am behind with orders."[33] Pagel obviously sent the requested payment. In the Pagel set, Talking God has his arm raised in what appears to be a wartime salute. He is depicted in traditional loose white muslin pants and the kilts of the dancers are more colorful, both features typical of Clitso's subsequent classic style.

Although Clitso spent most of his time filling orders for the popular four-figure Nightway sets, he would occasionally experiment with new interpretations. Around 1944, he carved a pair of Female Yei dancers impersonated by women in form-fitting velveteen blouses, long calico skirts, and white leather leggings, which he gave as a gift to Cozy McSparron (fig. 57). Actually, by the

FIG. 57. Clitso Dedman, McSparron pair of Female Yei dancers with raised arms, ca. 1944. Photo by John Jacobsen. Lars Garrison Collection.

mid-1940s, it had become increasingly common to find women impersonating the Female Yeis. Both of his new figures hold their arms up away from their bodies, as they would while performing during the Nightway. Clitso never again created similar figures, probably because the upraised arms were difficult to carve and could easily break.

In another artistic experiment around the same time period, Clitso carved two Female Yei dancers in kilts with their arms hanging at their sides in a position of repose (fig. 82). He apparently never carved others in this style either, preferring his original interpretation of Female Yeis with their arms

FIG. 58. Clitso Dedman, Noble first Yeibichai set: Talking God, Male Patient, Female Yei, Male Yei, ca. 1944. Courtesy Indiana University Museum of Archaeology and Anthropology, Mathers Ethnographic Collections 1962-06-0082, 0084, 0094, 0086.

held at waist level. These two original carvings were not created for sale, but were given as gifts to the McSparrons.

In summer 1945, Dr. Thomas Noble, a frequent prewar visitor from Indiana and a volunteer anthropologist at Canyon de Chelly, was finally able to return to Chinle after a four-year hiatus. Having long been interested in Navajo culture, he had years earlier attended a Nightway ceremony and recorded the chants of the dancers.[34] At the time, he had acquired a carving of a Female Yei figure with a ceremonial basket (fig. 80, second from left), similar to the one Clitso had given to Laramie. On his postwar visit, he was so delighted to discover that the artist had carved a sixteen-piece Yeibichai set, like the one pictured in *Arizona Highways*, that he immediately purchased it. Before returning home, he also strongly encouraged Clitso Dedman to continue carving the larger Yeibichai scenes.

In this first Noble set (fig. 58), the figures have round silver conchas. Talking God and the Male Yeis wear ring-shaped ruffs. Male Yeis are depicted with white rattles in their right hands. The Male Patient, with delicately carved features and a red bandana on his head, is depicted wearing typical nineteenth-century white calico pants.

FIG. 59. Clitso Dedman, Sallie Wagner pair of Enemyway figures, ca. 1945. Courtesy Toh-Atin Gallery.

In 1945, McSparron asked Clitso to carve two figures from the Enemyway for Bill Lippincott, who had returned to Wide Ruins after having served in the U.S. Navy (fig. 59).[35] During that three-day curative ceremony, which is performed to mitigate the harmful effects of war on returning veterans, a young woman—a virgin—brings a decorated cedar staff with a rattle on top from the home of the patient to the site of the concluding Squaw Dance, an event that attracts hundreds of participants.[36] Women invite men to dance to the accompaniment of a ceramic drum and expect a modest payment in return. In the Clitso carving, the woman's ceremonial staff is made of leather wrapped around a string core and decorated with ribbons. The man wears real feathers in

FIG. 60. Clitso Dedman, Elkus set of four Yeibichai participants, ca. 1945. Charles and Ruth Elkus Collection. Courtesy California Academy of Sciences, 0370–0501 A-D.

his hair and holds a willow drumstick fashioned from wire and a pipe cleaner. Both figures, presented in the stylized upright stance characteristic of his early style, are shown wearing silver squash blossom necklaces.

Clitso Dedman's Classic Period

In early 1945, Clitso Dedman began experimenting with more realistic renderings in a four-piece Yeibichai set with a Female Patient (fig. 60). The spruce ruffs worn by Talking God and Male Yei were sloped over the shoulders and notched to reflect the texture of the juniper branches. Female Yei had a longer, broader face mask. The leather belts, in brown paint, were decorated with silver and turquoise conchas. The straight legs of the Male and Female Yei were shaped to reveal the outline of the knees. The shirts of Talking God and the Female Patient were realistically depicted with wrinkled sleeves. However, the Talking God figure was still wearing the straight dark pants typical of earlier Clitso carvings. This set was acquired by Charles Elkus, an attorney whose San

Francisco law firm provided pro bono legal work for the Navajos and Pueblo tribes on issues relating to land and water rights and education.[37]

Once the war had come to an end, tourists again began visiting Canyon de Chelly. Many had read Wyatt's article in *Arizona Highways* about Clitso Dedman's "new Navajo art" and wanted to see Cozy McSparron's sixteen-piece Yeibichai set, which was on display in its special case in the dining room of the Thunderbird Ranch. These postwar collectors were eager to acquire the new large dance scenes, rather than the four-figure groups that Clitso had been producing until then.

Between 1945 and 1950, Clitso was extremely prolific and developed more realistic renderings of the participants in Nightway dance. In McSparron's estimation, he probably produced an average of two large Yeibichai sets per year.[38] In addition, he carved many smaller groups of figures. When carving a Yeibichai set, he would work on the figures as a group, carving them all, then sanding them, and finally painting them in an identical style.[39] Clitso would first produce a rough cut for each figure by clamping the upright cottonwood block to a special V-shaped vise with wooden brackets that he had built for his workbench. Then, with a chisel and mallet, he would define the general shape of the carving. He refined the rough cut, using gouges, knives, rasps, and files, until he obtained the desired final shape. After further finishing, he delicately painted each piece and provided a final touch by adding external elements, such as bits of down attached to the carved eagle feathers. In the hands of the Yei dancers, he placed bunches of dark green wool representing juniper branches; occasionally he incorporated feathers dyed green, and sometimes feathers dyed red to represent autumn sumac branches.[40] Some of the early Yeis, as mentioned, also held stiff wands of wire twisted green thread representing yucca wands.

In 1945, Carolyn Kelly discovered a newly carved Clitso Yeibichai set at Camillo Garcia's Canyon de Chelly trading post and immediately bought it. The Female Patient is holding a ceremonial basket. Her hair is parted down the middle and drawn back into a bun; her turquoise earrings are made of green yarn. Talking God has straight arms and is holding a pelt bag in the right hand. The Yeis are wearing colorful kilts with broad border designs. Water Sprinkler, with his knees slightly bent, has in his right hand a realistic fox pelt carved with four legs and a long tail. In July 1953, Kelly donated her set to the Museum of New Mexico in Santa Fe.

FIG. 61. Clitso Dedman, Lockett Yeibichai set, 1946. Photo by Ken Matesich. Courtesy Arizona State Museum, University of Arizona, E-2221 to E-2236.

In spring 1946, Tucson trader Clay Lockett drove to Chinle to purchase a sixteen-piece Clitso Yeibichai set (fig. 61). On returning home, he displayed his new acquisition in his store and publicized the set in the *Arizona Daily Star* issue of April 16, 1946. In his interview for the article, he exaggerated the rarity of the carvings as a potential museum piece, noting that Clitso Dedman, the creator of the figures, was in failing health and could no longer carve such beautiful Yeibichai scenes. The article proved an effective marketing ploy, since a generous donor decided to offer the set as a gift to the Arizona State Museum and purchased it for $250.[41]

The Clay Lockett Yeibichai set exhibits all the features of Clitso's classic style, many of which were already evident in the Elkus group of four figures. The spruce ruffs worn by the Male Yei impersonators are shaped over the shoulders and notched to reflect the texture of the juniper branches. The Male Yei dancers hold white gourd rattles in their right hands, in addition to feathers. Both Male and Female Yeis wear multicolored kilts with more complex borders. Water Sprinkler is depicted in a crouched stance with knees bent, holding a realistically carved fox pelt; the spruce branches on his torso and arms are painted in broad strokes. The Medicine Man, the Male Patient, and Talking God all wear flared white muslin pants. Over their creased shirts, the turquoise jacla necklaces are carved in relief. The Medicine Man and the Patient are depicted with striped trade blankets draped in a natural manner over their left shoulders.

Clitso Dedman had always been a perfectionist, continually experimenting with ways to improve his work, were it masonry, carpentry, or, now in his later years, the carving of the Yeibichai dancers. In the Clay Lockett set, and more noticeably in the set photographed for Wyatt's 1944 article in *Arizona Highways* (fig. 54), the Female Yei dancers were of somewhat different heights, as were the Male Yei dancers, since each figure had been carved out of a separate piece of cottonwood. In order to have each group of six dancers be of exactly the same size, Clitso came upon an ingenious solution: he would saw small trunks or large branches of seasoned cottonwood into sections of equal length, and then, with an ax, he would split each resulting cylinder into six long triangular pieces. He would then shape these triangular pieces into six rectangular blocks of the same length which could be carved "in the round" to produce six matching Yeis.

Clitso Dedman's daughter Mary Dedman Dodge, who frequently visited her father in his workshop, was able to observe him at work. She explained:

> Before beginning a Yeibichai dance set, he first prepared sixteen blocks of wood about 12 to 14 inches high. He then outlined the rough shapes of the figures using a pencil. Next he would start roughing out the blocks, first carving out the shape of the head. He would do this for all the blocks. Then he would rough out the torso for the entire set, and then continue down to the feet. After the rough cuts, he would again individually work across the set, chiseling and chipping in more detail. For the draping of the blanket for the medicine man, he would pencil in the folds and then carve the shapes with a small pocket knife so that the blanket would fall properly. In the course of his carving career, he wore out a lot of tools. He used sandpaper for the final finish work. At his workbench, he would have many different brushes and many small pots of paint of different colors.[42]

Laramie McSparron Jarvi recalled that as a child she would accompany her father on his regular visits to Clitso's workshop, delivering supplies, such as

FIG. 62. Clitso Dedman, Wallace Yeibichai set, ca. 1946–1947. Photo by Laura Shea. Valette Collection.

paint and brushes, and bringing him special dishes on holidays. Cozy McSparron and Clitso Dedman had become close friends over the years, and Laramie remembered their conversations as lively and full of humor. In reflecting on Clitso's approach to carving, she recalled: "On his work bench were always carvings in varying states of completion. In fact, sometimes Clitso did not like a figure and set it aside. He would work on one set at a time, but it was his habit to work on different figures at the same time. Sometime Clitso was disappointed in a figure and would not complete it."[43]

Zuni trader C. G. Wallace, today remembered for promoting the art of inlay jewelry, purchased an early classic Yeibichai set from Cozy McSparron and exhibited it in several of his trading posts, including his store in Gallup (fig. 62).[44] In this set, which was probably carved shortly after the Clay Lockett set, Clitso had standardized the heights of the dancers. Although the Female Yei dancers have much longer face masks, the colors and designs of the kilts and the silver concha belts in both sets are very similar. In the Wallace set, the Talking God and the Male Yei dancers have metal feathers. However, Clitso was not enamored with that new look, and in subsequent sets of the period, the feathers on the male headmasks were again carved in wood.[45]

FIG. 63. Clitso Dedman, Bradshaw Yeibichai set, ca. 1945–1947. Photo by Adobe Gallery. Private Collection.

FIG. 64. Clitso Dedman, Wheelwright Yeibichai set, ca. 1947. Photo by Herbert Lotz.

Another complete Yeibichai set of the same period, this one with a Female Patient, was donated to the Indian Pueblo Cultural Center in Albuquerque and later acquired by James and Rebecca Bradshaw (fig. 63).[46] In this set, Clitso again featured a Female Patient wearing a striped trade blanket with a delicately carved and painted fringe.

A colorful Clitso Yeibichai set dating from the same period was offered for sale at the March 1977 Wheelwright Museum benefit auction (fig. 64). It had had been donated by an anonymous supporter of the museum. The new owner, Rex Arrowsmith, displayed it at his Santa Fe store, Relics of the Old

West. In this set, the face masks of the Female Yeis are of medium length. In their hands, the dancers hold green- and red-dyed feathers, representing juniper and red sumac branches.

One of the regular summer guests at the Thunderbird Ranch, Dr. Leslie Eames, also ordered a sixteen-piece Yeibichai set at Cozy McSparron's suggestion. The Eames family lived in Glendale, California, and had hosted the McSparron daughters Laramie and Marion when they were in school in Claremont. In the Eames set, Clitso included a Transitional Style Talking God with a ring-shaped ruff and his right arm raised in salute, very similar to the Talking God he had carved for Corporal Pagel in 1944 (fig. 56). The other fifteen figures of the set are carved in the classic style: the Male Yeis have sculptured ruffs, and Water Sprinkler is depicted with bent knees. Dr. Eames later bequeathed his Yeibichai carvings to the Southwest Museum in Los Angeles.[47]

In 1956, Charles Elkus purchased a sixteen-piece Yeibichai set from Phoenix dealer Fred Wilson for $300 (fig. 65).[48] Wilson had exhibited the set in

FIG. 66. Thomas Noble, Clitso Dedman and His Carvings, ca. 1948. Courtesy Linda Wyatt.

1953 at the "Contemporary American Indian Arts and Crafts" show at the de Young Museum in San Francisco, pricing it at $250, but it did not sell at that time. Over the years, Ruth and Charles Elkus would amass a comprehensive collection of Southwestern Indian art, which they generously bequeathed to the California Academy of Sciences in 1972.[49]

Dr. Thomas Noble, the physician from Indianapolis who had bought one of Clitso's first Yeibichai sets, purchased a second one around 1948. A talented amateur photographer, Noble posed Clitso next to this set of carvings as it was being crated for shipment (fig. 66). These Yeibichai figures were later donated to the Indianapolis Museum of Art.

In the late 1940s, Clitso carved a pair of Yei dancers where the Female Yei is impersonated by a woman in traditional Navajo attire (fig. 67). The two figures were purchased at the Thunderbird Ranch by Utah lawyer John Boyden, who later donated them to the Nora Eccles Harrison Museum of Art in Logan, Utah.[50]

Cozy McSparron had been so delighted with this carving of a Female Yei in her velveteen blouse and pleated calico skirt that he commissioned his friend Clitso to carve a sixteen-piece Yeibichai set with women impersonators

FIG. 67. Clitso Dedman, Boyden pair of Yei dancers, ca. 1948–1950. Photo by Chris Soldt. Valette Collection.

FIG. 68. Clitso Dedman, McSparron second Yeibichai set: Six Female Yei dancers, ca. 1948–1950. Photo by John Jacobsen. Lars Garrison Collection.

(fig. 68). In this late classic set, both the Male Yeis and the Female Yeis wear sculpted necklaces and brown leather belts with raised conchas. The women's long hair is divided into strands.

Another Yeibichai set with women impersonating the Female Yeis was sold to Taos collector and philanthropist Helene Wurlitzer. Her signed set was probably carved around 1950. The figures themselves prefigure Clitso's late style, with necklaces and concha belts sculpted in relief and the male headdresses decorated with metal feathers. After Wurlitzer's death in 1963, an unnamed carver—perhaps a student at her Wurlitzer Foundation, which provided residencies for young artists—modified the male figures in the dance team by replacing the carved kit fox pelts attached to their belts with pieces of leather and giving them real hair. This person was obviously unfamiliar with Navajo ceremonies but had most likely attended Taos corn dances, where the men have short hair and are not masked. (The Navajo men traditionally

FIG. 69. Clitso Dedman, Wurlitzer Yeibichai set: Modified Water Sprinkler, ca. 1950. Courtesy William A. Smith Inc., Auctioneers & Appraisers.

FIG. 70. Clitso Dedman, McSparron pair of Yei dancers in movement, ca. 1948–1950. Photo by John Jacobsen. Lars Garrison Collection.

<small>FIG. 71.</small> *Devil Dance of the Apache Indians.* J. R. Willis postcard, 1937.

had long hair tied back in a bun, as depicted in the carvings of the Medicine Man and the Male Patient. The hair of the Male Yeis and Talking God would have been hidden under their headmasks.) After chiseling off Clitso's original wooden fox pelts, the carver added vertical "folds" to the kilts, and repainted them with designs that are not at all in the Clitso style. The painted garters of the Male Yeis were replaced by actual red ribbons. Water Sprinkler's painted juniper ruffs were rubbed out and replaced with green wool balls. The hem of his kilt was broken during the removal of the original wooden pelt in his right hand; his right hand was also reshaped and given much longer fingers (fig. 69).

While Clitso's output during his classic period consisted almost entirely of large sets of Nightway figures, he would occasionally deviate from this theme to create a more original, one-of-a-kind gift for the McSparrons. For example, as an experiment, he carved two Yei dancers in movement, each with an uplifted foot and wrinkled kilt (fig. 70).

In the late 1940s, Cozy McSparron showed Clitso a color postcard depicting four Apache dancers at the annual Gallup Intertribal Ceremonial (fig. 71). These four Crown Dancers, so named in English because of their impressive headdresses, impersonate the benevolent mountain spirits (*Gaan*) who bring healing to the Apache community. The participants represent the four quarters of the earth: north, east, south, and west.

As was typical at that time, the original photograph had been sent to the Curt Teich Company in Chicago for production as a postcard.[51] There it had been hand-tinted, with the result that the dancers' bare torsos with their elaborate body paint designs appeared to be clothed in light-colored shirts. Their plain black hoods with simple eyeholes had been retouched with the addition of frightening white pupils, an angular nose, and a threatening grin of white teeth. On viewing the resulting color proofs, New Mexico publisher and arts entrepreneur J. R. Willis ordered a print run of 12,500 and included on the back of the postcards the following text, designed to stir the imagination of the tourists: "Devil Dance of the Apache Indians. Terror! Treachery!! Cunning!!! are your first thoughts when you witness an Apache Devil Dance, regardless of whether seen at one of their New Mexico or Arizona Reservations or at the Intertribal Ceremonial at Gallup, where it is often performed at night by the light of huge bon-fires, producing the weirdest effect possible."

Since Clitso had never attended an actual Apache ceremony, he meticulously carved the dancers as they were depicted on the postcard, using metal to render their elaborate wooden headdresses and wands (fig. 72). It is quite amazing how skillfully he was able to transform a two-dimensional image into three-dimensional figures. The McSparrons were delighted with their "Devil Dancers" and included a photograph of the four carvings on their Christmas card the following December.[52]

Also in the late 1940s, probably as a change of pace from producing Yeibichai sets for sale, Clitso experimented with carving a cowboy figure in a yellow jacket, wearing leather chaps, cowboy boots, and a cowboy hat (fig. 73). He offered the carving as a gift to Cozy McSparron in appreciation of the latter's ongoing generous support. On their retirement from the Thunderbird Ranch, the McSparrons displayed the Clitso Cowboy, together with the four Apache dancers and the two Yeis with uplifted feet, on a shelf in their living room in Rimrock, Arizona (fig. 81). The Cowboy figure is unsigned, but definitely has been carved in Clitso's style.[53]

FIG. 72. Clitso Dedman, two Apache dancers, ca. 1948–1950. Valette Collection. Photo by Chris Soldt.

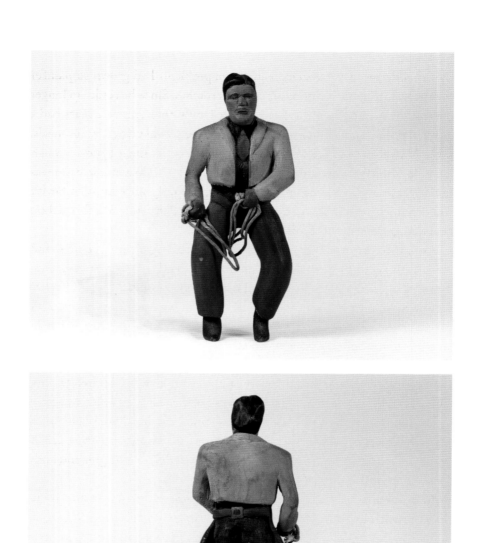

FIG. 73. Clitso Dedman, Cowboy, ca. 1948–1950. Courtesy California Academy of Sciences, 2007-0004-0001.

Final Years

By the early 1950s, Clitso Dedman's knee problems had grown so painful that he was reduced to getting around on crutches. Since he could no longer manage the stairs up to the bedroom in the family home, his wife Mary had a hospital bed installed in his workshop where she would bring him his meals. It was Mary who would market many of his late sets and single figures through Camillo Garcia's Canyon de Chelly Trading Post.[54] (Cozy McSparron was no longer actively promoting Clitso's work, not only since his own health was deteriorating but also because his attention at the time was focused on negotiating the sale of the Thunderbird Ranch.)[55]

As Clitso's arthritis began more seriously affecting his fingers, he found it increasingly difficult to manipulate his tools with his former precision. This lack of control could explain the more "expressionistic" look of his late figures. Since the carving of the wooden feathers became too great a technical challenge, he returned to metal feathers as a more feasible alternative. In an effort to render the figures with greater realism, the accoutrements of the dancers were embellished by the addition of ribbons attached to the wrists of the dancers. Mary would help with the final decorations.[56] Children Joe and Agnes assisted with the carving and did some of the painting, which was often rather imprecise with uneven brush strokes. Grandchildren Robert and Susan also helped occasionally, but their brushwork was not as meticulous, especially in the decoration of the kilts. The stocky figures, of different heights and body shapes, were finished in a high-gloss paint.

In the summer of 1954, Cozy and Inja McSparron retired from the Thunderbird Ranch and moved to Rimrock, Arizona, south of Flagstaff. They took with them their personal Clitso Dedman carvings, leaving an unsold late-style Yeibichai set (fig. 74) as a replacement for the classic set that had been on display in a special case in their dining room. When Emma Jean Bader arrived in Chinle in 1954 to manage the property for the new owners, the Babbitts, she immediately noticed the Clitso carvings. In 1960, when the LaFonts bought the Thunderbird Ranch, Bader left the Yeibichai set in its case, "thinking that guests and visitors would enjoy looking at them."[57] Twenty years later, in 1981, Roland LaFont acquired Goulding's Lodge in Monument Valley. He brought the figures with him to Utah, affixing them to a glass base so that they could be more safely displayed in his new office.[58]

FIG. 74. Clitso Dedman, LaFont Yeibichai set, ca. 1951. Goulding's Lodge, Monument Valley. Photo by author.

Ford dealer Clair Gurley acquired a similar late-style Clitso set from Camillo Garcia in partial payment for a car (fig. 75). For decades, he exhibited the carvings in his Gallup office.[59]

Gallup photographer Nello Guadagnoli was offered a late-style Yeibichai set in 1963 as partial payment for photographing Camillo Garcia's weavings (fig. 76).[60] The dancers are all of different heights and different builds. The Medicine Man and Patient are much stockier than their counterparts in the classic sets, and their facial features are not as delicate. The figures are finished in a high-gloss paint. Unfortunately, the set now has only fourteen pieces since, according to Nello's wife, two of the figures "jumped off the shelf" and got broken.[61]

Clitso was too weak to supervise the decoration of his final set (fig. 77) and left the task to his family members. They not only failed to paint juniper garlands on Water Sprinkler's arms and torso; they also took the initiative to outline triangular eyes on the Yei masks. This was something that Clitso had avoided throughout his career in his respect for Navajo tradition. (The grandchildren had been to many Yeibichai dances, helping Mary at her refreshment stand before watching the ceremony. They probably had been impressed by the eyes of the Yei impersonators, but, having been brought up as Catholics, they were unaware of the sacred nature of the masks.) The feet of the figures were

FIG. 75. Clitso Dedman, Gurley Yeibichai set, ca. 1951. Photo by Michael Schuelke.

FIG. 76. Clitso Dedman, Guadagnoli Yeibichai set of five figures, ca. 1952. Courtesy Bonhams.

signed "Clitso" in green paint, rather than pencil. This final set was purchased by Mormon trader Hugh Lee at Camillo Garcia's Canyon de Chelly Trading Post around 1955.

In the last years of his life, Clitso became eligible for welfare assistance. Since the Navajos of his generation were not on social security, it was the Bureau of Indian Affairs that had the responsibility for such support payments. In 1952, Bill Beaver, who later became owner of the Sacred Mountain Trading Post near Flagstaff, was working on the Navajo and Hopi Reservations bringing the older people in the Chinle and Ganado areas their welfare checks.[62] Beaver remembered that Clitso Dedman, whom he would visit every six months or so, would either be seated at his workbench or reclining in bed. Beaver was particularly impressed that Dedman spoke a very refined English and would politely say "I'm very much obliged" on receiving his payments. Beaver also was struck by Dedman's elegant Spencerian handwriting as he signed the required government receipt forms, especially since the other elderly Navajo welfare recipients with whom Beaver had contact at the time could only sign with thumbprints.

FIG. 77. Clitso Dedman, Lee Yeibichai set of five figures, 1953. Photo by Chris Soldt. Valette Collection.

FIG. 78. Clitso Dedman, four Yeibichai figures, 1953. Finished and painted by Phil Woodard. Photo by author.

FIG. 79. Joe Dedman, Male and Female Yei dancers, ca. 1953. Courtesy Arizona State Museum, University of Arizona, 1980-55-2 and 1980-55-4.

Bill Beaver never saw Clitso Dedman at work, but recalled that, on his last visit in spring 1953, he noticed four rough-cut figures on a shelf in the workshop. Beaver offered to buy the set, but the sale never went through since Clitso passed away before completing the pieces. In 1963, the unfinished figures were acquired by Gallup dealer Phil Woodard who sanded and painted them in the Clitso style (fig. 78).[63]

Clitso Dedman died on July 24, 1953, in Ganado after a brief hospitalization. His widow, Mary, arranged with the Franciscan friars for his burial in the community cemetery in Chinle. As was the practice at the time in Navajo cemeteries, no headstone was erected. There may have been a wooden marker, but, if so, it has been long gone.[64] At the initiative of grandson Robert Dedman, the town of Chinle revived his memory years later by naming Route 8162, which runs past Dedman Acres, as "Łitso Road."[65]

Joe Dedman did carve a pair Yeibichai figures reminiscent of his stepfather's late style, signing them with "Joe D" on one foot and "Dedman" on the other (fig. 79).[66] The Female Yei has an overly large face mask and an extremely short torso. The Male Yei has a much smaller headmask. Realizing that carving was not his forte, Joe Dedman quickly turned his attention to other activities. The Clitso Dedman era had come to an end.

9

A Forgotten Artist

During the last fourteen years of his life, Clitso Dedman, physically diminished by severe arthritis, had found a new occupation: woodcarving. With the
encouragement and promotion of mentor Cozy McSparron, Clitso's Yeibichai
carvings were sold almost as fast as they could be created. Between 1940 and
1945, his carvings consisted of pairs and single figures, plus thirteen sets of four:
Talking God, Water Sprinkler, and two Female Yeis. After World War II, Clitso
focused on carving more challenging full Yeibichai scenes, completing a total
of twenty-five such sets of sixteen figures. During less demanding periods, he
would carve one-of-a-kind figures for the McSparrons or their friend Sallie
Wagner Lippincott. His total production numbered about 500 carvings, over
two-thirds of which are in private collections.

Sadly, the memory of Clitso Dedman gradually faded after his death in 1953.
Unlike his Teller Institute classmate Jacob Morgan, Clitso had left no personal
writings. There was the brief article by Charles Wyatt in the 1944 *Arizona Highways* that described the Clitso carvings and concluded with a one-paragraph

biographical note. Two years later, an article in the *Arizona Daily Star*, which pictured the Clitso Yeibichai set that Tucson dealer Clay Lockett was displaying in his store, contained the following short reference: "The dolls in the collection are of museum importance, Lockett said, because their creator, Hosteen Klitso Dedman, is growing old, his eyesight is failing and his hands are no longer as firm as they need to be for the delicate carving and painting of the dolls."[1]

The Clitso Dedman contemporary with the most intimate knowledge of the man and his many talents was mentor and promoter Cozy McSparron, owner of the Thunderbird Ranch and Trading Post. However, in 1954, the year after Clitso's death, McSparron sold the Chinle property back to the Navajo Nation and moved two hundred miles southwest to the small town of Rimrock, located halfway between Flagstaff and Phoenix. By then, McSparron was already quite ill. He died five years later in 1959, without having published any personal memoirs in which he might have mentioned the carver.

Still living in Chinle in the late 1950s was Camillo Garcia, owner of the Canyon de Chelly Trading Post, who had been marketing the last Clitso Yeibichai sets. However, in 1962, Camillo and his son died in a plane crash, leaving nobody in Chinle to maintain the artist's memory.

Anthropologist Clara Lee Tanner, in her well-received 1968 book entitled *Southwest Indian Craft Arts*, did devote three pages to Navajo sculpture, including a photograph of the Clitso Yeibichai set at the Arizona State Museum. For lack of background information, however, she included only a short paragraph about the carver. She praised the "high standard" of his work and suggested that Tom Yazzie (to whom she devoted the remainder of the section) might have been inspired by the Clitso Dedman figures on display at the Navajo Arts and Crafts Guild at Window Rock (fig. 83).[2] In 1970, in his book *Southwestern Indian Ceremonials*, Tom Bahti included a photograph of two Clitso figures, Water Sprinkler and Female Yei, to illustrate the Yeibichai dance. In the caption, the carver was mistakenly identified as a "noted Navajo medicine man from Chinle."[3]

Over the next three decades, there was no mention of Clitso Dedman in print. Consequently, museums, collectors, and dealers had no references to consult in order to verify biographical details about the artist and the dating of his work. Moreover, if the figures had been glued to some sort of support, the signature on the feet was obliterated and the artist was sometimes either misidentified or not identified at all.

Museum Holdings

Less than one-third of Clitso Dedman's carvings are now housed in museum collections, and almost all of these are in storage and not on exhibit. Only one figure can be viewed today by the public: a Female Patient holding a ceremonial basket in the "Woven through Time" exhibit at the Arizona State Museum in Tucson. It is hoped that in the future more museums will opt to exhibit their Clitso holdings.

During Clitso Dedman's lifetime, four museums acquired his carvings.

1944, Museum of Indian Arts and Culture in Santa Fe: Early Female Begging God, gift of local dealer David Neumann

1945, Arizona State Museum in Tucson: Classic sixteen-piece Yeibichai set, purchased from local dealer Clay Lockett

1947, Wheelwright Museum in Santa Fe: Early four-figure Begging God set, gift of "DU"

1953, Museum of Indian Arts and Culture in Santa Fe: Classic sixteen-piece Yeibichai set, loaned by Caroline Kelly, and permanently bequeathed in 1970

In the four decades following Dedman's death, museums received donations of Clitso carvings, in sets of different sizes.

1956, Southwest Museum in Los Angeles (now Autry Museum of the American West): Classic sixteen-piece Yeibichai set, bequest of Dr. Leslie Eames

1959, Mathers Museum in Bloomington (now the Indiana University Museum of Archaeology and Anthropology): Fourteen transitional and classic figures, originally part of two distinct sixteen-piece sets collected by Dr. Thomas Noble

1962, Southeast Museum in Marathon, Florida; transferred in 1968 to the Denver Museum of Natural History (now the Denver Museum of Nature and Science): Early four-figure Begging God set, collected by Francis and Mary Crane

1967, Amon Carter Museum of American Art in Fort Worth: Mixed sixteen-piece set of Yeibichai figures, collected by Cozy McSparron

1972, California Academy of Sciences in San Francisco: Classic four-figure set, collected by Charles and Ruth Elkus and Classic sixteen-piece Yeibichai set, collected by Charles and Ruth Elkus

1972, Museum of Indian Arts and Culture in Santa Fe: Early four-figure Begging God set plus Female Yei with ceremonial basket, collected by Pansy Stockton, ca. 1942

1975, Arizona State Museum in Tucson: Early four-figure Begging God set, collected by Muriel Painter

1980, Arizona State Museum in Tucson: Pair of classic figures, collected by Dr. Edwin Wilde

1983, Indianapolis Museum of Art: Fourteen transitional and classic figures, originally part of two distinct sixteen-piece sets collected by Dr. Thomas Noble[4]

1984, Nora Eccles Harrison Museum of Art, Utah State University in Logan: Pair of classic figures, collected by John Boyden; deaccessioned in 2013

1992, Maxwell Museum, University of New Mexico in Albuquerque: Transitional seven-figure set, collected by Charles Freeman, 1950s

In the 1940s, Dr. Thomas Noble purchased two sixteen-piece Clitso sets, plus a single Female Yei holding a ceremonial basket. Over the years, five figures were lost or broken. After his death in 1958, his widow simply divided the remaining twenty-eight carvings into two groups of fourteen.[5] As a result, when the classic set that Dr. Noble photographed in 1948 (fig. 66) was donated to the Indianapolis Museum of Art, it consisted of only five Female Yeis and five Male Yeis. In fact, one of the Female Yeis (second from right in fig. 80) belongs to the earlier transitional set now at the Indiana University Museum in Bloomington. The missing Male Patient was replaced by the Female Yei with a ceremonial basket. The transitional set now in Bloomington has twelve of its original sixteen figures, plus a Female and Male Yei from the classic set now at the Indianapolis museum.

Dispersal of the McSparron Collection
When the McSparrons left the Thunderbird Ranch in Chinle and moved to Rimrock, Arizona, they took with them their private collection of Clitso

FIG. 80. Clitso Dedman, Nightway figures at the Indianapolis Museum of Art at Newfields, 2015.51 to 2015.64.

carvings. These included two large classic Yeibichai sets (one of which had been exhibited in a special case in their Thunderbird Ranch dining room; fig. 55) and several unique pieces that Clitso had carved especially for them over the years. Some of the latter were displayed on a crowded shelf in their new home, far away from the public eye (fig. 81).[6] Daughter Laramie inherited the two Apache figures on the left, plus the two Yeibichai dancers with raised legs. Daughter Marion received the other two Apache dancers, plus Fringe Mouth and the Cowboy.

After McSparron's death in 1959, his widow, Inja, would live another ten years in Rimrock. In 1967, prior to moving to Prescott to be closer to her daughter Laramie, Inja sold a sixteen-piece Clitso set to Mitchell Wilder, the energetic director of the Amon Carter Museum in Fort Worth, Texas, who was eager to expand the Navajo holdings. Unfortunately, Inja was not as knowledgeable as her husband had been, and the background information she provided to Wilder contained several errors.[7] The accession files state that Dedman died in 1954, not 1953. The date of the carvings is given as ca. 1937, rather than ca.

FIG. 81. Clitso Dedman carvings at the McSparron home in Rimrock, Arizona. Courtesy Laramie McSparron Jarvi.

1945. In her sketch as to how to display the figures, Inja misidentified Talking God as "Batachi."[8]

What is much more serious than the above errors is the fact that Inja mixed together figures from the two distinct McSparron Yeibichai sets.[9] They had most probably been packed together in the move from Chinle and perhaps had not been displayed in Rimrock for lack of space. The result is that she sold Mitchell Wilder nine figures from the transitional McSparron set: Female Patient, Medicine Man, Talking God, four Female Yeis and two Male Yeis. She then added four Male Yeis and Water Sprinkler from the classic set. She also included two Female Yeis with lowered arms, which were a unique pair of carvings that Clitso had made for Cozy McSparron as a gift (fig. 82). It is also possible that prior to 1967, Inja had sold the two Male Yeis and the two Female Yeis from the original transitional set to another collector; in any event, the whereabouts of those four figures is not known.

After Inja McSparron's death in 1977, the remaining Clitso Dedman carvings went to daughter Laramie. Around 1984, Laramie sold eighteen Clitso figures, including eleven from Cozy McSparron's classic Yeibichai set with its Female Yeis in long skirts (fig. 68), to collector Lars Garrison.[10] She also sold

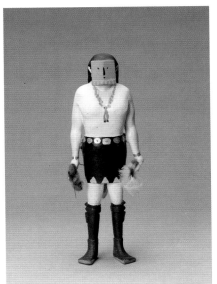

FIG. 82. Clitso Dedman, pair of Female Yei dancers with lowered arms, ca. 1943. Courtesy Amon Carter Museum of American Art, 1967-26-8 and 1967-26-9.

him Meredith Guillet's oil portrait of Clitso Dedman (fig. 33). Laramie kept the Water Sprinkler from the transitional McSparron set, which had been displayed in the dining room at the Thunderbird Ranch, as a souvenir of her childhood.

From Oblivion to Belated Recognition

By twenty years after Clitso Dedman's death, his name had faded into oblivion. In November 1975, Sotheby Parke Bernet in New York held a special auction of Native American artifacts that belonged to Zuni dealer C. G. Wallace. Among the lots was a sixteen-piece Clitso set that Wallace had displayed for many years in a special case in his Gallup trading post. It attracted little attention among the uninformed buyers and remained unsold. In March 1977, at the annual Wheelwright Benefit Auction, a sixteen-piece Clitso set drew little interest and was acquired by a Santa Fe dealer Rex Arrowsmith who, finding himself unable to market it, subsequently passed it on to Tobe Turpen, a Gallup colleague. In December 1981, when Southwest trader Tom Woodard put his collection of Navajo art up for auction at Christie's in New York, his eight-piece Clitso set failed to meet its reserve.

In 1983, Chuck and Jan Rosenak's discovery of the wood carvings of Navajo Johnson Antonio in the Wheelwright Museum became a catalyst inspiring them to spend the next decade traveling throughout Navajoland exploring the development of Navajo folk art, research that culminated in the publication of their book *Navajo Folk Art* (1994). In their introduction, they state that Tom Yazzie was "one of the first to carve a set of Yeibichai dancers," dating the figures to 1957 or 1958.[11] Unfortunately, and in a sense understandably, the Rosenaks make no mention of Clitso Dedman, because during the decade of their exploration, the latter's carvings were hidden from the general public in museum storage vaults and private collections.

With the publication of Rebecca and Jean-Paul Valette's article "The Life and Work of Clitso Dedman, Navajo Woodcarver" in the Spring 2000 issue of *American Indian Art Magazine*, researchers and collectors finally had in their hands a brief biography of this innovative carver together with photographs of his work. Thus Clitso Dedman finally received belated recognition for his pioneering contribution to the development of Navajo carving. Today his carvings bring on the average of $1,000 to $2,000 per figure. It is hoped that this new comprehensive biography and catalog will stimulate even broader awareness of the remarkable career of this Navajo man and of his distinctive carvings.

Epilogue

A NEW NAVAJO ART

In his 1944 article in *Arizona Highways*, Charles Wyatt had written: "A new form of Navajo art is possibly beginning at Canyon de Chelly National Monument, in northeastern Arizona. If the opposition of the elders is not too strong, woodcarving may take its place with the well-established crafts of weaving and silversmithing. The new work is being pioneered by Klitso Dedman under the tutelage of Cozy McSparron, Chinle Indian trader."[1] It was not until ten years after the publication of Wyatt's short piece that this prediction would begin to be realized.

In the mid-1950s, the Navajo Arts and Crafts Guild in Window Rock acquired one of Clitso Dedman's late-style sixteen-piece Yeibichai sets (fig. 83). Around 1960, when the Guild (renamed the Navajo Arts and Crafts Enterprise in 1972) moved into its current facility, the Clitso carvings were prominently displayed, thus signaling to those Navajos visiting the store that woodcarving was indeed a Navajo art form to be developed and promoted.[2]

FIG. 83. Clitso Dedman, Navajo Nation Yeibichai set, ca. 1951. Navajo Arts and Crafts Enterprise. Photo by author.

Today, among the best-known woodcarvers to continue the "new form of Navajo art" are Charlie Willeto, Tom Yazzie, and Sheldon Harvey.

Charlie Willeto

Charlie Willeto (1897–1964), a Blessing Way medicine man who had led a pastoral life northeast of Chaco Canyon, began carving simple figures in 1961, inspired by the small figurines he had occasionally used in his healing ceremonies.[3] Using only hatchet, saw, and knife, without sandpaper, he fashioned old pieces of board into rough human and animal shapes, decorating them with unused paint left by road crews (fig. 84).[4] He would exchange his carvings, one or two at a time, for foodstuffs and other merchandise at the Mauzy Trading Post at Lybrook thirteen miles east of Nageezi. After his death, his carvings were discovered by Santa Fe trader Rex Arrowsmith and became highly collectible.[5] His wife Elizabeth, who had helped her husband in painting his figures, encouraged sons Leonard, Harold, and Robin to continue the family carving tradition.[6]

FIG. 84. Charlie Willeto, Male Yei dancer, 24 in. Marti Streuver Collection. Courtesy Adobe Gallery.

FIG. 85. Tom Yazzie, Yeibichai dancers in rehearsal, 10 in. to 12 in., 1971. Valette Collection. Photo by Chris Soldt.

Tom Yazzie

Tom Yazzie (1930–2019) began carving single Yeibichai figures in 1957, but soon began recreating scenes of Navajo ceremonies as they might have appeared around 1900.[7] Some of his realistic larger sets contain as many as thirty figures. In order to assure the accuracy of his carvings, he attended numerous dances and events, observing ritual details, and also consulted frequently with his brother Alfred who was a medicine man. While Yazzie focused his attention on the actual carving, his wife Marie would paint the figures, paying careful attention to their ceremonial attire and accoutrements. Tom Yazzie is represented in many museum collections, with over 125 of his figures having been donated to the Navajo Nation Museum in 1972 by the Navajo Arts and Crafts Enterprise.

At the Gallup Intertribal Ceremonial in 1971, his eight-piece Yeibichai set (fig. 85) won not only first prize but also the Elkus Memorial Special Award.[8] The scene depicts six male Yei dancers (without masks) rehearsing their steps in the presence of Talking God and Calling God, prior to the last night of the Nightway. Each of the figures is glued to a thin sandy board, signed underneath "Tom Yazzie."

FIG. 86. Sheldon Harvey, *Air-Spirit Being*, 21 in., 2007. Valette Collection. Photo by author.

Sheldon Harvey

Sheldon Harvey (b. 1978) was originally trained as a medicine man by his grandfather, but then opted for an artistic career with the goal bringing to life the ancient Navajo stories he had known since childhood. In August 2005, and again in 2007 and 2008, he won first place in the Sculpture division at the Santa Fe Indian Market. Many of his carvings are inspired by the Emergence Story and the description of the first dark underworld, which was inhabited by insect-like Air-Spirit Beings (fig. 86). A prolific sculptor and painter, Sheldon Harvey continues to explore new interpretations and new subject matter.[9]

Beginning in the 1970s and 1980s, woodcarving was adopted as an artistic medium by numerous Navajo folk artists. In 1994, Chuck and Jan Rosenak published *Navajo Folk Art*, a generously illustrated book featuring numerous Navajo carvers of the preceding forty years. Although they failed to mention the then-forgotten pioneer Clitso Dedman, it is clearly evident that the latter's legacy has today been firmly established.

APPENDIX

INVENTORY OF CLITSO DEDMAN CARVINGS

The following inventory lists all the Clitso Dedman carvings that we have been able to study, plus pictures of carvings that have been advertised by dealers or auction houses. Although there are definitely still a few Clitso carvings in private hands of which we are unaware, these pages list the quasi-entirety of his output. In order to facilitate reference, we have named the sets for their original owners, if known, or for subsequent owners. Where possible, we have also provided references to auction lots, dealer offerings, publications, exhibits, and museum holdings. We have also noted instances in which, over the decades, figures in some sets have been lost and/or replaced by others from different sets.

Clitso's cottonwood carvings of Yeibichai dancers vary in height from eight to thirteen inches. Of his known production, there are twenty-two sets of sixteen-piece Yeibichai dance scenes consisting of a Medicine Man, a Patient (man or woman), Talking God, six Male Yei dancers, six Female Yei dancers (impersonated by men, unless otherwise indicated), and Water Sprinkler. There are also forty-one smaller sets, ranging from single dancers to groups of eight. In addition, Clitso Dedman occasionally carved other figures, such as Navajo participants on the Eighth Day of the Nightway or in the Enemyway, as well as Apache dancers and even a cowboy.

Clitso Yeibichai figures are all carved in a very characteristic style, thus making them easily recognizable. Most of the carvings are signed "Clitso" on both feet, as in figure 87. With his very earliest figures, Clitso also penciled the year. Occasionally the signatures are now difficult or impossible to discern, especially if the figures were once affixed to a baseboard.

Clitso carvings were created over a span of fifteen years, during which time subtle changes occurred in his style, reflecting developments in his carving skill, the availability of different types of paint and, ultimately, the effects of old age which diminished his ability to control the chisel and the paintbrush, leading him to enlist the help of family members.

The entries below are divided into four sections representing the evolution of Clitso Dedman's carving technique: Early style (1939–43), Transitional style (1943–45), Classic style (1945–50), and Late style (1951–53). Within each section, the entries are listed according to the number of figures in each set, from one to sixteen.

ABBREVIATIONS

E.	Early style: Nightway Begging Gods
T.	Transitional style: Nightway figures and Yeibichai dancers
T. EW.	Transitional style: Enemy Way
C.	Classic style: Yeibichai dancers
C.A.	Classic style: Apache dancers
C.C.	Classic style: Cowboy
L.	Late style: Yeibichai dancers
L. PW.	Late style: Yeibichai dancers, finished by Phil Woodard

FIG. 87. Clitso signature. Photo by author.

FIG. 88. Clitso Dedman, early style: E.4-C. Koenig set of four Begging Gods. Courtesy Cowan's Auctions.

Early Style (1939–43)

Clitso Dedman's first carvings are of the masked Nightway participants who as Begging Gods go out on the Sixth Day of the ceremony to solicit donations of food from those living in the surrounding area. Talking God and Water Sprinkler, both carrying large fawnskin bags, are accompanied one or two Yeis waving yucca wands made of wire or stiffened plied green yarn. Clitso portrays Talking God in long pants with a sacred white deerskin over his left shoulder. He is shown holding a small pollen pouch in his right hand and a tan spotted fawnskin bag in his left hand. Water Sprinkler similarly carries a fawnskin bag for collecting donations. The Female Yeis, and also Water Sprinkler, are depicted with yucca wands. Sometimes they also hold green clumps of yarn or feathers representing juniper and sumac twigs.

Clitso's Begging Gods are solidly planted upright figures with a proud bearing and broad stance. The figures have been sanded and the lines smoothed to convey an almost idealized representation of the Nightway participants. All his figures stand on straight thin legs and hold their arms away from their bodies. They wear brown moccasins and blue stockings with sculpted red garters. The painting of the figures is highly stylized and almost two-dimensional in the simplicity of its line. The necklaces and jaclas are delicately indicated with fine brush strokes of red and dark blue. The kilts are generally painted a matte ocher or a rusty red-brown with simple geometric black border designs; hanging down the back is a kit fox pelt. The concha belts are suggested by a row of simple white circles outlined in black and with a central black dot. The spruce ruffs of Talking God and Water Sprinkler are represented by green rings. Toward the end of this period, Clitso began using more glossy paints in a broader range of colors. The figures are signed "Clitso" on the bottom of each foot. On the earliest figures, Clitso added the date 1940 or 1941.

Occasionally, during this period, Clitso Dedman would carve a masked Female Yei who appears in the Nightway on the Eighth Day. She is depicted in traditional dress, holding a ceremonial basket. By 1943, Clitso also began carving the first Male Yeis, not as Begging Gods with yucca wands but as Yeibichai dancers with gourd rattles.

Clitso Dedman's known production in the early style consists of fifty-seven carvings grouped in twenty-three sets ranging from one to five figures.

E.1-A David Neumann Female Yei

Female Yei wears a rusty red-brown kilt with white conchas and holds a wire yucca wand and green wool tufts representing juniper sprigs. The feet are not signed.

> Description: Cottonwood, green wool tufts, wire; 10 in.; ca. 1942.
> History: Santa Fe trader David L. Neumann donated this early carving to the Museum of New Mexico in December 1944, referring to the Wyatt article in the April 1944 issue of *Arizona Highways*.
> Current Location: Museum of New Mexico, Lab of Anthropology, Santa Fe, cat. no. 14279/12.

E.1-B Water Sprinkler

Erect Water Sprinkler holds a wire yucca wand in his right hand and a pelt bag in his left hand. He wears a rusty red-brown kilt with white conchas. The green ring around his neck represents the spruce ruff.

> Description: Cottonwood, green wool tufts, wire; 11 in.; ca. 1942.
> History: Collected by an Arkansas family.
> Dealer: Offered on eBay (2014); price $3,250.
> Current Location: Unknown.

E.1-C Laramie McSparron Female Yei with Ceremonial Basket

The Female Yei, impersonated by a woman with long, sleek black hair, wears a short blue mask and jacla earrings. The white, black, red, and orange striped trade blanket draped over her dark orange blouse and skirt is attached in front with a rectangular silver clasp. She has white conchas on her red sash belt. (See fig. 47.)

> Description: Cottonwood; 8 in.; 1941.
> History: Gift from Clitso Dedman to Laramie McSparron, daughter of
>   Cozy McSparron, Christmas 1941.
> Publication: Valette and Valette, "The Life and Work of Clitso Dedman," 55.
> Current Location: Unknown.

E.1-D Marion McSparron Fringe Mouth

Fringe Mouth stands erect with both arms outstretched above his shoulders. In his left hand, he holds a curved pipe cleaner "rope." The right side of his body is painted red, and the left side black. His black and red headdress is topped with pipe cleaner "rope" and feathers. His dark blue kilt is decorated with white circular conchas. (See figs. 48 and 81.)

> Description: Cottonwood, feathers, pipe cleaner; 8 in.; 1941.
> History: Gift from Clitso Dedman to Marion McSparron, daughter of
>   Cozy McSparron, Christmas 1941
> Auction: Bonhams & Butterfields, June 4, 2007, one of two carvings in
>   lot 4027; price of lot $650.
> Current Location: California Academy of Sciences, San Francisco, cat. no.
>   2007-0004-0002.

E.1-E Sallie Wagner Talking God

Talking God wears a brown shirt and blue pants. His light green ring-shaped ruff has distinctive black dots. He holds a pouch in his right hand and a spotted fawnskin bag in the left. The feet are signed "Clitso 1941" in pencil. (See fig. 49.)

Description: Cottonwood, feathers; 10 in.; 1941.

History: Gift from Clitso Dedman to Cozy McSparron, Christmas 1941. Given to Sallie Wagner Lippincott in the early 1940s.

Dealer: Offered by Toh-Atin Gallery, Durango, Colorado (2020); price $2,000.

Current Location: Jackson Clark Collection.

E.1-F Charles Wyatt Water Sprinkler

Erect Water Sprinkler holds a wire yucca wand in his right hand. In his left hand, he has a spotted fawnskin bag. He wears a dark kilt with a white design. His oversized headmask with a green ring-shaped ruff around the neck is missing its feathers. (See fig. 50.)

Description: Cottonwood, feathers, wire; 8 in.; 1941.

History: Gift from Clitso Dedman to Cozy McSparron, Christmas 1941. Given to Charles Wyatt in the early 1940s.

Current Location: Private Collection.

E.1-G Thomas Noble Female Yei with Ceremonial Basket

The Female Yei, impersonated by a woman with long sleek black hair, wears a short blue mask and jacla earrings. The blue, red, and brown striped trade blanket draped over her brown blouse and skirt is attached in front with an oval silver clasp. She has white conchas on her red sash belt. (See fig. 80.)

Description: Cottonwood; 8 in.; ca. 1941.

History: Acquired by Dr. Thomas Noble in the 1940s. Donated to the Indianapolis Museum of Art by his daughter Patricia Noble in 1983.

Current Location: Indianapolis Museum of Art, cat. no. 2015.59.

Note: This figure is inappropriately mixed with the Noble Classic Yeibichai set C.16-G.

E.1-H Valette Female Yei

Female Yei has smooth black hair and wears a glossy red-brown kilt with a simple black border design. The belt is indicated by silver painted conchas with turquoise stones. The fox pelt hanging down her back is dark and light gray with tan highlights and a white tip on the tail. She holds tufts of white down. The piece is signed "Clitso" on both feet.

> Description: Cottonwood, feathers; 11 in.; ca. 1943.
> History: Unknown.
> Auction: Butterfield & Butterfield, November 23, 1998, one of "Four Southwest Items" in lot 3473; price $650. (The description in the catalog did not identify the carver.)
> Dealer: Sold by Jed Foutz, Shiprock Trading Company (December 1998); price $1,000.
> Current Location: Valette Collection.

E.2-A Pair of Female Yeis as Begging Gods

Both Female Yeis in dark blue face masks hold wire yucca wands in their hands. They wear light brown kilts with black border designs and white circular conchas, also outlined in black. The red garters on their blue stockings are simply painted, and not sculpted as in later carvings. The feet are signed "Clitso 1940." These may be the first known Clitso carvings. (See fig. 45.)

> Description: Cottonwood, wire; 9 in. and 9.5 in.; 1940.
> History: Unknown.
> Current Location: Private Collection.

E.2-B Tom Bahti Set of Two: Female Yei and Water Sprinkler as Begging Gods

Water Sprinkler stands erect, with white (rather than black) decorations on his kilt. His large headmask has a green ruff collar. In his right hand, he holds green wool tufts and a wire yucca wand. In his left hand, he holds a brown spotted fawnskin bag. Female Yei wears a red-brown kilt with silver conchas. In her right hand, she also has green wool tufts and a wire yucca wand. She holds red "sumac" feathers in her left hand.

Description: Cottonwood, feathers, green wool tufts, wire; 10 in. and 11 in.; ca. 1943.

History: Tom Bahti purchased the two figures from Bill Cousins in the 1960s.

Publication: Bahti, *Southwestern Indian Ceremonials*, 14.

Current Location: Bahti family.

E.2-C John Malloy Pair of Female Yeis as Begging Gods

The one Female Yei, in a light brown kilt, holds green wool tufts and wire yucca wands. The other Female Yei, in a red-brown kilt, has feathers in her hands. Belts are painted as a row of round silver conchas with turquoise center stones.

Description: Cottonwood, feathers, green wool tufts, wire; 10 in.; ca. 1942.

History: Unknown.

Dealer: Offered by the John Malloy Gallery, New York (2008); asking price $3,200.

Current Location: Unknown.

E.2-D Cozy McSparron Set of Two Female Yeis with Lowered Arms

These are the only known Clitso Female Yeis with lowered arms lightly attached at the waist. Both figures have dark kilts with round silver conchas and ivory border designs. In their right hands, they hold green wool tufts and wire yucca wands. In their left hands, they hold white feathers. (See fig. 82.)

Description: Cottonwood, green wool tufts, wire; 10 in.; ca. 1943.

History: Cozy McSparron Collection. Sold by widow Inja McSparron to the Amon Carter Museum in 1967 as part of a reconstituted 16-piece Yeibichai set (T.16-B.).

Current Location: Amon Carter Museum of American Art, Fort Worth, cat. nos. 1967.26.8–9.

E.2-E Phil Woodard Set of Two: Talking God and Male Yei

Talking God, in a ring ruff, wears a dark shirt and dark pants. He holds a small pouch in his right hand and a light tan pelt bag in his left. The feathers of his headdress are topped with white down. Male Yei, in a dark blue kilt with a white border design and round silver conchas, has a large headmask with a ring ruff. He holds a white gourd rattle and small green tufts.

> Description: Cottonwood, feathers green wool tufts; 11 in.; ca. 1943.
> History: Acquired by Gallup dealer Phil Woodard in 1963.
> Current Location: Unknown.

E.2-F Russell Hartman Set of Two Male Yeis

The two Male Yeis are of somewhat different heights and builds. Both have similar ring ruffs and wear simple straight kilts with white border designs and silver conchas with turquoise. Their hands are held away from the waist with a wooden support. They each have a white gourd rattle and gray feathers in the right hand and a combination of gray and red feathers in the left. The kit fox pelt attached to the back of the shorter Yei is long and gray; the pelt worn by the taller Yei is brown and not as long.

> Description: Cottonwood, feathers; 11 in.; ca. 1943.
> History: Unknown.
> Dealer: Offered on eBay (2020); asking price $920.
> Current Location: Russell Hartman Collection.

E.3 Mark Bahti Set of Three Begging Gods:
Talking God, Water Sprinkler, Female Yei

Talking God wears a red-orange shirt with silver buttons and dark pants. He holds a spotted fawnskin bag in his right hand. Erect Water Sprinkler holds a fox pelt in his right hand and feathers in his left. This is one of the rare groupings in which Talking God and Water Sprinkler hold the pelts in their right rather than left hands. Both Talking God and Water Sprinkler have simple green ring ruffs. The hands of Female Yei are empty; originally she was probably also holding feathers. The dark green kilts of Water Sprinkler and Female Yei have white border designs and large silver conchas.

> Description: Cottonwood, feathers; 10 in. and 11 in.; ca. 1943.
> History: Unknown.
> Dealer: Offered by Mark Bahti Indian Arts, Santa Fe (2010); asking price
> $3,450.
> Current Location: Unknown.

E.4-A Francis Crane Set of Four Begging Gods: Talking
God, Two Female Yeis, Water Sprinkler

Talking God has an orange shirt and green pants. He holds an orange-brown pouch in his right hand and a tan fawnskin bag in his left. Water Sprinkler holds a large spotted fawnskin bag. His headdress has lost its two feathers. The ring ruffs of Talking God and Water Sprinkler are light brown, rather than green as they will be with later Clitso figures. Female Yeis hold green wool tufts and wire yucca wands. Concha belts are shown as a row of white circles outlined in black. The feet are not signed. (See fig. 46.)

> Description: Cottonwood, feathers; green wool tufts, wire; 10 in. and 11 in.; ca. 1941.
>
> History: Sold to Lupton dealer Al Frick in the early 1940s by Reed Winnie. Purchased by Francis Crane in 1962 from Gallup dealer J. W. Kennedy for $185. Exhibited at the Southeast Museum in Marathon, Florida. Donated to the Denver Museum of Natural History in 1968.
>
> Note: The Denver Museum accession file erroneously dated the set to 1925 and ascribed it to Reed Winnie.
>
> Publication: Valette and Valette, "Clitso Dedman," 62.
>
> Current Location: Denver Museum of Nature and Science, cat. nos. 6203 to 6206.

E.4-B Sallie Wagner Set of Four Begging Gods: Talking
God, Two Female Yeis, Water Sprinkler

Talking God, in a gray shirt and red-brown pants, holds a small pouch in his right hand and a brown spotted fawnskin bag in the left. His feathers of his headdress are tipped with white down. His green ring ruff has dark green dots, as does the ring ruff of Water Sprinkler. The Female Yeis each hold green wool twigs and two wire yucca wands. Erect Water Sprinkler has green wool twigs and a yucca wand in the right hand and a spotted fawnskin bag in the left. The orange-brown kilts have simple black border designs and round white conchas. The feet are signed "Clitso 1941." (See fig. 51.)

> Description: Cottonwood, feathers, green wool tufts, wire; 10 in. and 12 in.; 1941.
>
> History: Original owner: Sallie Wagner Lippincott.

Dealer: Offered by Toh-Atin Gallery, Durango, Colorado (2020); asking price $8,000.

Current Location: Jackson Clark Collection.

E.4-C Koenig Set of Four Begging Gods:
Talking God, Two Female Yeis, Water Sprinkler
Talking God has a light brown shirt and light-blue pants. He holds a small pouch in his right hand and a spotted fawnskin bag in his left hand. Water Sprinkler holds a spotted fawnskin bag. Female Yeis hold green wool tufts and wire yucca wands. The ochre kilts have black border designs with silver conchas. The feet are signed "Clitso 1941." (See fig. 88.)

Description: Cottonwood, feathers, green wool tufts, wire; 10 in. and 12 in.; 1941.

History: Purchased by Harriet and Seymour Koenig at the Parke Bernet Auction, December 17, 1968.

Auction: Cowan's, April 5, 2019; lot 355. Sold for $2,952.

Publication: Koenig and Koenig, *Acculturation*: Water Sprinkler and Female Yei, cover illustration; Talking God, 3.

Current Location: Unknown.

E.4-D Muriel Painter Set of Four Begging Gods:
Talking God, Two Female Yeis, Water Sprinkler
Talking God wears a red shirt and dark blue pants; his bent arms are close to his body. He has a pouch in his right hand and a tan spotted fawnskin bag in his left. Female Yeis, in olive-green kilts with silver conchas and white border designs, hold green wool tufts and wire yucca wands. Erect Water Sprinkler wears a dark red kilt with a black border design and holds a spotted fawnskin bag in his left hand.

Description: Cottonwood, feathers, green wool tufts, wire; 10 in. and 12 in.; ca. 1943.

History: Purchased by Muriel Thayer Painter. Bequeathed to Arizona State Museum in 1975.

Current Location: Arizona State Museum, Tucson, cat. nos. 1975-13-1 to 4.

E.4-E Wheelwright Set of Four Begging Gods: Talking
God, Two Female Yeis, Water Sprinkler

Talking God, in a red-orange shirt and dark pants, holds a small pouch in his right hand and a gray and tan fawnskin bag in his left. Female Yeis have glossy colored kilts with silver conchas, typical of the transitional style. They hold green tufts and wire yucca wands. Erect Water Sprinkler, in a dark green kilt with white triangular decorations, holds a large spotted fawnskin bag in his left hand. In his right hand, he has a green tuft and a yucca wand.

Description: Cottonwood, feathers, green wool tufts, wire; 10 in. and 12 in.; ca. 1943.

History: Original owner, indicated simply as "DU," donated the set to the Wheelwright in 1947.

Current Location: Wheelwright Museum, Santa Fe, cat. nos. 2-59-309 to 312.

E.4-F Alan Edison Set of Four Begging Gods: Talking
God, Two Female Yeis, Water Sprinkler

Talking God, in an orange shirt and blue pants, holds a small pouch in his right hand and a gray and tan spotted fawnskin bag in his left. Female Yeis have red-orange kilts with simple black border decorations and silver conchas. They hold green tufts and wire yucca wands. Erect Water Sprinkler, in a similar red-orange kilt, holds a large spotted fawnskin bag in his left hand. In his right hand, he has a green tuft and a yucca wand. The feet of the figures are signed "Clitso 1941, Chin Lee Ariz." On the back of Talking God's white deerskin, an earlier owner has written "Canyon de Chelly, Navajo Res. 1941, by 100 yr. Navajo cottonwood root."

Description: Cottonwood, feathers, green wool tufts, wire; 10 in. and 12 in.; 1941.

History: Purchased by Alan Edison in 2018.

Dealer: Offered by Adobe Gallery, Santa Fe NM (2023); asking price $6,000.

Current Location: Unknown.

E.5-A Pansy Stockton Set of Five: Talking God, Water Sprinkler, Two Female Yeis, Female Yei with Ceremonial Basket

This set has the typical four Begging God figures of the early sets with the addition of a Female Yei impersonated by a woman. Talking God, in a blue shirt and olive-green pants, holds a pouch in his right hand and a spotted fawnskin bag in the left. Female Yei dancers have orange-brown kilts with white border designs. They hold green tufts and yucca wand wires. Their shiny black hair hangs straight down their backs. Erect Water Sprinkler also has a green tuft and a wand in his right hand, and a gray and tan spotted fawnskin bag in the left. The fifth figure is a Female Yei holding a ceremonial basket away from her body, but connected by a wooden support. The red, orange, black, white, and light-blue striped trade blanket draped over her dark orange blouse and skirt is attached in front with a silver clasp. She has silver conchas on her red sash belt. (See fig. 53.)

> Description: Cottonwood, feathers, green wool tufts, wire; 9 in., 10 in., and 12 in.; ca. 1942.
> History: Purchased by Colorado artist Pansy Stockton, ca. 1942. Bequeathed to the Museum of Indian Arts and Culture in 1972.
> Exhibit: Bosque Redondo Memorial, Fort Sumner, New Mexico, 1992–2005.
> Publication: *New Mexico Magazine Calendar*, 1973; and Valette and Valette, "Clitso Dedman," 62.
> Current Location: Museum of Indian Arts and Culture, Santa Fe, cat. no. 46170/12.

E.5-B James Solomon Set of Five: Talking God, Male Yei, Female Yei, Water Sprinkler, Female Yei with Ceremonial Basket

Talking God wears a dark shirt and pants; he has a small pouch in his right hand and a spotted fawnskin bag in the left. All male figures have ring ruffs. The three dancers have straight kilts with simple black border designs and silver conchas. Erect Water Sprinkler holds a spotted fawnskin bag in his left hand. The Female Yei with the ceremonial basket has short feathers in her hair.

> Description: Cottonwood, feathers, green wool tufts, wire; 9 in., 10 in., and 12 in.; ca. 1943.
> History: Unknown.
> Current Location: Unknown.

FIG. 89. Clitso Dedman, transitional style: T.5-A. Begner set of five Yeibichai participants. Courtesy Turkey Mountain Traders.

Transitional Style (1943–45)

During his transitional period, Clitso Dedman begins carving the participants in the Yeibichai dance that is held on the Ninth Night. The ceremonial attire of the figures becomes increasingly colorful. The kilts of the Yeis, with their kit fox pelts down the back, have broader varied border designs. Brown belts have conchas rendered more realistically in silver aluminum paint. Female Yeis have longer masks and often hold twigs of red and green chicken feathers in addition or in place of bunches of green wool. As in the early style, Talking God is often depicted with long dark pants, but in later carvings, he is carved with flared white muslin pants. His arms are carved close to his body; in his right hand, he holds an Abert's squirrel medicine pouch, and in the left hand, he has a fox pelt, which he waves while directing the Yeibichai dance. Water Sprinkler, who stands erect with straight legs, also often is depicted holding a large, tattered fox skin. The ruffs of the male impersonators are often, but not always, contoured in a more realistic manner. Depicted in traditional attire are the unmasked participants in the Nightway ceremony: the Medicine Man and the Patient, the latter with a ceremonial basket. Figures are signed "Clitso" on both feet, without dates.

Clitso Dedman's known production in the transitional style consists of ten sets of single figures and small groupings, plus three Yeibichai dance scenes, for a total of ninety-five individual carvings.

T.2-A Cobbs Auctioneers Set of Two: Male Yei and Female Yei

The two figures are of different styles. The Female Yei is shorter and stockier with dark brown moccasins. The Male Yei is thinner with tan moccasins. The Female Yei has a glossy green kilt with white border designs, and wears a gray-brown kit fox pelt. Her hands are empty. The Male Yei has a matte orange kilt with yellow and white border designs and wears a light gray fox pelt down his back. He has a sculpted ruff and is missing one of his feathers on his headdress. He has a white rattle in his right hand and feathers and brown wool tufts in his left hand.

> Description: Cottonwood, feathers, brown wool tufts; 10 in. and 11 in.; ca. 1944.
> History: Unknown.
> Auction: Offered at Cobbs Auction, January 14, 2017, lot 142A. Estimate $700–$900; did not sell. The figures were not identified as Clitso carvings, but simply as "Late Period Kachina Dolls, unsigned."
> Current Location: Unknown.

T.2-B Cozy McSparron Set of Two: Female Yeis with Raised Arms

These are the only known Clitso Female Yeis with raised arms. One dancer has a smooth, fitted dark orange shirt and a dark blue pleated skirt with a white border design. The other has a smooth, fitted light orange shirt and a dark green skirt, also with a white border design. Both wear red sashes with silver conchas and turquoise stones. (See fig. 57.)

> Description: Cottonwood, feathers; 11 in.; ca. 1944.
> History: Cozy McSparron Collection. Sold by daughter Laramie McSparron in the 1980s to Lars Garrison.
> Current Location: Lars Garrison Collection.

T.16-A *Arizona Highways* Yeibichai Set of Sixteen with Male Patient

Talking God with straight arms holds a spotted fawnskin bag in his right hand. He is dressed in nineteenth-century white calico pants. The figures wear early style white conchas. Male Patient and Medicine Man carry bandolier bags. This is probably the first sixteen-piece Yeibichai set carved by Clitso. (See fig. 54.)

Description: Cottonwood, feathers; 10 in. to 12 in., 1943.

History: Photographed by Charles Wyatt in Chinle in 1944.

Publication: Wyatt, "A New Navajo Art," 35; and Valette and Valette, "Clitso Dedman," 61.

Current Location: Unknown.

T.16-B Cozy McSparron First Yeibichai Set of Sixteen with Female Patient

Talking God, in a dark shirt, white pants, and a sculpted concha belt, holds a pelt bag in his right hand. Both arms are at his sides. Medicine Man is in a dark red shirt, white pants, and a dark green striped trade blanket. Female Patient has a dark red skirt and a dark striped trade blanket. Male Yeis with large headmasks and green ring ruffs hold gourd rattles in their right hands and red feathers in their left hands. Female Yeis hold green wool tufts and red feathers. Water Sprinkler, with knees slightly bent, holds a ragged fox pelt in his right hand. The belts are represented by silver circular conchas with single turquoise stones.

Description: Cottonwood, feathers; 10 in. to 12 in.; ca. 1945.

History: Cozy McSparron displayed this set in the Thunderbird Ranch dining room. (See fig. 55.) In 1967, McSparron's widow, Inja McSparron, sold a composite sixteen-piece Yeibichai set to the Amon Carter Museum in Fort Worth, which included nine figures from this first Cozy McSparron set.

Current Location: Amon Carter Museum of American Art: Talking God, Medicine Man, Female Patient, four Female Yeis, and two Male Yeis, cat. nos. 1967.26.1–3, 5–7,10–12. In the 1980s, Laramie McSparron sold two of the Male Yeis to Lars Garrison. The location of the other four figures (two Male Yeis, two Female Yeis) is unknown. Laramie kept Water Sprinkler in her private collection, but its current location is unknown.

Note: The Amon Carter Yeibichai set also includes two Female Yeis with lowered arms (E.2-D), and five figures from the Cozy McSparron Second Set (C.16-L).

T.16-c Thomas Noble First Yeibichai Set of Sixteen with Male Patient

This Yeibichai set consisted of sixteen slender figures. Yeis wear colored kilts and silver conchas. Male figures have simple green ring ruffs. Talking God, in a fitted dark red shirt and long pants, holds a pouch in his slightly lowered right hand and a felt bag in his left. His right arm is slightly bent and held somewhat away from his body. Male Patient, in a dark blue fitted shirt and white pants, has a bandolier bag over his shoulder. Medicine man, in a dark green shirt and white pants, holds a medicine pouch in his right hand. He, too, has a bandolier bag, but it is mainly hidden under his gray, white, and red trade blanket. Male Yeis with large headmasks are holding white rattles and red feathers. Female Yeis are holding green tufts and red or gray feathers. Water Sprinkler, in a broad upright stance, holds a large fox pelt in his left hand, and wool tufts and a wire yucca wand in his right. (See four pieces of this set in fig. 58.)

> Description: Cottonwood, feathers; 11 in. and 12 in.; ca. 1944.
>
> History: This is the first of two Clitso sets that Dr. Thomas Noble (1895–1958) purchased from Cozy McSparron. After Noble's death, his two Yeibichai sets were equally divided between his heirs. Unfortunately, two Male Yeis and two Female Yeis of this first set were lost or broken over time. In 1959, the twelve remaining figures of the first set were donated to the Mathers Ethnographic Collection at Indiana University. Also included in the donation were a Male Yei and a Female Yei that originally belonged to Dr. Noble's second classic set, which is now at the Indianapolis Museum of Art (C.16-G).
>
> Current Location: Indiana University Museum of Archaeology and Anthropology, Bloomington, cat. nos. 1962-06-0082 to 86, 88 to 91, 93–95.

T.EW2 Sallie Wagner Enemyway Set:
Male Drummer and Woman with Ceremonial Stick

The Male Drummer, with a feather in his hair, wears a fitted navy-blue shirt and dark khaki pants, and is wrapped in an orange and black trade blanket. He is in the act of striking a black pottery drum with a shaped willow drumstick. The Woman, wearing a green skirt and wrapped in a pink and blue blanket, carries a beribboned ceremonial stick made of leather wrapped around a string core. Both are depicted with delicately painted silver squash blossom necklaces. (See fig. 59.)

Description: Cottonwood, feathers, ribbon, string, leather; 10 in.;
    ca. 1945.
History: Given to Sallie Wagner Lippincott by Cozy McSparron.
Dealer: Offered by Toh-Atin Gallery, Durango, Colorado (2020); asking
    price $4,000.
Current Location: Jackson Clark Collection.

FIG. 90. Clitso Dedman, classic style: C.16-B. Five figures from the Wallace Yeibichai set. Photo by Chris Soldt. Valette Collection.

Classic Style (1945–50)

These refined and carefully painted figures represent Clitso Dedman's finest production. In his sixteen-piece Yeibichai dance sets, all six Male Yeis and all six Female Yeis are of the same height and identically carved, with the only variation being their colorful kilts. Their brown belts have silver conchas with turquoise stones. The necklaces of Talking God, Medicine Man, and the Patient are carved in relief, rather than simply being painted. The green spruce ruffs of the male dancers follow the contour of the shoulders. The Male Yeis carry gourd rattles. The masks of the Female Yeis extend below the chin hiding the neck and are partially separated from the face. Small wooden pegs, rather than paint, are used to render the turquoise earring studs. Anatomical features, such as knees and wrists, pectoral and dorsal muscles, are realistically represented. Talking God is depicted wearing traditional white muslin pants and typically he carries only a pelt bag and no medicine pouch. His arms hang straight down, next to his body. Water Sprinkler is portrayed in a crouched position with a fox pelt in his right hand. The Medicine Men and the Patients have delicately carved and painted features. Their shirtsleeves are creased and their trade blankets are realistically draped. Clitso's known production in the classic style consists of six sets of single figures and small groupings plus thirteen Yeibichai dance scenes for a total of 222 individual carvings.

C.2-A Sallie Wagner Set of Two: Male and Female Patients

Male Patient, in a green shirt and white pants, wears a bandolier bag over his right shoulder. Female Patient, in a blue-gray blouse and yellow skirt, has a fringed red and white trade blanket draped unevenly across her body. Both figures have smooth facial features and sculpted necklaces.

> Description: Cottonwood; 11 in. and 10 in.; ca. 1947.
> History: Original owner: Sallie Wagner Lippincott.
> Dealer: Offered by Toh-Atin Gallery, Durango, Colorado (2020); asking price $4,000.
> Current Location: Jackson Clark Collection.

C.2-B Cozy McSparron Set of Two: Male and Female Yeis in Movement

Each Yei dancer, on a supporting base, has a wrinkled kilt and a raised leg, as if in motion. These are the only known Clitso carvings in this stance. Both figures, with feathers in their hands, have sculpted necklaces and contoured concha belts. Male Yei holds a white rattle. He is missing one of the feathers on his headdress.

> Description: Cottonwood, feathers; 10 in. and 11 in.; ca. 1948–50.
> History: Original owner Cozy McSparron. Sold by daughter Laramie McSparron in the 1980s to Lars Garrison.
> Current Location: Lars Garrison Collection.

C.2-C Edwin Wilde Set of Two: Talking God and Female Patient

Talking God wears an orange shirt and white pants. In his right hand, he holds a pelt bag. Female Patient has a red blouse and an orange skirt and holds a ceremonial basket. She has a straight green striped trade blanket over her left shoulder.

> Description: Cottonwood, feathers; 11 in. and 10 in.; ca. 1950.
> History: Collected by Dr. and Mrs. Edwin Wilde in the early 1950s. Bequeathed to Arizona State Museum in 1980.
> Exhibit: Female Patient is on permanent exhibit at the museum in the basketry gallery.
> Current Location: Arizona State Museum, Tucson, cat. nos: 1980-55-3, 1980-55-5.

C.2-D John Boyden Set of Two:

Male Yei and Female Yei (Impersonated by a Woman)

Male Yei wears a contoured ruff and a sculpted turquoise necklace. His black kilt has yellow and white border designs. Female Yei, with a long mask, wears a dark green blouse and a dark orange skirt. Both figures have painted brown belts with silver and turquoise conchas. (See fig. 67.)

> Description: Cottonwood, feathers; 12 in. and 10 in.; ca. 1948–50.
> History: The original owner was John S. Boyden (1906–80), a lawyer who represented Indian tribes in Utah and Arizona. His heirs donated the figures to the Nora Eccles Harrison Museum of Art at Utah State University in Logan, Utah, cat. no. 1984.126. They were deaccessioned 2013.
> Auction: Cowan's, September 20, 2013, lot 268; price $1,560.
> Publication: Female Yei is pictured in Valette and Valette, *Navajo Weavings,* 231.
> Current Location: Valette Collection.

C.2-E Robert Bauver Set of Two: Medicine Man and Male Patient

Medicine Man, in a gray shirt and white pants, has a gray and black trade blanket realistically draped over his right shoulder. In his left hand, he holds a medicine pouch. Male Patient, in an orange shirt and white pants, has a blue and black trade blanket over his right shoulder. The ends of his feet and part of the ceremonial basket are broken.

> Description: Cottonwood; 11 in.; ca. 1948.
> Dealer: Offered by Robert Bauver (ca. 2000).
> Current Location: Unknown.

C.4 Elkus Set of Four: Talking God, Female Patient, Male and Female Yei

Talking God wears a red shirt and long gray pants (typical of the early style) and carved conchas on his belt. He holds a brown pouch in his right hand and a pelt bag in the left. Female Patient wears a red blouse, with a sculpted necklace, and a dark blue skirt. A light purple trade blanket with white stripes and a dark green fringe is draped over her left shoulder. Both Yei dancers have green kilts with painted silver conchas on their belts. Female Yei is unsigned. (See fig. 60.)

> Description: Cottonwood, feathers, wool; 10 in. to 12 in.; ca. 1945.

History: Purchased by Charles and Ruth Elkus at Freeman's store near
Winslow, Arizona, on August 21, 1956. The group originally consisted
of six figures. This set of four was bequeathed to the California
Academy of Sciences in 1972.
Current Location: California Academy of Sciences, cat. nos. 0370–0501A-D.

C.16-A Clay Lockett Yeibichai Set of Sixteen with Male Patient

Talking God, in a dark green shirt, holds a pelt bag. He has a sculpted concha
belt. Medicine Man has a red-brown shirt and has a gray striped trade blanket
draped over his left shoulder. Male Patient has a red shirt and a dark blue striped
trade blanket. Male and Female Yeis wear colorful kilts with broad border
designs and brown belts with flat silver conchas. Water Sprinkler, with bent
knees, holds a tattered fox pelt in his right hand. (See fig. 61.)

Description: Cottonwood, feathers; 10 in. to 12 in.; 1946.
History: Dealer Clay Lockett sold the set on May 23, 1946, for $250 to
Ann Allen Danson, who subsequently donated it to the Arizona State
Museum, Tucson.
Exhibit: Set was on public exhibit in the museum until the 1980s.
Publication: *Arizona Daily Star*, April 16, 1946; LaFarge, *Pictorial His-
tory*, 127; Tanner, *Southwest Indian Craft Arts*, 167; Lindig and Teiwes,
Navajo, 190–91; and Valette and Valette, "Clitso Dedman," 63.
Current Location: Arizona State Museum, cat. nos. E-2221 to E-2236.

C.1B-B C. G. Wallace First Yeibichai Set of Sixteen with Male Patient

Talking God, in an orange shirt, holds a pelt bag. He has a sculpted concha belt.
Medicine Man has a green shirt and wears a light gray striped trade blankets
draped over the left shoulder. Male Patient has a light green shirt and a brown
striped trade blanket. Yeis wear colorful kilts with broad border designs and
brown belts with flat silver conchas. Female Yeis have long face masks. Male
Yeis have metal feathers. Water Sprinkler, with bent knees, has a tattered fox
pelt in his right hand. (See figs. 62 and 90.)

Description: Cottonwood, tin, feathers; 10 in. to 12 in.; ca. 1946–47.
History: Original owner C. G. Wallace displayed this set in his Gallup
store.

Auction: Sotheby Parke Bernet, November 14, 1975, lot 144; in the
catalog, the carver's name was spelled "Klitso Deadman." An accompanying description by aging C. G. Wallace erroneously dated the set
to 1927.

Dealer: Sold by Adobe Gallery (1997); price $16,000.

Exhibits: Museum of our National Heritage, Lexington, Massachusetts,
2000; Mount Holyoke College, South Hadley, Massachusetts, 2016.

Publication: Talking God is pictured in Valette and Valette, *Navajo
Weavings*, 230.

Current Location: Valette Collection.

C.16-c Caroline Kelly Yeibichai Set of Sixteen with Female Patient

Talking God, in an orange shirt, holds a pelt bag. He has a sculpted concha
belt. Medicine Man has a dark red shirt and wears a gray striped trade blanket
draped over the left shoulder. Female Patient has a green blouse and a brown
skirt. She wears a beige fringed trade blanket. Yeis wear colorful kilts with
broad border designs and brown belts with flat silver conchas. Water Sprinkler, with bent knees, has a realistic fox pelt in his right hand. He is missing a
feather on his headdress.

Description: Cottonwood, feathers; 10 in. to 12 in.; ca. 1945.

History: Caroline Kelly purchased the set at Camillo Garcia's Trading
Post, ca. 1945. She loaned it to the Museum of Indian Arts and
Culture, July 1953, and it was donated permanently to the museum by
her son Dan Kelly in 1970.

Publication: Valette and Valette, "Clitso Dedman," 63.

Current Location: Museum of Indian Arts and Culture, Lab of Anthropology, Santa Fe, cat. nos. 37161 to 37176.

Note: Museum file contains a 1954 letter from Cozy McSparron, in which
he writes that on seeing the Yeibichai set, the medicine men "were quite
concerned. It is supposed that they wished a curse on him [Clitso]."

C.16-d Bradshaw Yeibichai Set of Sixteen with Female Patient

Talking God, in a dark shirt, holds a pelt bag. He has a sculpted concha belt.
Medicine Man has a dark blue shirt and wears a light brown striped trade

blanket draped over his left shoulder. Female Patient has a maroon blouse and a dark skirt. She wears a beige fringed trade blanket. Yeis wear colorful kilts with broad border designs and brown belts with flat silver conchas. Female Yeis have long masks. Water Sprinkler, with bent knees, has a realistic fox pelt in his right hand and a large feather in the left. (See fig. 63.)

> Description: Cottonwood, feathers; 10 in. to 12 in.; ca. 1945–47.
> History: Donated to the Indian Pueblo Cultural Center, Albuquerque, and later deaccessioned. Acquired by James and Rebecca Bradshaw in the early 1990s for $5,800.
> Dealer: Sold by Adobe Gallery (2022); price: $22,000.
> Current Location: Private Collection.

C.16-E Wheelwright Auction Yeibichai Set of Sixteen with Male Patient
Talking God, in a light gray shirt, holds a pelt bag. He has a sculpted concha belt. Medicine Man has a yellow shirt and wears a light gray striped trade blankets draped over the left shoulder. Male Patient has a red shirt and a dark green striped trade blanket. Yeis wear colorful kilts with broad border designs and brown belts with flat silver conchas. Female Yeis have square masks. Water Sprinkler, with bent knees, has a tattered fox pelt in his right hand and a large feather in the left. (See fig. 64; also fig. 43 and the two carvings center and right in fig. 44.)

> Description: Cottonwood, feathers; 10 in. to 12 in.; ca. 1947.
> History: Unknown.
> Auction: Sold at the Wheelwright Museum benefit auction, March 1977.
> Dealers: Rex Arrowsmith, 1978 catalog, price $3,250. Sold by Tobe Turpen (1999); price $13,600.
> Publication: Valette, "Yeibichai Weavings," 53; and Rebecca Valette, Navajo Weavings, 230–31.
> Current Location: Valette Collection.

C.16-F Leslie Eames Yeibichai Set of Sixteen with Female Patient
Talking God, in a fitted blue shirt, is carved in the earlier transitional style with a ring-shaped ruff and holding a pelt bag. He has his right arm raised, as in the Pagel set (fig. 56). The other fifteen figures are carved in the classic

style. Medicine Man has a brown shirt and wears a red striped trade blanket draped over his left shoulder. Female Patient has a green blouse and a brown skirt. She wears a tan fringed trade blanket. Yeis are portrayed in colorful kilts with broad border designs and brown belts with flat silver conchas. Female Yeis have broad, long face masks. Water Sprinkler, with bent knees, has a tattered fox pelt in his right hand and a large feather in the left hand.

Description: Cottonwood, feathers; 10 in. to 12 in.; 1945–48.
History: Acquired by Dr. Leslie Eames from Cozy McSparron.
Bequeathed to the Southwest Museum in 1956, cat. no. 1437.G.1A-P.
Current Location: Autry Museum of the American West, Los Angeles,
California.

C.16-G Elkus Yeibichai Set of Sixteen with Male Patient

Talking God, in a red shirt, holds a pelt bag. He has a sculpted concha belt. Medicine Man has a dark orange shirt and wears a gray striped trade blanket draped over the left shoulder. Male Patient has a red shirt and wears a bandolier bag with silver buttons. Yeis wear colorful kilts with border designs. Their belts are painted in the transitional style with flat silver conchas. Water Sprinkler, with slightly bent knees, has a tattered fox pelt in his right hand and a green tuft in the left hand. (See fig. 65.)

Description: Cottonwood, feathers; 10 in. to 12 in.; ca. 1945–47.
History: Dealer Fred Wilson exhibited the set at the "Contemporary
American Indian Arts and Crafts" show at the de Young Museum in
San Francisco, October to December 1953. The set, priced at $250,
did not sell. Charles and Ruth Elkus purchased the set in 1956 from
Wilson for $300. They bequeathed it to the California Academy of
Sciences in 1972.
Exhibit: California Academy of Sciences, 1999–2003/2004.
Publication: Valette and Valette, "Clitso Dedman," 59; and Valette and
Valette, *Navajo Weavings,* 229.
Current Location: California Academy of Sciences, San Francisco, cat.
nos. 0370–0503A-P.
Note: Museum file contains a letter from Fred Wilson, dated 1956, in
which he describes the carver as "Chief Clitso."

C.16-H Thomas Noble Second Yeibichai Set of Sixteen with Male Patient

Talking God, in a red shirt, holds a pelt bag. He has a sculpted concha belt. Medicine Man has a yellow shirt and wears a green striped trade blanket draped over his left shoulder. Male Patient has a light-colored shirt and wears a gray striped trade blanket. Yeis wear colorful kilts with broad border designs and brown belts with flat silver conchas. Female Yeis have large, long face masks. Male Yeis have semi-contoured lightly sculpted ruffs. Water Sprinkler, with slightly bent knees, has a tattered fox pelt in his right hand and red feathers in the left hand. (Fig. 66 shows the original set; fig. 80 contains only thirteen pieces from the original set.)

> Description: Cottonwood, feathers; 10 in. to 12 in.; ca. 1946–47.
>
> History: Purchased in Chinle by Dr. Thomas Noble, who photographed the set prior to shipment. Dr. Noble owned two Yeibichai sets, the figures of which were mixed by his heirs. Fourteen figures were donated to the Indianapolis Museum of Art by daughter Patricia Noble in 1983 in memory of her brother John Noble.
>
> Current Location: Indianapolis Museum of Art, thirteen figures of the photographed set: cat. nos. 2015.51 to 2015.58 to 2015.60 to 2015.64. A Male and Female Yei from the original set are at the Indiana University Museum of Archaeology and Anthropology, Bloomington: cat. nos. 1962-06-87 and 1962-06-92. The Female Yei, cat. no 2015.53, second from the right in figure 80, belongs with the Noble First Set at Indiana University. The location of the Male Patient is unknown; it may have been lost or broken.
>
> Note: The Indianapolis Museum set also has a Female Yei with a ceremonial basket, cat. no. 2015–59, which Dr. Noble acquired separately (see E.1-G).

C.16-I Davis Yeibichai Set of Sixteen with Female Patient

Talking God, in a dark shirt, with his arms at his sides, wears a sculpted concha belt. Medicine Man has a green shirt and wears a light brown striped trade blanket draped over one shoulder. Female Patient has a maroon blouse and a dark skirt. She wears a green fringed trade blanket. Yeis wear colorful kilts with broad border designs and brown belts with flat silver conchas. Female Yeis have long masks. Water Sprinkler, with slightly bent knees, has a tattered fox pelt in his right hand and red feathers in the left.

Description: Cottonwood, feathers; 10 in. to 12 in.; ca. 1945–47.
History: Original owner: Reverend Davis, Presbyterian minister.
Dealer: Offered by Robert Gallegos (2010); asking price $25,000.
Current Location: Unknown.

C.16-J Santa Fe Art Auction Yeibichai Set of Sixteen with Male Patient

Talking God, in a green shirt, holds a pelt bag. He has a sculpted concha belt. Medicine Man has a red shirt and wears a light gray striped trade blanket draped over the left shoulder. Male Patient wears an orange shirt and a light-blue trade blanket with vertical stripes. Yeis are shown in colorful kilts with broad border designs and brown belts with flat silver conchas. Female Yeis have long facemasks. Male Yeis have metal feathers. Water Sprinkler, with bent knees, holds a tattered fox pelt in his right hand and feathers in his left hand.

Description: Cottonwood, feathers; 10 in. to 12 in.; ca. 1945–48.
History: Private New Mexico Collection.
Auction: Santa Fe Art Auction, November 14, 2015, lot 8; estimate
$15,000 to $20,000. Sold for $16,000.
Current Location: Unknown.

C.16-K C. G. Wallace Second Yeibichai Set of Sixteen with Two Patients

Talking God wears a dark green shirt and blue pants, in the transitional style. He has a small pouch in his right hand and a pelt bag in the left. He has a sculpted concha belt. Medicine Man has a dark blue shirt and wears an orange striped trade blanket draped over one shoulder. Male Patient has a red shirt and wears a bandolier bag with silver buttons. Female Patient has a dark green blouse and skirt, and wears a brown striped trade blanket with a maroon fringe. Yeis wear colorful kilts and brown belts with flat silver conchas. Water Sprinkler, with a large headmask and slightly bent knees, holds a wire yucca wand in his right hand and a spotted fawnskin bag in the left.

Description: Cottonwood, feathers; 10 in. to 12 in.; ca. 1945–47.
History: C. G. Wallace displayed the original set in the trading post of his
De Anza Motor Lodge in Albuquerque. It was purchased by a private
collector in 1974, and sold to the Atkinson Trading Company (Gallup)
in the early 1980s. At some point, one Female Yei was lost or broken,

of the dancers. Clitso Dedman's known production in the late style consists of six Yeibichai dance scenes plus a single figure and an unfinished set of four for a total of 101 individual carvings.

L.1 Valette Water Sprinkler
Water Sprinkler wears a red kilt and is crouched. In his right hand, he holds a realistically carved fox pelt, with a white spot on the end of its tail. Red and green ribbons are attached to his left wrist.

> Description: Cottonwood, feathers, brown wool tufts, ribbons; 10 in.;
>   ca. 1951.
> History: Unknown.
> Current Location: Valette Collection.

L.16-A Roland LaFont Yeibichai Set of Sixteen with Female Patient
Talking God wears a bright red shirt with his arms close to his body. In his right hand, he holds a pelt bag. Medicine Man wears a dark green shirt and white pants, with a light gray striped trade blanket. Female Patient, in a pink blouse and a dark green skirt, wears jacla earrings. Over her left shoulder, she has a red and gray striped trade blanket with a maroon fringe. Attached to their left wrists, Male and Female Yei dancers have double streamers: a red ribbon and a gold and silver metallic ribbon. Water Sprinkler holds a fox pelt in his right hand. (See fig. 74.)

> Description: Cottonwood, tin, feathers, ribbons, brown wool tufts; 10 in.
>   to 12 in.; ca. 1951.
> History: In 1954, original owner Cozy McSparron had this set on display
>   in a glass case at his Thunderbird Ranch. The Babbitts acquired the
>   set when they purchased the property, and subsequently sold it to the
>   LaFonts. Roland LaFont attached the figures to a glass base for display
>   at his Goulding's Lodge.
> Current Location: Goulding's Lodge, Monument Valley, Utah.

L.16-B Clair Gurley Yeibichai Set of Sixteen with Female Patient
Talking God wears a dark green shirt with his arms close to his body. In his right hand, he holds a pelt bag. Medicine Man wears an orange shirt, white

pants, and a dark gray striped trade blanket. Female Patient, in a light red blouse and a dark red skirt, wears jacla earrings. Over her left shoulder, she has a light gray striped trade blanket. Male and Female Yeis have red and gold ribbons on the left wrists. Water Sprinkler, in a gray kilt, holds a realistic fox pelt in his right hand. He also has ribbons tied to his left wrist. (See fig. 75.)

Description: Cottonwood, tin, feathers, ribbons, brown wool tufts; 10 in. to 12 in.; ca. 1951.

History: Gallup Ford dealer Clair Gurley purchased the set in the mid-1950s and displayed the carvings in a special glass case in his office. When Clair Gurley retired, he gave the set to his grandson Michael Schuelke.

Current Location: Schuelke Collection.

L.16-c Nello Guadagnoli Yeibichai Set of Sixteen with Female Patient

Talking God, with a very uneven, flat metal headdress, wears a dark red shirt with his arms close to his body. In his right hand, he holds a pelt bag. Medicine Man wears a dark green shirt and white pants with a gray-green striped trade blanket. Female Patient, in an orange blouse and skirt, has long looped earrings. She has a fringed green striped trade blanket over her left shoulder. Yei dancers have purple and pink ribbons attached to their left wrists. Water Sprinkler has a realistic fox pelt in his right hand. (Fig. 76 shows five of the pieces.)

Description: Cottonwood, tin, feathers, ribbons, brown wool tufts; 10 in., 11 in.; ca. 1952.

History: Gallup photographer Nello Guadagnoli acquired the set from Camillo Garcia at the Canyon de Chelly Trading Post in Chinle between 1965 and 1968 in exchange for photography services. At the time of his acquisition, the set had sixteen figures. However, over the years a Male Yei and a Female Yei broke and were discarded. In 1998, the set had only fourteen figures.

Dealer: Offered by John Hill Antique Indian Art, Scottsdale (2009).

Auction: Bonhams, December 9, 2013, lot 1015. Estimate $10,000–$15,000. Did not sell.

Publication: Valette and Valette, "Clitso Dedman," 65.

Current Location: Mark and Linda Winter Collection.

L.16-D Navajo Nation Yeibichai Set of Sixteen with Male Patient

Talking God wears a light green shirt with his arms close to his body. In his right hand, he holds a pelt bag. Medicine Man wears an orange shirt and white pants. Over his left shoulder is a dark green striped trade blanket. Female Patient, in a purple blouse and green skirt, has jacla earrings painted in turquoise and coral. Over her left shoulder is a light-blue striped trade blanket. Male and Female Yei dancers have red, white, and gray ribbons attached to their left wrists. (See fig. 83.)

> Description: Cottonwood, tin, feathers, ribbons, brown wool tufts; 10 in. to 12 in.; ca. 1952.
>
> History: Acquired in the late 1950s by the Navajo Arts and Crafts Guild. Originally displayed above the entry door, and later moved to a shelf behind the counter.
>
> Current Location: Navajo Arts and Crafts Enterprise, Window Rock, Arizona.

L.16-E Tobe Turpen Yeibichai Set of Sixteen with Male Patient

Talking God, with an uneven metal feathered headdress, wears a dark green shirt with his arms close to his body. In his right hand, he holds a pelt bag. Medicine Man wears a red shirt and white pants, with a blue striped trade blanket over his left shoulder. Male Patient wears a dark orange shirt and white pants with a gray striped trade blanket. Male Yeis, with red ribbons on their left wrists, have tufts of brown wool and metal feathers on their headmasks. Female Yeis, with red and green ribbons on their right wrists, hold red and gray feathers. Water Sprinkler has a large realistic fox pelt in his right hand and red and gray feathers in his left hand. All figures are finished in high-gloss paint. The lower sections of the kilts are decorated with complex geometric designs. (Fig. 91 shows four of the pieces.)

> Description: Cottonwood, tin, feathers, ribbons, brown wool tufts; 10 in. to 12 in.; ca. 1953.
>
> History: Purchased by Tobe Turpen at Camillo Garcia's Canyon de Chelly Trading Post in the 1950s.
>
> Current Location: Unknown.

L.16-F Hugh Lee Yeibichai Set of Sixteen with Female Patient

Talking God wears an orange shirt with his arms close to his body. In his right hand, he holds a pelt bag. Medicine Man wears a yellow shirt and white pants. Over his left shoulder, he has a green trade blanket with a single stripe down the back. Female Patient wears a light orange blouse with a dark red skirt and has a gray striped trade blanket. She wears jacla earrings. Water Sprinkler, in an orange kilt, has a realistic fox pelt in his right hand. His upper body is plain white and he is missing the typical green painted juniper garlands on his arms and across his torso. Yei dancers have red ribbons on their left wrists. Their eyes are highlighted with irregular triangles. All the figures wear roughly sculptured turquoise necklaces. The feet are signed "Clitso" in green paint, rather than pencil. (Fig. 44 shows the Female Patient on the left; fig. 77 shows five of the pieces.)

> Description: Cottonwood, tin, feathers, ribbons, brown wool tufts; 9 in. to 12 in.; 1953. Probably Clitso's last set; finished with the assistance of his family.
> History: Mormon trader Hugh Lee acquired the set around 1955.
> Dealer: Sold by son Art Lee through Bill Beaver at his Sacred Mountain Trading Post (2000); price $10,500.
> Current Location: Valette Collection.

LPW.4 Phil Woodard Set of Four: Medicine Man, Female Yei, Two Male Yeis

Medicine Man wears a solid green blanket, rather than the usual striped design. Necklaces are painted blue, rather than Clitso's typical turquoise. (See fig. 78.)

> Description: Cottonwood, tin, feathers, green wool tufts; 10 in. and 11 in.; 1953.
> History: In 1963, Phil Woodard of Gallup acquired the four unfinished figures, which he sanded and painted in his own style.
> Current Location: Unknown.

NOTES

PREFACE

1. Wyatt, "A New Navajo Art," 35.
2. Tanner, *Southwestern Indian Craft Arts*, 166–67.
3. Roosevelt, *A Book-Lover's Holidays*, 226–27.
4. Valette and Valette, "The Life and Work of Clitso Dedman," 54–67.

1. EARLY YEARS IN CHINLE

1. Since Navajos at the time had no calendars and no written records, Clitso Dedman himself did not know his exact date of birth. In 1943, he told Charles Wyatt, then a park ranger at Canyon de Chelly National Monument, that he was sixty-seven years old. Therefore, he most likely would have been born in 1876. See Wyatt, "A New Navajo Art," 35.
2. For a detailed description of Navajo life in the thirty years following the return from Bosque Redondo in 1868, see Bailey and Bailey, *History of the Navajos*, 25–73.
3. The full text of the treaty can be found in Iverson, *Diné*, 325–34.
4. Bailey and Bailey, *History of the Navajos*, 27.
5. Mindeleff, "Navaho Houses," 484.
6. Mindeleff, "Navaho Houses," 487–88, 491–505.
7. There were, of course, no written records at the time. The Navajo census conducted by Peter Paquette in 1915 was limited to the Southern Navajo/Fort Defiance jurisdiction.
8. The complexities of the clan system and the current legal interpretations are explained in detail in Austin, *Navajo Courts*, 137–98.
9. Marcellus Troester, OFM (1878–1936), was a Franciscan friar from St. John the Baptist Province in Cincinnati. After his ordination in 1906, he was sent to the Navajo Reservation where he was first assigned to missions in Chinle and Lukachukai. In the 1920s, having become fluent in the Navajo language, he decided to establish a

census of the Navajos residing in the Franciscan "sphere of influence." To this end, he traveled widely to trading posts, fairs, Yeibichai dances, and other ceremonials, interviewing thousands of informants. On separate cards, he recorded each Navajo's name or nickname, clan affiliation, spouse(s), and children, together with vital dates and information regarding baptism, schooling, and marriages. As the files grew, individuals were assigned identification numbers for easy reference. Although not "official," Father Marcellus's census cards still today provide invaluable biographical and genealogical information for the Navajo families of the area.

10. The Tótsohnii clan is grouped under the Hashtł'ishnii clan.

11. For more on Navajo clans and Navajo names, see Kluckhohn and Leighton, *The Navaho*, 111–17. Also see Girdner, *Diné Tah*, 268–72; and Reichard, *Social Life*, 96–107.

12. Troester, *Navajo Census Cards*. Apparently Clitso's mother assumed the surname "Dine" (or "Navajo"), which she transmitted to the children of her second husband. This name would subsequently be modified as "Denny."

13. The war names for girls, often ending in *paa* or *baa*, were occasionally disclosed, especially in census reports. For a list of war names, see Reichard, *Social Life*, 97–100.

14. See Jett, "Territory and Hogan," 119–23. Also see Schwarz, "Unraveling the Anchoring Cord," 43–48.

15. Chisholm, *Navajo Infancy*, 74. The hoop at the top of the cradleboard supports a fawnskin or blanket as protection from sun or wind without touching the child's face or interfering with the child's breathing.

16. Hrdlička, *Physiological and Medical Observations*, 81.

17. Mitchell, *Tall Woman*, 30–34.

18. Girdner, *Diné Tah*, 12.

19. Dyk, *Left Handed*, 8–9.

20. The herd was a cooperative enterprise and a symbol of social integration within the family group. Around age five, when children were old enough to share in tasks of caring for the herd, they were given their own lamb. In this way, they learned the importance of communal life. See Witherspoon, "Navajo Social Organization," 527–30. For a Navajo child's view of herding, see Wetherill, *Wolfkiller*, 1–5. Also see Mitchell, *Tall Woman*, 37–40; Mitchell and Allen, *Miracle Hill*, 4–5; and Nez and Avila, *Code Talker*, 23–33. For an anthropologist's overview of the relationship of Navajos to their sheep, see Hall, *West of the Thirties*, 125–141.

21. For the names of Navajo constellations, see Griffin-Pierce, *Earth Is My Mother*, 142–173.

22. For a selection of stories that a Navajo grandfather would tell his children, see Wetherill, *Wolfkiller*, 1–61.

23. Matthews, *Navaho Legends*, 224–25.

24. For an excellent description of Hózhó, see Austin, *Navajo Courts*, 53–62.

25. For a brief introduction to the Navajo ceremonial system, see Parezo, *Navajo Sandpainting*, 11–21.

26. This description of the Yeibichai dance is based on the nineteenth-century accounts by Stevenson, "Ceremonial of Hasjelti Dailjis," 270–75; and Matthews, *Night Chant*, 146–52. For a twentieth-century description, see Waters, *Masked Gods*, 228–38.

27. In the nineteenth century, medicine men from the Lukachukai and Chinle area were traditionally of the Táchii'nii clan. See Faris, *Nightway*, 105, 108.

28. For more detailed accounts of the Nightway initiation ceremony, see Stevenson, "Ceremonial of Hasjelti Dailjis," 266–69; and Matthews, *Night Chant*, 116–20.

29. In a 1944 interview, Clitso Dedman told Charles Wyatt that he had started school in 1884. Wyatt erroneously concluded that Dedman had been enrolled in the Grand Junction School that year, but it did not open until 1887. See Wyatt, "A New Navajo Art," 35. The year 1884 would have stuck in Dedman's memory, because it was only when he went to school in Fort Defiance that he was introduced to the American calendar, with its months, days, and years. At the time, the Navajos had no calendar and simply followed the seasons.

30. Liebler, *Boil My Heart for Me*, 36–37.

31. Dedman's recruitment experience was probably similar to that of Jacob Morgan. See Morgan, "Evangelist J. C. Morgan's Life-Story: I. My Start," 297–99. See also Morgan, "A Retrospect," 76–81.

2. BOARDING SCHOOL

1. Adams, *Education for Extinction*, chapter 7.

2. Iverson, *Diné*, 328.

3. Adams, *Education for Extinction*, 7.

4. Gaston, "Navajo Agency 1870," 153–54.

5. Menaul, "Defiance, Navajo Agency 1871," 375.

6. Locke, *Book of the Navajo*, 408–9.

7. Young, *Navajo Yearbook 1951–1960*, 8.

8. Quoted in Young, *Navajo Yearbook 1951–1960*, 10.

9. Iverson, *Diné*, 82.

10. The assigning of English names and surnames became part of Indian boarding school policy in the effort to "Americanize" the students. See Child, *Boarding School Seasons*, 28–30. Also Littlefield and Underhill, "Renaming the American Indian."

11. Dedman may have been given an Anglo first name during his school years, but if so, no records exist. In his post-school contacts, he always referred to himself as "Clitso Dedman."

12. Leroy Dedmon has spent years researching the origins of the Dedmon/Dedman/Deadman families. See his "Dedmon Connection," vol. 93, where he explores the possible Navajo link: www.dedmon.org.

13. In the *Census of the Navajo Reservation under Jurisdiction of Peter Paquette, Super-intendent. Year 1915*, the name is spelled "Clitsoi Dedman" on page 11 and "Clitso Deadman" on page 54.

14. Nez and Avila, *Code Talker*. 46. Chester Nez was one of the first Navajo Code Talk-ers in World War II. Bilingual Navajo young men were recruited by the Marines in 1942 to develop a secret code for relaying messages back and forth from the ships to the island landing beaches in the Pacific. The Japanese never managed to break the code, which was labeled top secret and only declassified in 1968.

15. Mitchell, *Navajo Blessingway Singer*, 57–67.

16. See Nez and Avila, *Code Talker*, 101–15, 271–91.

17. In 1910, Franciscan missionary Berard Haile published *An Ethnologic Dictionary of the Navaho Language*, using approximate English transcriptions of Navajo words. The Navajo alphabet was not formalized until 1937. In 1958, Leon Wall, who was in charge of the literacy program on the reservation, and William Morgan, a Navajo translator, published their *Navajo-English Dictionary*. In 1980, linguist Robert Young and William Morgan completed their monumental reference work *The Navajo Language: A Grammar and Colloquial Dictionary*.

18. Mitchell, *Navajo Blessingway Singer*, 63, 67.

19. By the 1920s, the discipline at the Fort Defiance boarding school had grown much more severe. As Chester Nez recounts in his autobiography *Code Talker*, "I'd been caught speaking Navajo three days before. The Pima matron brushed my teeth with brown Fels-Naptha soap. I still couldn't taste food, only the acrid, bitter taste of the lye soap. Teachers at the school were encouraged to be strict, and the smaller children were frequently targeted by slaps or kicks. But the lingering taste of the soap was worse than either of those punishments" (50). "Two boys, who had run away from school, were brought back and humiliated in front of the student body by being dressed as girls" (59).

20. See "Ch'ahádiniini' Bináli," in Johnson, ed., *Stories*, 228.

21. Patterson, "Report of Navajo Agency, 1888," 194.

22. Vandever, "Report of the Navajo Agency, 1889," 285.

23. Morgan, "A Retrospect," 77–78.

24. Vandever, "Report of the Navajo Agency, 1890," 163.

25. In the late nineteenth century, the upper section of the Colorado River, with its headwaters in the Rocky Mountains, was frequently referred to as the Grand River. It was only in 1921, by an act of Congress, that this section was officially named the Colorado River.

26. For more on the Meeker Massacre at the White River Agency, see Ruland-Thorne, *Historic Tales*, 20–27.

27. For a more detailed early history, see MacKendrick, "Cesspools, Alkali and White Lily Soap," 4–11. See also Blackman, "The Story of the Ute and the Grand Junction Indian School."

28. For a complete overview, see Adams, *Education for Extinction*.

29. Adams, *Education for Extinction*, 60–70.

30. Breen, "Report of School at Grand Junction, 1888," 251.

31. Davis, "Report of School at Grand Junction, 1887," 111–13.

32. Breen, "Report of School at Grand Junction, 1888," 250–54.

33. Wheeler, "Report of School at Grand Junction, 1889," 349.

34. Denver, at the time, had a population of 107,000, and Salt Lake City a population of 44,000.

35. The Leadville to Glenwood Springs portion of the trip had been built by the Colorado Midland Railroad, and only became part of the AT&SF system in 1890.

36. Morgan, "Evangelist J. C. Morgan's Life-Story: II. My First Step," 493.

37. Morgan, "A Retrospect," 78.

38. After the Grand Junction School (Teller Institute) closed in 1911, all records were sent to Leavenworth, Kansas, where soon afterward they were lost in a fire. Therefore, we cannot determine under which spelling of his surname Clitso was enrolled.

39. Record, "Report of Training-School at Grand Junction, 1890," 282.

40. Gjeltema, "Jacob Casimera Morgan," 53.

41. In 1890, the area through which the Navajo boys traveled home to Chinle was far different from what it would be in 2020. With a population of 1,100, Montrose would grow to almost 20,000. Rico, a semi-ghost town of 200 people, had a population of 1,100 in 1890, which by 1892 had increased to nearly 5,000. Cortez was a small settlement of irrigation workers (population 300), while Dolores was a much larger town (population 1,500). By 2020, the reverse was true, with Cortez at almost 9,000 and Dolores down to 900.

42. The story of these runaway Navajo students would inspire a highly fictionalized account that appeared in a popular youth magazine. See Otis, "Across the Range," 370–84.

43. Plummer, Letter to the Commissioner of Indian Affairs in Washington, dated December 20, 1893, Fort Defiance AZ.

44. Record, "Report of Training-School at Grand Junction, 1890," 282.

45. The Spencerian script was the penmanship style of nineteenth-century business letters. Today's Coca-Cola and Ford logos are examples of this once-popular script. It was replaced in schools in the twentieth century by the easier-to-master and less ornate Palmer Method. For an example of Dedman's handwriting, see fig. 15.

46. Record, "Report of Training-School at Grand Junction, 1890," 283.

47. Lemmon, "Report of the Teller Institute, Grand Junction, 1891," 559.

48. MacKendrick, "Cesspools, Alkali and White Lily Soap," 7–8. For more on Morgan's work as commissioner, see Prucha, "Thomas Jefferson Morgan 1889–93," 193–203.

49. Morgan, "Report of the Commissioner of Indian Affairs, 1891," 56.

50. Lemmon, "Report of the Teller Institute, Grand Junction, 1891," 558.

51. Gjeltema, "Jacob Casimera Morgan," 55–56. The Navajos and Apaches were both originally Athapaskan tribes that migrated to the Southwest from what is now western Canada. Their languages are linguistically quite similar.

52. Most American schools in the nineteenth century used only the first two levels of the McGuffey readers. The level of the third reader was at about today's sixth-grade level. Since the lessons reflected American culture of the period, they often included vocabulary and situations that were totally foreign to children on the Indian reservations.

53. Lemmon, "Report of Apache Indian Boarding School, San Carlos, 1890," 12.

54. Lemmon, "Report of School at Grand Junction, 1892," 658.

55. Mary Dedman Dodge, personal communication, August 8, 1999. Dedman's daughter Mary was in her eighties at the time of our meeting, and could not remember the year of her father's trip home from Grand Junction. It would have been either winter 1891–92 or 1892–93, since the railroad spur from Telluride to Dolores was not completed until 1891. She was also unsure who accompanied Clitso from Chinle to Cortez, whether his father or another family member.

56. Lemmon, "Report of School at Grand Junction, 1893," 410.

57. It is not known whether Clitso Dedman received a school-leaving certificate. As mentioned earlier, all Teller Institute records have been lost.

58. Reyhner, "American Indian Boarding Schools," 68.

59. Thornton, "Report of the Governor of New Mexico," 376.

3. RAILROAD APPRENTICE

1. For a history of Navajo railroad workers, see Youngdahl, *Working on the Railroad*.

2. Nickelson, *One Hundred Years of Coal Mining*, 12.

3. Williams, *C. N. Cotton*, 30–34.

4. Ducker, *Men of the Steel Rails*, 10–16, 112.

5. The amounts of $2.60 and $1.70 would be the equivalent in 2023 of about $87 and $56, respectively.

6. This description of the Santa Fe division center in Gallup is extrapolated from Ducker, *Men of the Steel Rails*, 48–50, 71–72.

7. Roosevelt, *A Book-Lover's Holidays*, 226.

4. TRADING POST YEARS

1. "Cloudcroft Season Opens," *El Paso Herald*, June 2, 1902.

2. For a detailed and informative introduction to Navajo trading posts, see McPherson, *Both Sides of the Bullpen*; Kelley and Francis, *Navajoland Trading Post Encyclopedia*, 1–37; Kelley and Francis, *A Diné History*, 181–208; Powers, *Navajo Trading*, 3–100.

3. Wilkins, *Patterns of Exchange*, 120. Indian agents discouraged barter and already in the late 1800s required traders to conduct business in cash "in an effort to assimilate Navajo people into private property ownership and the capitalist economy."

4. For a description of "Navvy" trader talk, see Adams, *Shonto*, 212–13.

5. Kelley and Francis, *Navajoland Trading Post Encyclopedia*, 495.

6. For a full biography, see Blue, *Indian Trader*.

7. For a history of the Hubbell Trading Post, see Brugge, *Hubbell Trading Post National Historic Site*; Cottam, *Hubbell Trading Post*. See also Kelley and Francis, *Navajoland Trading Post Encyclopedia*, 169–74.

8. Graves, *Thomas Varker Keam*, 109–38.

9. Kelley and Francis, *Navajoland Trading Post Encyclopedia*, 25–28.

10. For a list of Hubbell's over thirty trading business sites with dates, see Blue, *Indian Trader*, 284.

11. Blue, *Indian Trader*, 149–55.

12. Blue, *Indian Trader*, 256.

13. For a more detailed biography of Burbank, including his relationship with J. L. Hubbell, see Padget, *Indian Country*, 137–68.

14. Burbank reminisced about this period in his autobiographical memoir, *Burbank among the Indians* (1944).

15. Letter of November 21, 1897, E. A. Burbank Timeline, Harvard-Diggins Library, Harvard IL. Transcribed for the Montana Historical Society.

16. The value of $50 in 1897 would be the equivalent of $1,800 in 2023.

17. Letter of November 25, 1897, E. A. Burbank Timeline, Harvard-Diggins Library, Harvard IL. Transcribed for the Montana Historical Society.

18. Letter from E. A. Burbank to J. L. Hubbell, Los Angeles CA, May 15, 1913. University of Arizona Special Collections, Hubbell Archives, AZ375.

19. McNitt, *Indian Traders*, 73–75.

20. Although gambling was outlawed on the Navajo Reservation, Hubbell apparently tolerated such games as long as they were not public.

21. Blue, *Indian Trader*, 210.

22. For a description of Coon Can (also known as Conquian), see Parlett, *Penguin Book of Card Games*.

23. Clitso was identified in the painting by Edward Chamberlin, curator of the exhibit "Portraits of the People: E. A. Burbank at Hubbell Trading Post," August 9 to December 21, 2002.

24. See Kelley and Francis, "Rough Rock Trading Post," *Navajoland Trading Post Encyclopedia*, 329–32.

25. See Adams, *Shonto*, 152.

26. Klara Kelley, personal communication, August 1, 2020.

27. For a detailed description of Rough Rock buildings, see Anderson, "Nomination Form for Rough Rock Trading Post," sections 7 and 8.

28. Anderson, "Nomination Form for Rough Rock Trading Post," section 7, page 4.

29. Troester, "Clitso Dedman, Census No. 70142," *Navajo Census Cards*. Clitso Dedman's census card lists his wives and children.

30. For a more detailed description of the traditional Navajo marriage ceremony, see Austin, *Navajo Courts*, 149–51.

31. Troester, "Clitso Dedman, Census No. 70142," *Navajo Census Cards*.

32. Hadzizbaa was her war name, given to her as a young child. Although this is the name that appears in Anglo records, and is the name we will use in this biography, Clitso Dedman and other Navajos would have only referred to her by her nicknames.

33. Troester, "Hadzizbaa, Census No. 54070," *Navajo Census Cards*.

34. Bahr, *Navajo as Seen by the Franciscans*, 204.

35. The date of the wedding license appears in "Clitsoe Dedman vs. Sonnie Dedman Complaint." Filed Jan. 4, 1918, John H. Udall, Clerk of the Superior Court of the State of Arizona in and for Apache County, by Deputy Clerk Levi S. Udall.

36. Jimmy Dedman is listed with his birthdate on Clitso Dedman's census card and he appears on the official 1910 U.S. census. Jimmy would have died before 1915, since his name does not figure on the Paquette census of that year.

37. Kelley and Francis, *Navajoland Trading Post Encyclopedia*, 104, 330.

38. Mary Dedman Dodge, personal communication, August 8, 1999.

39. See Long, *Big Eyes*, 7–17. In 1909, Schwemberger would leave the Franciscan order and open his own studio in Gallup.

40. For a biography of J. S. Candelario, see Batkin, *Native American Curio Trade*, 50–75.

41. Batkin, *Native American Curio Trade*, 63. R. G. Dun & Company merged with John M. Bradstreet to form today's Dun & Bradstreet.

42. The value of $1 in 1910 would be the equivalent of $31.50 in 2023.

43. In a letter to Hubbell, dated October 11, 1913, Dedman wrote, "I just came back from Santa Fe last night." Hubbell Trading Post Records, University of Arizona Libraries, Special Collections, AZ375, box 23.

44. John W. Kennedy, interview with Karen Underhill, December 16, 1998. Special Collections, Northern Arizona University. In 1915, George Kennedy sold his Salina Springs Trading Post and moved his family to Chinle. See Kennedy, *Tales of a Trader's Wife*, 1–20.

45. Paquette, *Census of the Navajo Reservation 1915*, 10. Although the Salt Springs Trading Post did not officially close until spring 1915, it had probably become a very small operation and thus did not figure in the census that was taken in late 1914.

46. Mary Dedman Dodge, personal communication, August 8, 1999.

47. Robert Dedman, personal communication, May 1999. For a graphic description of the challenge of using dynamite to clear boulders on the Navajo Reservation, see Hall, *West of the Thirties*, 13–20.

48. Ann Cummings, U.S. National Archives, personal communication, October 29, 1998.

49. Kelley and Francis, *Navajoland Trading Post Encyclopedia*, "Nazlini Trading Post," 277–79. Also Kelley and Nabahe, "An Archaeological Survey."

50. These items are all listed in the "Inventory of C.D. Dedman's effects—April 15, 1915." Hubbell Trading Post Records, University of Arizona Libraries, Special Collections, AZ375, Box 491 folder 1.

51. The photograph of Clitso Dedman on horseback in front of the Nazlini Trading Post had been taken by Frederick Melville DuMond in July 1910. See chapter 5 of the present volume.

52. For a more complete history, see Aigner, *Swastika Motif*, chapters 3 and 7.

53. See Clitso Dedman correspondence with J. L. Hubbell. University of Arizona Special Collections, Hubbell Archives, AZ375, Box 23.

54. Kelley and Francis, *Navajoland Trading Post Encyclopedia*, 13. Dedman's shotgun is listed in the "Inventory of C.D. Dedman's effects—April 15, 1915." University of Arizona Special Collections, Hubbell Archives, AZ375, Box 491 folder 1.

55. Letter from Clitso Dedman to J. L. Hubbell, June 26, 1910. University of Arizona Special Collections, Hubbell Archives, AZ375, box 23.

56. The value of $1 in 1914 would be the equivalent of $30 in 2023.

57. *Arizona Republic*, December 19, 1913, p. 10.

58. Letter from Clitso Dedman to J. L. Hubbell, March 3, 1913. University of Arizona Special Collections, Hubbell Archives, AZ375, box 23.

5. FROM WAGON TO AUTOMOBILE

1. Paquette, *Census of the Navajo Reservation 1915*, 11.

2. There is a Hosteen Yazza listed in the 1920 U.S. census as having been born in 1876 and residing in Tohatchi.

3. Charlie Day was Sam Day's oldest son. For more on Charlie's automobile business and photographs of the Ford Touring cars on the Navajo Reservation, see Link, *Navajo Country Pioneers*, 125–39. The amount of $900 in 1910 would be the equivalent of $2,835 in 2023. The amount of $690 in 1912 would be the equivalent of $2,140 in 2023.

4. University of Arizona Archives, Hubbell Collection, AZ375, Box 23, Clitso Dedman Correspondence, 67.

5. University of Arizona Archives, Hubbell Collection, AZ375, Box 23, Clitso Dedman Correspondence, 69.

6. Bodo, *Tales of an Endishodi*, 69–70.

7. Kennedy, *Tales of a Trader's Wife*, 28.

8. Quoted in Cottam, *Hubbell Trading Post*, 89.

9. Wagner, *Wide Ruins*, 31–47. The difficulties of driving a car on the Navajo Reservation in 1915 are dramatically described in Curtis Zahn's account of the trip his five uncles made in their Franklin car from Los Angeles to Flagstaff, Arizona, and from there to Kayenta and the San Juan River, over steep terrain and primitive wagon trails. In preparation,

they had fuel drums placed strategically along their route. They took along dynamite for blasting rocks and heavy cable with a winch to maneuver steep inclines. When their transmission broke near Monument Valley, Navajos with horses helped pull the car to Kayenta. One brother rode on horseback to Tuba City to pick up replacement parts sent by train from Los Angeles. Miraculously, the group had not a single flat tire on their 2,000-mile round trip. Zahn, "The Automobile Is Here to Stay."

10. University of Arizona Archives, Hubbell Collection, Box 23, Clitso Dedman Correspondence, letters from Nazlini dated January 2, 1914, January 27, 1914, June 17, 1914, June 23, 1914, August 1, 1914.

11. University of Arizona Archives, Hubbell Collection, AZ375, Box 384, Ledgers, Clitzo Account No. 30, entry for January 1, 1914. The amount of $85 in 1913 would be the equivalent of $258 in 2023.

12. Golden, *Red Moon Called Me*, 152.

13. The passenger in the backseat wearing a hat is most likely Chee Dodge.

14. University of Arizona Archives, Hubbell Collection, AZ375, Box 23, Clitso Dedman Correspondence, December 8, 1913. At the time, Polarine Motor Oil was a "baby brand" of Standard Oil.

15. McKenna and Travis, *Archeological Investigations*, 7.

16. For a full biography, see Panofsky, *Art and Ambition*.

17. The Canyon de Chelly paintings in the exhibition included: No. 17. The White Man, Painted Desert, Nazlini Canyon, Arizona; no. 18. The Captains at Sunset, Detail of Erosion, Canyon de Chelly, Arizona; and No. 19. "Theck-i-o-see" The Chimney, Canyon de Chelly, Arizona.

18. Bradley, "An Artist's Two Years Alone in the Desert," 35.

19. Alan Carson visit, August 18, 1999. He showed us the painting at his store in Farmington, New Mexico. His father, Fred Carson, had acquired it in 1937 when he took over the Nazlini Trading Post.

20. Panofsky, *Art and Ambition*, 119–20.

21. J. L. Hubbell also asked Sammie Day, Sam Day's second son who frequently acted as his chauffeur, to drive Roosevelt's two sons on a quick day trip to Canyon de Chelly. See Link, *Navajo Country Pioneers*, 148.

22. Roosevelt, *Letters*, 1481.

23. Saunders, *The Indians of the Terraced Houses*, 204–205. In the early twentieth century, the location of the Snake Dance alternated between Walpi in the uneven years (e.g., 1911, 1913) and Oraibi in the even years (e.g., 1912, 1914).

24. "Hopi Indians Dance for Theodore Roosevelt at [Walpi, Ariz.] 1913," video. Washington DC: Library of Congress, Digital ID: trmp 4121.

25. *Arizona Republic,* December 19, 1913, 10. Earlier that year, in February, Mr. Graves had hired Clitso Dedman for two days to chauffeur him from Fort Defiance to the Crystal Trading Post; *Arizona Republic,* February 28, 1913.

26. Roosevelt, *A Book-Lover's Holidays*, 226–27.

27. In 1910, Father Berard Haile published the first edition of his 500-page *Ethnologic Dictionary of the Navajo Language* in which vocabulary was grouped by theme. The second half of the book contained descriptions of Navajo culture and religious practices.

28. Fischer, "A Sick Call to Crystal," 360–64.

29. Weber, "Congressional Committee Visit," 40.

30. McPherson, *Navajo Land*, 95.

6. AN UNANTICIPATED CAREER SHIFT

1. Paquette, *Census of the Navajo Reservation 1915*. The spellings of names, places, and clans varies slightly with each entry, since most of these were recorded phonetically.

2. Golden, *Red Moon Called Me*, 142–43.

3. Golden, *Red Moon Called Me*, 153.

4. Golden, *Red Moon Called Me*, 153–56. It is Golden who refers to the student with pseudonym "Ada."

5. According to Mitchell, *Navajo Blessingway Singer*, 113, fn. 17: "Dr. Wigglesworth was the first good doctor the People ever had. He taught the People about tuberculosis and the contagious diseases."

6. Arizona Territorial Board of Health, Bureau of Vital Statistics, Supplementary Report of Birth, March 22, 1915. See also Arizona State Board of Health, Bureau of Vital Statistics, Original Certificate of Death, State Index No. 6, County Registered No. 81.

7. Estelle Aubrey Brown, then working at the Phoenix Indian School, provides a second account of the young woman's story, giving her the pseudonym "Lucy." See Brown, *Stubborn Fool*, 224–26.

8. The Franciscan missionary priest in Fort Defiance at the time was Father Egbert Fischer, who had been providing religious instruction for the students since 1911. The Fort Defiance church, dedicated as Our Lady of the Blessed Sacrament, was built in fall 1915. Clitso Dedman had been one of the more generous local donors with a gift of $25 (equivalent of $750 in 2023). Most gifts, which were acknowledged in the 1914 issue of *Franciscan Missions of the Southwest*, ranged from $1 to $10.

9. Golden, *Red Moon Called Me*, 156.

10. Golden, *Red Moon Called Me*, 155.

11. Klara Kelley, personal communication, October 15, 2021.

12. "Inventory of C. D. Dedman's effects—April 15, 1915." Hubbell Trading Post Records, University of Arizona Libraries, Special Collections, AZ375, Box 491 folder 1. This inventory consists of nine ledger pages of personal items and one page of Navajo accounts.

13. The amounts of $25, $50, and $1,322 in 1915 would be the equivalent of $750, $1,500, and $39,700 in 2023.

14. Letter from Clitso Dedman to J. L. Hubbell, El Paso TX, May 4, 1915. University of Arizona Special Collections, Hubbell Archives, AZ375, box 23. The amounts of $146 and $175 in 1915 would be the equivalent of $4,380 and $5,250 in 2023.

15. Letter from Clitso Dedman to J. L. Hubbell, El Paso TX, May 6, 1915. University of Arizona Special Collections, Hubbell Archives, AZ375, box 23. "Moki Indians dolls" are kachina carvings.

16. Letter from Clitso Dedman to J. L. Hubbell, El Paso TX, June 1915. University of Arizona Special Collections, Hubbell Archives, AZ375, box 23.

17. Letter from Clitso Dedman to J. L. Hubbell, El Paso TX, June 17, 1915. University of Arizona Special Collections, Hubbell Archives, AZ375, box 23. The amounts of $16, $200, and $916 in 1915 would be the equivalent of $480, $5,960, and $27,480 in 2023.

18. Letter from Clitso Dedman to J. L. Hubbell, El Paso TX, July 17, 1915. University of Arizona Special Collections, Hubbell Archives, AZ375, box 23. "Sam" is Clitso's younger brother who was handling his affairs in Nazlini.

19. Letter from A. H. Logan, 800 Texas St., El Paso TX, to J. L. Hubbell, September 20, 1915, written on Clitso Dedman's old Salt Springs letterhead. University of Arizona Special Collections, Hubbell Archives, AZ375, box 23.

20. It is not known when Clitso acquired title to the 160 acres, or whether it was his mother who did so. According to Klara Kelley (personal communication, May 27, 2020), Navajo Indian agents took applications for most allotments between about 1905 and the mid-1930s. What is certain is that by 1915 the land was listed as Clitso Dedman's property; see Paquette, *Census of the Navajo Reservation 1915*, 54.

7. BACK TO CHINLE

1. For a photographic tour of the region, see Simonelli and Winters, *Crossing between Worlds*.

2. Kelley and Francis, *Navajoland Trading Post Encyclopedia*, 102–9.

3. The Gormans were parents of Code Talker Carl Gorman (1907–1998) and grandparents of artist R. C. Gorman (1931–2005).

4. Frisbie, "On the Trail of Chinle's 'Big House,'" 70–72.

5. Koper and Ostermann, "Life at Chin Lee Mission, 1917–1918," 409.

6. Beadle, *The Undeveloped West*, 546–60.

7. For a detailed account of Charlie and Sammie Day's assistance to Edward Curtis, see Link, *Navajo Country Pioneers*, 66–82, 96–99. See also "A Seattle Man's Triumph," *Seattle Sunday Times*, Part V, May 22, 1904; and Faris, "The Navajo Photography of Edward S. Curtis," 377–89. The actual Nightway ceremony is only performed at night in winter months, and Curtis was in Chinle in the spring; therefore, all his Nightway scenes needed to be staged.

8. Curtis, "The Navaho," 73–130; plus Portfolio 1, plates 1, 26–39.

9. Wyatt, "A New Navajo Art," 35.

10. Holmström and Holford, *American Blacksmithing*.

11. This photograph was taken at the Upper Canada Village, a living history site southeast of Ottawa that replicates a rural nineteenth-century town. Clitso Dedman's blacksmith shop would have been similarly equipped, but on a much smaller scale.

12. By 1915, it would have been possible to replace the cumbersome leather bellows with its heavy wooden shaft by a metal blower that could be simply cranked by hand.

13. For a detailed description of the structure of a forge at that time, see Watson, *Blacksmith*, 101–27.

14. Rather than Sears Roebuck, it is possible that Dedman ordered his supplies from Montgomery Ward, which he had used in the past. See Clitso Dedman letter dated October 28, 1910, Arizona Archives, Hubbell Collection AZ375, box 23.

15. *Tools, Machinery Blacksmiths' Supplies*, 72–84.

16. The amount of $58.25 in 1915 would be the equivalent of $1,750 in 2023.

17. Clitso Dedman 1915 ledgers, University of Arizona Special Collections, Hubbell Archives, AZ375, box 384. The amount of $85 in 1915 would be the equivalent of $2,500 in 2023.

18. For more on forging, see Watson, *Blacksmith*, 32–52.

19. For more on Navajo horseshoes and bridles, see Clark, "Early Horse Trappings," 233–48.

20. For more on the art of shoeing horses, see Watson, *Blacksmith*, 68–79.

21. Robert Dedman Sr., personal communication, May 1999.

22. Clitsoe Dedman vs. Sonnie Dedman Complaint. Filed Jan. 4, 1918, John H. Udall, Clerk of the Superior Court of the State of Arizona in and for Apache County, by Deputy Clerk Levi S. Udall. Note that in the file Hadzizbaa is referred to by her Navajo nickname Sonnie.

23. Troester, "Clitso Dedman, Census No. 70142," *Navajo Census Cards*.

24. Troester, "Clitso Dedman, Census No. 70142," *Navajo Census Cards*. Clitso Dedman was baptized in the Annunciation Mission in Chinle on September 30, 1947.

25. Ostermann, "Shortcoats and Longgowns," 343.

26. In traditional matrilineal Navajo culture, it was the mother's clan, and by extension the mother's surname, that was transmitted to her children. Although named "Dedman," these later Hadzizbaa children and their offspring were not Clitso Dedman descendants.

27. Troester, "Hadzizbaa, Census No. 54070," *Navajo Census Cards*.

28. For more on repairing wagons, see Watson, *Blacksmith*, 80–91. The complex factors in building wagons are explained in detail in Sturt, *Wheelwright's Shop*.

29. Mary Dedman Dodge, personal communication, August 8, 1999.

30. Kirk, "The Kirk Clan," 147–57. Actually it was not in Ganado, but in Cienega Amarillo, near St. Michaels that Dedman helped remodel a trading post for Sam Day and his

wife Anna. In 1909, the Days added a second story for living quarters and renamed the building "Two Story Trading Post." See Kelley and Francis, "St. Michaels (Two Story Trading Post)," *Navajoland Trading Post Encyclopedia*, 338–39.

31. Ostermann, "Chin Lee in Retrospect," 184. In the citation, the older spelling "Chin Lee" is replaced by the current "Chinle."

32. Wilken, *Anselm Weber*, 119.

33. Frisbie, *Chinle Franciscan Mission Historic District Registration Form*, sect. 7, 3–5; sect. 8, 13–18.

34. Mary Dedman Dodge, personal communication, August 8, 1999.

35. Bodo, *Tales of an Endishodi*, 73.

36. Laramie McSparron Jarvi, personal communication, April 11, 1999.

37. Wagner, *Wide Ruins*, 2–3. After her divorce from Bill Lippincott, Sallie Wagner went back to using her maiden name.

38. Day, "Canyon de Chelly," Somatology is a branch of anthropology that studies the science of the human body.

39. Kennedy, *Tales of a Trader's Wife*, 22.

40. Stella Elizabeth Laughlin (1884–1969) married Cozy McSparron in 1916 in Wind River, Wyoming, where she was teaching on the Indian Reservation. After the wedding, the couple moved to Chinle. www.wikitree.com/wiki/Laughlin-449#Biography. Laramie McSparron Jarvi thought that the couple had married in 1918; personal communication, April 11, 1999.

41. See Brady and Bahr, "The Influenza Epidemic of 1918–1920 among the Navajos," 459–491.

42. For a more detailed history, see Kelley and Francis, "Chinle (Day Trading Post, Thunderbird Ranch)," *Navajoland Trading Post Encyclopedia*, 105–8. After McSparron sold the Thunderbird Ranch in the 1950s, it was renamed the Thunderbird Lodge.

43. Jarvi, "Oral History Project Interview," 8–9. Laramie is Cozy's daughter by his second wife, Inja.

44. Harrison and Spears, *Historic Structure Report*, 10.

45. Morris, *Digging*, 142.

46. For details on these buildings and their subsequent modernization, see Harrison and Spears, *Historic Structure Report*, 108–24. See also McKenna and Travis, *Archeological Investigations*, 6–10, 28, 33.

47. See Harrison and Spears, *Historic Structure Report*, 97.

48. Harrison and Spears, *Historic Structure Report*, 11, fn. 31.

49. The amount of $2,000 in 1928 would be the equivalent of $35,200 in 2023.

50. Quoted in Harrison and Spears, *Historic Structure Report*, 10, fn. 23.

51. Laramie McSparron Jarvi, personal communication, April 11, 1999.

52. Jarvi, "Oral History Project Interview," 4–5. Inja (1900–1977) was so named because of her grandmother's pronunciation of Indiana as "Inja-yana."

53. Jarvi, "Oral History Project Interview," 12.

54. Meredith Guillet entered the National Park Service in the 1930s. Upon leaving Canyon de Chelly, he served at Walnut Canyon National Monument near Flagstaff Arizona. From 1966 to 1972, he was superintendent at Mesa Verde National Park in Colorado.

55. Laramie McSparron Jarvi, personal communication, September 29, 1998. Laramie said that the former ranch house had become a gift shop and that the fireplace was hidden behind a display case.

56. Jarvi, "Oral History Project Interview," 21.

57. Laramie McSparron Jarvi, personal communication, September 14, 1999.

58. Laramie McSparron Jarvi, visit, October 14, 1998.

59. Armer, *Southwest*, 134.

60. Blue Canyon is a remote section of the Moenkopi Wash, twenty miles east of Tuba City, with stunning eroded rock formations in red and white sandstone.

61. For more on *Waterless Mountain* and an accompanying biographical sketch, see Palmquist, "Waterless Mountain," 118–23.

62. Armer, *Southwest*, 106. In her books, Armer spelled Clitso with a *K* as "Klitso."

63. Armer, *Southwest*, 108.

64. Armer, *In Navajoland*, 105.

65. Armer, *Southwest*, 38–40.

66. Armer, *Southwest*, 171.

67. Kelley and Francis, *Navajoland Trading Post Encyclopedia*, 59.

68. Mary Brown's clan affiliation is not noted on the St. Michaels census cards.

69. Susan Dedman Yazzie, personal communication, October 25, 1998.

70. Laramie McSparron Jarvi, personal communication, September 29, 1998. Unfortunately the house no longer exists, nor does the blacksmith shop.

71. Robert Dedman, personal communication, May 1999. This letter is the source of information for the following section describing life at Dedman Acres.

72. Smith, "Trader at Thunderbird," 9–10.

73. For more on the Chinle style, see Rodee, *One Hundred Years of Navajo Rugs*, 143–49.

74. Robert Dedman, personal communication, May 1999.

75. Robert Dedman, personal communication, May 1999.

8. WOODCARVER

1. Walsh, *Great Tradition of Hopi Katsina Carvers*, 1.

2. Wright, *Hopi Kachinas*, 66.

3. For a description of the evolution of Kachina dolls in the 1910–1945 period, see Walsh, *Great Tradition of Hopi Katsina Carvers*, 21–29; see also Erickson, *Kachinas*, 53–71.

4. Offered for sale by John Moran auctioneers, Monrovia CA, April 16, 2016, lot 1042; price $5,460.

5. Kluckhohn, Hill, and Kluckhohn, *Navaho Material Culture*, 415–18.

6. The lack of a tradition of secular carving among the Navajos was mentioned by the Franciscan Fathers in Haile, *Ethnologic Dictionary*, 495–96.

7. See Kelly, Lang, and Walters, *Navaho Figurines Called Dolls*, 58–63.

8. For a detailed description of sacred sandpaintings and their depiction in secular art forms, see Parezo, *Navajo Sandpainting*.

9. For a complete history, see Valette and Valette, *Navajo Weavings with Ceremonial Themes*.

10. For a 1905 photograph and description of the Begging Gods, see Long, *Big Eyes*, 63–64.

11. Matthews, *Night Chant*, 136.

12. Matthews, *Night Chant*. Simon Schwemberger was permitted to film a Nightway ceremony in 1905; see Long, *Big Eyes*, 39–75.

13. For a more detailed description of the last day of the Nightway, see Matthews, *Night Chant*, 136–50. A briefer account of a 1992 ceremony is described in Rosenak and Rosenak, *Navajo Folk Art*, 8.

14. Accession file, MIAC, Lab of Anthropology, cat. no. 37161/12.

15. For the Hopi, a prime function of the Kachinas was to bring rainfall; Erickson, *Kachinas*, 10. Therefore, a Kachina doll could only be carved "from the root of the water-seeking cottonwood tree, and it [had to be] thoroughly dried and seasoned." Wright, *Hopi Kachinas*, 10.

16. Matthews, *Night Chant*, 9–10, 126–27. Wyman, *Southwest Indian Drypainting*, 87.

17. At some point, the male figure of Water Sprinkler lost the two feathers of his headdress.

18. "Christmas Toys," *Life Magazine*, December 9, 1940, 102–3. Cozy McSparron subscribed to both *Time* and *Life* magazines.

19. The Alexander Doll Company, which was founded by Beatrice "Madame" Alexander in 1923, specialized in the creation of dolls replicating famous personalities, as well as characters from popular books and films.

20. Laramie McSparron Jarvi, personal communication, September 29, 1998. Marion's figure is the only carving that Clitso made of a stylized Fringe Mouth impersonator. It was sold from her estate in lot 4027 at the Bonhams & Butterfields auction of June 4, 2007, and acquired by the California Academy of Sciences in San Francisco.

21. This figure that Cozy McSparron gave to Sallie Wagner was probably part of the 1941 Christmas set. Given its distinctive ruff in light green with black dots, this carving is definitely one of Clitso's earliest representations of Talking God.

22. Cozy McSparron gave this early single Water Sprinkler with his smooth round ruff to Canyon de Chelly Ranger Charles Wyatt.

23. For more on the Eighth Day ceremony, see Matthews, *Night Chant*, 131–35.

24. Laramie McSparron Jarvi, personal communication, October 14, 1998. Sallie Wagner wrote that Cozy McSparron had given her the set of Yei dancers "not too long after Clitso began making them. I do remember that Cozy was excited at having found

the old man doing such things." Sallie Wagner, personal communication, February 3, 1999.

25. Inja McSparron, letter to Mitchell Wilder of the Amon Carter Museum, February 1, 1967, describing a sixteen-piece Yeibichai set, cat. nos. 2667/1 to 16. Inja was sixty-seven years old at the time and erroneously wrote that the early set of four carvings dated to Christmas 1937, rather than 1940.

26. Sallie Wagner, personal communication, August 16, 1999. In addition to the set of four Begging Gods, there was also a second smaller carving of Talking God. Bill Lippincott and wife Sallie first came to Canyon de Chelly in summer 1936 when he was hired as a summer ranger. Cozy McSparron helped them acquire the trading post at Wide Ruins, which they owned from 1938 to 1950.

27. The Koenigs purchased the set at a Parke-Bernet Auction in December 1968.

28. Bill Beaver, personal communication, October 13, 1998. He also provided the description of the workbench and the vise.

29. A similar set of five, but with only one Female Yei dancer and a Male Yei, was collected by James Solomon.

30. Cozy McSparron sold this first set to "someone in Scarsdale." Laramie McSparron Jarvi, personal communication, September 14, 1999.

31. Some years later, McSparron would replace this set with a second one in Dedman's more realistic classic style.

32. The amount of $15.30 in 1956 would be the equivalent of $168 in 2023.

33. Clitso-Pagel correspondence, Skinner Auction 26368, February 11, 2013, lot 310.

34. According to a typed note (possibly by a curator) in the files at the Indianapolis Museum of Art, Dr. Noble had "recorded the chant and explained the ceremony on eight-track tape."

35. Sallie Wagner, personal communication, February 3, 1999.

36. For a description of the Enemyway, see Gilpin, *Enduring Navaho*, 227–35; Downs, *Navajo*, 103–7. At the end of the final Squaw Dance, the ceremonial stick is taken away and hidden or buried so that nobody will be harmed. See Kelly, Lang, and Walters, *Navaho Figurines Called Dolls*, 60.

37. These services were funded by the Indian Rights Association, a national organization in which Elkus was active. For a biography, see Ben Elkus, "Prologue," in Washburn, *Elkus Collection*, 7–11.

38. Cozy McSparron, 1954 letter, Caroline Kelly accession file, Museum of Indian Arts and Culture, Laboratory of Anthropology, Santa Fe, New Mexico. The copy of the letter in the file states that Clitso Dedman had started carving in 1934, an obvious typographical error. In parentheses, the curator added that McSparron thought Clitso had carved "22 sets" in his lifetime.

39. Description provided by Mary Dedman Dodge, personal communication, August 8, 1999.

40. James Faris, personal communication, October 22, 1998.

41. The amount of $250 in 1946 would be the equivalent of $3,875 in 2023.

42. Mary Dedman Dodge, personal communication, August 8, 1999.

43. Laramie McSparron Jarvi, personal communication, October 14, 1998.

44. Zuni trader Charles Garrett Wallace (1898–1993) purchased this set from Cozy McSparron and exhibited it in his trading posts, including his store in Gallup. In 1975, he donated 500 items from his collection to the Heard Museum in Phoenix and auctioned the remainder through Sotheby Parke Bernet. At age seventy-six, with a failing memory, Wallace wrote the following rather imaginary description for the auction house: "These 16 Navajo Yebachi Dancers were made by Hostien Deadmond and finished in 1927. . . . These were all hand-carved. [To dry the paints,] Deadmond used solar heat from atop the canyon where he made hand-made ladders. He slept there in the cave during the winter months. During the summer he would come back down to the river where he raised all his crops, beans, corn and squash. He spent spring, summer and fall down there."

45. Although Clitso was not pleased with the look of the metal feathers, he realized that they were much easier to produce. During the last years of his life, as his manual dexterity diminished, he would again use metal feathers for his figures.

46. This set was deaccessioned by the Indian Pueblo Cultural Center in Albuquerque in the early 1990s since it did not fit the theme of their collection.

47. Cat. no. 1437G. The Southwest Museum merged with the Autry Museum of the American West in 2003. The collections, including the Clitso set, were formerly housed at the Mount Washington Campus location and are now in storage in Burbank.

48. The amount of $300 in 1956 would be the equivalent of $3,300 in 2023.

49. See the 1984 publication of the California Academy of Sciences entitled *The Elkus Collection*. This was not a comprehensive catalog, however, and focuses on only the jewelry, textiles, pottery, and paintings in the collection. It does not include baskets or carvings.

50. John Boyden advised the Navajos on judicial matters and spent some time on the Navajo Reservation. The Utah museum decided to deaccession the two Clitso figures, selling them at Cowan's Auction, September 20, 2013, lot 268.

51. J. R. Willis (1876–1960) operated a camera store in Gallup from 1917 to 1931, before moving to Albuquerque. Over the years, he worked closely with the Gallup Inter-tribal Ceremonial and published hundreds of postcards of the Southwest with Curt Teich in Chicago. In the 1930s, Curt Teich & Company was the largest producer of postcards in the world. All their cards were retouched and repainted to meet the specifications of the client. According to Albuquerque historian Joe Sabatini, Willis ordered 12,500 copies of the "Devil Dance" postcard from Teich on June 27, 1937; personal communication, September 1, 2022.

52. Laramie McSparron Jarvi, personal communication, October 14, 1998. In speaking of the carvings, she used the phrase "Devil Dancers."

53. Russell Hartman, who arranged the purchase of the figure for the California Academy of Sciences, also ascribed the carving to Clitso Dedman. At the time of purchase, the Cowboy no longer had his hat.

54. According to Margaret Delaney, daughter of Camillo Garcia, Clitso Dedman's wife would sometimes sell his carvings directly to tourists. Margaret Delaney, personal communication, September 11, 1998.

55. Brugge and Wilson, *Administrative History*, chapter 7. Cozy McSparron fell seriously ill in spring 1954, just as the sale was being consummated. He died in 1959.

56. Robert Dedman, personal communication, October 25, 1998.

57. Emma Jean Bader, personal communication, December 10, 1998.

58. Rosetta LaFont, personal communication, October 24, 1998.

59. Pat Gurley (Clair Gurley's son), personal communication, September 8, 1998. The set was subsequently willed to Clair's grandson, Michael Schuelke.

60. Camillo Garcia's widow had asked Nello Guadagnoli to photograph the trading post holdings after her husband and son had been killed in a 1962 plane crash.

61. Nello Guadagnoli, personal communication, September 8, 1998.

62. Bill Beaver, personal communication, November 16, 1998. Public Law 474, which became effective on July 1, 1950, provided federal assistance for needy Navajo and Hopi Indians residing on their reservations.

63. Phil Woodard, personal communication, October 23, 1998.

64. See Jett, "Modern Navajo Cemeteries," 3–6.

65. Susan Dedman Yazzie, personal communication, August 23, 2022.

66. See Valette and Valette, "The Life and Work of Clitso Dedman," 57. These figures were collected by Dr. and Mrs. Edwin Wilde and bequeathed to the Arizona State Museum in 1980. One foot is signed "Joe D" and the other is signed "Dedman."

9. A FORGOTTEN ARTIST

1. *Arizona Daily Star*, April 16, 1946.

2. Tanner, *Southwest Indian Craft Arts*, 166–69. The Navajo Arts and Crafts Guild was subsequently renamed the Navajo Arts and Crafts Enterprise.

3. Bahti, *Southwestern Indian Ceremonials*, 14.

4. In 2015, the set was given a new catalog number, which is confusing since most museums would have given the accession date, in this case 1983.

5. See details in the appendix: T.16-C (Transitional Noble set) and C.16-H (Classic Noble set).

6. Missing on the shelf are the two Female Yeis with upraised arms, T.2-A.

7. Accession file, #26.67/3, Amon Carter Museum.

8. The Amon Carter accession file lists Clitso Dedman's ethnicity as Eskimo; however, this annotation may be due to a secretarial error. Inja McSparron definitely knew that Clitso was Navajo.

9. See details in the appendix: T.16-B (Transitional McSparron set) and C.16-L (Classic McSparron set).

10. Lars Garrison, personal communication, September 2, 2020.

11. Rosenak and Rosenak, *Navajo Folk Art*, 7, 100.

EPILOGUE

1. Wyatt, "A New Navajo Art," 34.

2. Russell Hartman, personal communication, February 5, 2021. According to Hartman, former director of the Navajo Tribal Museum, this display of the Clitso set would have been in place around 1955. In 1972, the Navajo Arts and Crafts Guild was renamed the Navajo Arts and Crafts Enterprise.

3. For more background on these ceremonial figurines plus numerous illustrations, see Kelly, Lang, and Walters, *Navaho Figurines Called Dolls*, 13–45. See also McGreevy, "Charlie Willeto."

4. Rosenak and Rosenak, *Navajo Folk Art*, 50–51. See also Begay et al., *Collective Willeto*.

5. McGreevy, "Charlie Willeto," 108.

6. Rosenak and Rosenak, *Navajo Folk Art*, 52–58. Apparently Harold Willeto was at first fearful that his brother Leonard's van accident and later suicide were due to "breaking taboos by making carved figures."

7. Hartman and Heyser, *Navajo Ceremonies*, 5; Rosenak and Rosenak, *Navajo Folk Art*, 98–100.

8. Charles Elkus sponsored a $50 award to "encourage the younger generation to enter the craft field." Washburn, *Elkus Collection*, 10. After Elkus's death in 1962, the Elkus Memorial Award was established in recognition of his longtime support of Native artists.

9. "Indian Market: Best of Show Winner Refused to Quit," *New Mexican*, August 18, 2009. See also "Mythical Abstraction: Sheldon Harvey."

BIBLIOGRAPHY

Adams, David Wallace. *Education for Extinction: American Indians and the Boarding School Experience, 1875–1928*. Lawrence: University Press of Kansas, 1995.

Adams, William Y. *Shonto: A Study of the Role of the Trader in a Modern Navaho Community*. Bureau of American Ethnology Bulletin, no. 188. Washington: Smithsonian Institution, 1963.

Aigner, Dennis J. *The Swastika Motif: Its Use in Navajo and Oriental Weaving*. Laguna Beach CA: DAI Press, 2018.

American Museum of Natural History. Invitational flyer to "An Exhibition of Paintings Made in the Cañons, Deserts and Cliff Dwellings and in the Moki and Navajo Country of the Southwest by F. Melville DuMond, March Ninth to Twenty-Third, 1912." New York, 1912.

Anderson, Michael F. "National Register of Historical Places Nomination Form for Rough Rock Trading Post." Window Rock AZ: Navajo Nation Historic Preservation Department, 2000.

Armer, Laura Adams. *In Navajoland*. New York: McKay, 1962.

———. *Southwest*. London: Longmans, Green, 1935.

Austin, Raymond D. *Navajo Courts and Navajo Common Law: A Tradition of Tribal Self-Governance*. Minneapolis: University of Minnesota Press, 2009.

Bahr, Howard M., ed. *The Navajo as Seen by the Franciscans, 1898–1921: A Sourcebook*. Lanham MD: Scarecrow, 2004.

Bahti, Tom. *Southwestern Indian Ceremonials*. Las Vegas: KC Publications, 1970.

Bailey, Garrick, and Roberta Glenn Bailey. *A History of the Navajos: The Reservation Years*. Seattle: University of Washington Press, 1986.

Batkin, Jonathan. *The Native American Curio Trade in New Mexico*. Santa Fe: Wheelwright Museum, 2008.

Beadle, J. H. *The Undeveloped West; or Five Years in the Territories*. Philadelphia: National, 1873.

Begay, Shonto, Walter Hopps, Lee Kogan, Greg LaChapelle, and John and Stephanie Smither. *Collective Willeto: The Visionary Carvings of a Navajo Artist*. Albuquerque: Museum of New Mexico Press, 2002.

Berkholz, Richard C. *Old Trading Posts of the Four Corners: A Guide to Early-Day Trading Posts Established on or Around the Navajo, Hopi, and Ute Mountain Ute Reservations*. Lake City CO: Western Reflections, 2007.

Blackman, Craig H. "The Story of the Ute and the Grand Junction Indian School." *Whispering Wind* 37, no. 3 (January–February 2008): 14.

Blue, Martha. *Indian Trader: The Life and Times of J. L. Hubbell*. Walnut CA: Kiva, 2000.

Bodo, Murray, OFM, ed. *Tales of an Endishodi: Father Berard Haile and the Navajos, 1900–1961*. Albuquerque: University of New Mexico Press, 1998.

Bowman, John H. "Navajo Agency, August 31, 1885." *Annual Report of the Commissioner of Indian Affairs*. Washington DC: Office of Indian Affairs, 1885: 379–82.

———. "Navajo Agency, September 3, 1884." *Annual Report of the Commissioner of Indian Affairs*. Washington DC: Office of Indian Affairs, 1884: 177–80.

Bradley, Eleanor. "An Artist's Two Years Alone in the Desert." *True West* 26, no. 1 (September–October 1978): 30–38.

Brady, Benjamin R., and Howard M. Bahr. "The Influenza Epidemic of 1918–1920 among the Navajos: Marginality, Mortality, and the Implications of Some Neglected Eyewitness Accounts." *American Indian Quarterly* 38, no. 4 (Fall 2014): 459–91.

Breen, Thos. H. "Report of School at Grand Junction, Colo., October 2, 1888." *Annual Report of the Commissioner of Indian Affairs*. Washington DC: Office of Indian Affairs, 1888: 250–54.

Brown, Estelle Aubrey. *Stubborn Fool: A Narrative*. Caldwell ID: Caxton, 1952.

Brugge, David M. *Hubbell Trading Post National Historic Site*. Tucson: Southwest Parks and Monuments Association, 1993.

Brugge, David M., and Raymond Wilson. *Administrative History: Canyon de Chelly National Monument Arizona*. Washington DC: National Park Service, January 1976.

Bryant, Keith L., Jr. *History of the Atchison, Topeka and Santa Fe Railway*. New York: Macmillan, 1974.

Bulow, Ernie. "Roughing It in Indian Country." *Gallup Journey Magazine* 10, no. 11 (November 2013): 26–27.

Burbank, E. A., and Ernest Royce. *Burbank among the Indians*. Caldwell ID: Caxton Printers, 1944.

"Canyon de Chelly of Arizona: A Monument of Prehistoric America." *Scientific American Supplement* 2250 (February 15, 1919): 100–101.

Child, Brenda. *Boarding School Seasons: American Indian Families, 1900–1940*. Lincoln: University of Nebraska Press, 1998.

Chisholm, James S. *Navajo Infancy: An Ethological Study of Child Development*. Hawthorne NY: Aldine, 1983.

Clark, Laverne Harrell. "Early Horse Trappings of the Navajo and Apache Indians." *Arizona and the West* 5, no. 1 (Spring 1963): 233–48.

Clifford, Casey Jones, Sr. "Carrying Our History Forward." *Leading the Way: The Wisdom of the Navajo People* 15, no. 1 (January 2017): 14–18.

Colton, Harold S. *Hopi Kachina Dolls with a Key to their Identification*. Albuquerque: University of New Mexico Press, 1949; rev. ed. 1959.

Cottam, Erica. *Hubbell Trading Post: Trade, Tourism, and the Navajo Southwest*. Norman: University of Oklahoma Press, 2015.

Crane, Leo. *Indians of the Enchanted Desert*. Boston: Little, Brown, 1927.

Curtis, Edward S. "The Navaho." *The North American Indian: Volume One*. Cambridge MA: University Press, 1907. Portfolio 1, Plates 1, 26–39.

Dalrymple, Larry. "Stewart Hatch: A Lifetime Trading with the Navajo and Ute." *Journal of the Southwest* 55, no. 4 (Winter 2013): 495–505.

Davenport, Kristen. "The First People and First Seeds." *Mother Earth Gardener* (Winter 2015–16). Topeka KS: Odgen.

Davis, Barbara A. *Edward S. Curtis: The Life and Times of a Shadow Catcher*. San Francisco: Chronicle, 1985.

Davis, Carolyn O'Bagy. *Arizona's Historic Trading Posts*. Charleston SC: Arcadia Publishing, 2014.

Davis, W. I. "Report of School at Grand Junction, Colo., September 1, 1887." *Annual Report of the Commissioner of Indian Affairs*. Washington DC: Office of Indian Affairs, 1887: 111–13.

Day, S[am] E., Sr. "Canyon de Chelly." *Gallup New Industrial Independent*, 1916. Arizona Archives Online, Day Family Collection, Box 2, Folder 6.

Downs, James F. *The Navajo*. New York: Holt, Rinehart and Winston, 1972.

Ducker, James H. *Men of the Steel Rails: Workers on the Atchison, Topeka & Santa Fe Railroad, 1869–1900*. Lincoln: University of Nebraska Press, 1983.

Dyk, Walter. *Left Handed, Son of Old Man Hat: A Navajo Autobiography*. Lincoln: University of Nebraska Press, 1995. First published 1938 by Harcourt Brace (New York).

Eastman, Galen. "Navajo Agency, September 1, 1882." *Annual Report of the Commissioner of Indian Affairs*. Washington DC: Office of Indian Affairs, 1882: 127–29.

Erickson, Jon T. *Kachinas: An Evolving Hopi Art Form?* Phoenix: Heard Museum, 1977.

Evaneshko, Veronica. "Life among the Navajo." Cline Library, Digital Collection NAU. PH.2003.19.2. Flagstaff: Northern Arizona University, 2003.

Faris, James C. "The Navajo Photography of Edward S. Curtis." *History of Photography* 17, no. 4 (1993): 377–89.

———. *The Nightway: A History and a History of Documentation of a Navajo Ceremonial*. Albuquerque: University of New Mexico Press, 1990.

Fewkes, Jesse Walter. "Hopi Katcinas, Drawn by Native Artists." *Twenty-First Annual Report of the Bureau of American Ethnology*, vol. 21, 1899–1900. Washington DC: Government Printing Office, 1903.

Fischer, Egbert, OFM. "A Sick Call to Crystal." In *The Navajo as Seen by the Franciscans, 1898–1921: A Sourcebook*, edited by Howard M. Bahr, 360–65. Lanham MD: Scarecrow, 2004.

Franciscan Fathers. *An Ethnologic Dictionary of the Navaho Language*. St. Michaels AZ: Franciscan Fathers, 1910.

Frisbie, Charlotte J. *Chinle Franciscan Mission Historic District Registration Form*. Washington DC: National Park Service, April 25, 2007.

———. *Food Sovereignty the Navajo Way: Cooking with Tall Woman*. Albuquerque: University of New Mexico Press, 2018.

———. "On the Trail of Chinle's 'Big House.'" In *Diné Bikeyah: Papers in Honor of David M. Brugge*, edited by Meliha S. Duran and David T. Kirkpatrick, 69–85. Albuquerque: Archaeological Society of New Mexico, Publication 24, 1998.

Gaston, Charity A. "Navajo Agency, Fort Defiance, New Mexico, August 23, 1870." *Annual Report of the Commissioner of Indian Affairs*. Washington DC: Office of Indian Affairs, 1870: 153–54.

Geneste, Eric, and Eric Mickeler. *Kachina, Messagers des Dieux Hopis et Zuñis/Kachina, Messengers of the Hopi and Zuñi Gods*. Paris: Somogy Art Publishers, 2011.

———. *100 Masques Pueblos (et même un peu plus) des Indiens Hopis, Zuñis, Lagunas/ Hopi, Zuni and Laguna Pueblo Indian Masks*. Paris: Somogy Art Publishers, 2013.

Gilpin, Laura. *The Enduring Navaho*. Austin: University of Texas Press, 1974.

Girdner, Alwin J. *Diné Tah: My Reservation Days 1923–1939*. Tucson: Rio Nuevo Publishing, 2015.

Gjeltema, Bruce James. "Jacob Casimera Morgan and the Development of Navajo Nationalism." PhD dissertation. Albuquerque: University of New Mexico, 2004.

Golden, Gertrude. *Red Moon Called Me: Memoirs of a School Teacher in the Government Indian Service*. San Antonio TX: Naylor, 1954.

Graves, Laura. *Thomas Varker Keam, Indian Trader*. Norman: University of Oklahoma Press, 1998.

Griffin-Pierce, Trudy. *Earth Is My Mother, Sky Is My Father: Space, Time, and Astronomy in Navajo Sandpainting*. Albuquerque: University of New Mexico Press, 1992.

Guillet, Meredith. "Nature and Man in Canyon de Chelly." *National Parks Magazine* 39 (July 1965): 9–11.

Haile, Berard, OFM. *An Ethnologic Dictionary of the Navaho Language*. St. Michaels AZ: Franciscan Fathers, 1910.

———. *Navajo Sacrificial Figurines*. Chicago: University of Chicago Press, 1947.

Hall, Edward T. *West of the Thirties: Discoveries among the Navajo and Hopi*. New York: Doubleday, 1994.

Harrison, Laura Soullière, and Beverley Spears. *Historic Structure Report: Chinle Trading Post, Thunderbird Ranch and Custodian's Residence, Canyon de Chelly National Monument, Arizona*, Southwest Cultural Resources Center, Professional Papers No. 17. Santa Fe NM: National Park Service, 1989.

Hartman, Russell P., and Richard Heyser. *Navajo Ceremonies: Carvings by Tom Yazzie*. Lakewood CO: Jefferson County Public Library, 1979.

Holmström, John Gustaf, and Henry Holford. *American Blacksmithing, Toolsmiths' and Steelworkers' Manual*. Chicago: Sears, Roebuck & Co., 1911.

Hoxie, Frederick E. *A Final Promise: The Campaign to Assimilate the Indians, 1880–1920*. Lincoln: University of Nebraska Press, 1984.

Hrdlička, Aleš. *Physiological and Medical Observations among the Indians of Southwestern United States and Northern Mexico*, Smithsonian Institution, Bureau of American Ethnology, Bulletin 34. Washington DC: Government Printing Office, 1908.

Hubbell, J. L., as told to J. E. Hogg. "Fifty Years an Indian Trader; the Dean of all Indian traders of the Southwest Relates His Experiences during Half a Century of Contact with Utes, Navajos, and Hopis." *Touring Topics* 22 (December 1930): 24–29.

Hutchinson, Elizabeth. *The Indian Craze: Primitivism, Modernism, and Transculturation in American Art, 1890–1915*. Durham NC: Duke University Press, 2009.

Iverson, Peter. *Diné: A History of the Navajos*. Albuquerque: University of New Mexico Press, 2002.

Iverson, Peter, ed. *"For Our Navajo People": Diné Letters, Speeches & Petitions 1900–1960*. Albuquerque: University of New Mexico Press, 2002.

Jacobs, Margaret D. "A Battle for the Children: American Indian Child Removal in Arizona in the Era of Assimilation." *Journal of Arizona History* 45 (2004): 31–62.

James, George Wharton. *Indian Blankets & Their Makers*. New York: Dover, 1974. First published 1914 by McClurg (Chicago).

Jarvi, Laramie McSparron. "Oral History Project Interview." Prescott AZ: Sharlot Hall Museum, November 9, 2002.

Jett, Stephen C. "Modern Navajo Cemeteries." *Material Culture* 28, no. 2 (Summer 1996): 1–23.

———. "The Navajo Homestead: Situation and Site." *Yearbook of the Association of Pacific Coast Geographers* 42 (1980): 101–17.

———. "Territory and Hogan: Local Homelands of the Navajo." In *Diné Bikeyah: Papers in Honor of David M. Brugge*, edited by Meliha S. Duran and David T. Kirkpatrick, 117–28. Albuquerque: Archaeological Society of New Mexico, Publication 24, 1998.

Johnson, Broderick H., ed. *Stories of Traditional Navajo Life and Culture by Twenty-Two Navajo Men and Women*. Tsaile AZ: Navajo Community College Press, 1977.

Johnston, Denis Foster. *An Analysis of Sources of Information on the Population of the Navaho*. Smithsonian Institution, Bureau of American Ethnology Bulletin 197. Washington DC: US Government Printing Office, 1966.

Keane, Maribeth, and Bonnie Monte. "Katsina or Kachina? Barry Walsh on the Spiritual Roots of Native American Dolls." *Collectors Weekly*, September 10, 2010.

Kelley, Klara, and Harris Francis. *A Diné History of Navajoland*. Tucson: University of Arizona Press, 2019.

———. *Navajoland Trading Post Encyclopedia*. Window Rock AZ: Navajo Nation Heritage and Historic Preservation Department, 2018.

Kelley, Klara, and Rolf Nabahe. "An Archaeological Survey of the Nazlini Trading Post Compound, Nazlini, Arizona." NNCRMP-87-161. Window Rock AZ: Navajo Nation Historic Preservation Department, 1987.

Kelly, Roger E., R. W. Lang, and Harry Walters. *Navaho Figurines Called Dolls*. Santa Fe: Museum of Navajo Ceremonial Art, 1972.

Kennedy, John D. *A Good Trade: Three Generations of Life and Trading around the Indian Capital Gallup, New Mexico*. Gallup NM: Kennedy Traders, 2013.

Kennedy, Mary Jeanette. *Tales of a Trader's Wife: Life on the Navajo Indian Reservation, 1913–1938*. Albuquerque: Valliant, 1965.

Kirk, Tom. "The Kirk Clan, Traders with the Navaho." In *People of the Far West*, edited by Horace L. Dodd and Robert W. Long, 147–57. Brand Book no. 6. San Diego, CA: Corral of the Westerners, 1979.

Kluckhohn, Clyde, and Dorothea Leighton. *The Navaho*, rev. ed. Garden City NY: Doubleday, 1962.

Kluckhohn, Clyde, W. W. Hill, and Lucy Wales Kluckhohn. *Navaho Material Culture*. Cambridge MA: Harvard University Press, 1971.

Koenig, Seymour H., and Harriet Koenig. *Acculturation in the Navajo Eden: New Mexico, 1550–1750*. New York: YBK Publishers, 2005.

Koper, Fidelis, OFM, and Leopold Ostermann, OFM. "Life at Chin Lee Mission, 1917–1918: Contrasting Views." In *The Navajo as Seen by the Franciscans, 1898–1921: A Sourcebook*, edited by Howard M. Bahr, 400–411. Lanham MD: Scarecrow Press, 2004.

Kvasnicka, Robert, and Herman Viola, eds. *The Commissioners of Indian Affairs*. Norman: University of Oklahoma Press, 1979.

LaFarge, Olivier. *A Pictorial History of the American Indian*. New York: Crown Publishers, 1956.

Lemmon, Theo G. "Report of Apache Indian Boarding School, San Carlos, Ariz., August 31, 1890." *Annual Report of the Commissioner of Indian Affairs*. Washington DC: Office of Indian Affairs, 1890: 12–14.

———. "Report of School at Grand Junction, Colo., August 20, 1892." *Annual Report of the Commissioner of Indian Affairs*. Washington DC: Office of Indian Affairs, 1892: 657–59.

———. "Report of School at Grand Junction, Colo., August 27, 1894." *Annual Report of the Commissioner of Indian Affairs*. Washington DC: Office of Indian Affairs, 1894: 375–78.

———. "Report of School at Grand Junction, Colo., September 4, 1893." *Annual Report of the Commissioner of Indian Affairs*. Washington DC: Office of Indian Affairs, 1893: 410–14.

———. "Report of Teller Institute, Grand Junction, Colo., August 31, 1891." *Annual Report of the Commissioner of Indian Affairs.* Washington DC: Office of Indian Affairs, 1891: 58–59.

Liebler, H. Baxter. *Boil My Heart for Me.* Jericho NY: Exposition, 1969.

Lindig, Wolfgang, and Helga Teiwes. *Navajo: Tradition and Change in the Southwest.* New York: Facts on File, 1993. [Originally published in German in Zurich, Switzerland: U. Bär Verlag, 1991, with the title *Navajo.*]

Link, Martin A., ed. *Navajo: A Century of Progress 1868–1968.* Window Rock AZ: Navajo Tribe, 1968.

———. *Navajo Country Pioneers: Four Generations of the Day Family.* Santa Fe: Clear Light, 2012.

Littlefield, Daniel, Jr., and Lonnie E. Underhill. "Renaming the American Indian: 1890–1913." *American Studies* 12 (1971): 33–45.

Locke, Raymond Friday. *The Book of the Navajo.* Los Angeles: Mankind, 1976.

Lockwood, Frank C. *The Life of Edward E. Ayer.* Chicago: McClurg, 1929.

Long, Paul V. *Big Eyes: The Southwestern Photographs of Simeon Schwemberger, 1902–1908.* Albuquerque: University of New Mexico Press, 1992.

M'Closkey, Kathy. *Swept under the Rug: A Hidden History of Navajo Weaving.* Albuquerque: University of New Mexico Press, 2002.

MacKendrick, Donald A. "Cesspools, Alkali and White Lily Soap: The Grand Junction Indian School 1886–1911." *Journal of the Western Slope* 8, no. 3 (Summer 1993).

Matthews, Washington. *The Mountain Chant: A Navajo Ceremony.* Salt Lake City: University of Utah Press, 1997. First published 1887 in the *U.S. Bureau of American Ethnology Fifth Annual Report 1883–1884.*

———. *Navaho Legends.* Salt Lake City: University of Utah Press, 1994. First published 1897 by Houghton Mifflin (Boston).

———. *The Night Chant: A Navaho Ceremony.* Salt Lake City: University of Utah Press, 1995. First published 1902 by Knickerbocker (New York).

McGreevy, Susan Brown. "Charlie Willeto: Incantations, Transformations." In *Vernacular Visionaries: International Outsider Art*, edited by Annie Carlano, 96–111. New Haven CT: Yale University Press, in association with the Museum of International Folk Art, Santa Fe, 2003.

McKenna, Peter J., and Scott E. Travis. *Archeological Investigations at Thunderbird Lodge, Canyon de Chelly, Arizona.* Southwest Cultural Resources Center Professional Papers, Number 20. Santa Fe: National Park Service, 1989.

McNitt, Frank. *The Indian Traders.* Norman: University of Oklahoma Press, 1962.

McPherson, Robert S. *Both Sides of the Bullpen: Navajo Trade and Posts.* Norman: University of Oklahoma Press, 2017.

———. *Navajo Land, Navajo Culture: The Utah Experience in the Twentieth Century.* Logan: Utah State University Press, 2001.

————. *Traders, Agents, and Weavers: Developing the Northern Navajo Region.* Norman: University of Oklahoma Press, 2020.

McPherson, Robert S., ed. *The Journey of Navajo Oshley: An Autobiography and Life History.* Logan: Utah State University Press, 2000.

Menaul, Charity A. G. "Defiance, Navajo Agency, August 29, 1871." *Annual Report of the Commissioner of Indian Affairs.* Washington DC: Office of Indian Affairs, 1871: 375–76.

Mindeleff, Cosmos. "Navaho Houses." *Seventeenth Annual Report of the Bureau of American Ethnology, 1895–1896.* Washington DC: Government Printing Office, 1898.

Mitchell, Emerson Blackhorse, and T. B. Allen. *Miracle Hill: The Story of a Navaho Boy.* Norman: University of Oklahoma Press, 1967.

Mitchell, Frank. *Navajo Blessingway Singer: The Autobiography of Frank Mitchell, 1881–1967.* Edited by Charlotte J. Frisbie and David McAllester. Tucson: University of Arizona Press, 1978. First published 2003 by University of New Mexico Press (Albuquerque).

Mitchell, Rose. *Tall Woman: The Life Story of Rose Mitchell, a Navajo Woman, c. 1874–1977.* Edited by Charlotte J. Frisbie. Albuquerque: University of New Mexico Press, 2001.

Moore, J. B. "How Shall We Aid the Navajos?" *Indian Craftsman* 1, no. 4 (1909): 29–38.

Morgan, Jacob C. "A Retrospect." *The Southern Workman* 62 (May 1933): 76–81.

————. "Evangelist J. C. Morgan's Life-Story: I. My Start." *Missionary Monthly Reformed Review* 33, no. 387 (August 1929): 297–99.

————. "Evangelist J. C. Morgan's Life-Story: II. My First Step." *Missionary Monthly Reformed Review* 33, no. 391 (December 1929): 492–94.

Morgan, T. J. "Report of the Commissioner of Indian Affairs, October 1, 1891." *Annual Report of the Commissioner of Indian Affairs.* Washington DC: Office of Indian Affairs, 1891.

Morris, Ann Axtell. *Digging in the Southwest.* Chicago: Hale, 1933.

"Mythical Abstraction: Sheldon Harvey (Navajo)." *Native American Art* 18 (December–January 2019): 122–25.

Newcomb, Franc. *Hosteen Klah: Navaho Medicine Man and Sand Painter.* Norman: University of Oklahoma Press, 1964.

Newcomb, Franc J., and Gladys A. Reichard. *Sandpaintings of the Navajo Shooting Chant.* New York: Dover, 1975. First published 1937 by J. J. Augustin (New York).

Nez, Chester, and Judith Schiess Avila. *Code Talker: The First and Only Memoir by One of the Original Navajo Code Talkers of WWII.* New York: Penguin, 2011.

Nickelson, Howard B. *One Hundred Years of Coal Mining in the San Juan Basin, New Mexico.* Bulletin 111, New Mexico Bureau of Mines & Mineral Resources. Socorro NM: New Mexico Institute of Mining & Technology, 1988.

Noe, Sally. *Gallup, New Mexico, U.S.A: Our Story.* Virginia Beach: Donning, 1997.

Ostermann, Leopold, OFM. "Chinle in Retrospect." In *The Navajo as Seen by the Franciscans, 1898–1921: A Sourcebook,* edited by Howard M. Bahr, 182–92. Lanham MD: Scarecrow, 2004.

————. "Shortcoats and Longgowns." In *The Navajo as Seen by the Franciscans, 1898–1921: A Sourcebook,* edited by Howard M. Bahr, 335–48. Lanham MD: Scarecrow, 2004.

Otis, James. "Across the Range." *Harper's Young People* 15 (March 31, 1894): 370–84.

Padget, Martin. *Indian Country: Travels in the American Southwest 1840–1935*. Albuquerque: University of New Mexico Press, 2004.

Palmquist, Peter E. "Waterless Mountain." In May Castleberry, *Perpetual Mirage: Photographic Narratives of the Desert West*, 118–23. New York: Whitney Museum of Art, 1996.

Panofsky, Richard J. *Art and Ambition, 1887–1927: Frederick Melville DuMond, An American Painter of His Times*. Raleigh NC: Lulu, 2010.

Paquette, Peter. *Census of the Navajo Reservation under Jurisdiction of Peter Paquette, Superintendent. Year 1915*. Amherst: University of Massachusetts, Microfilm D-111, Reel 273.

Parezo, Nancy J. *Navajo Sandpainting: From Religious Act to Commercial Art*. Albuquerque: University of New Mexico Press, 1983.

Parlett, David. *The Penguin Book of Card Games*. London: Penguin, 2008.

Patterson, S. S. "Report of Navajo Agency, N. Mex., September 1, 1888." *Annual Report of the Commissioner of Indian Affairs*. Washington DC: Office of Indian Affairs, 1888.

Pattison, James William. "E.A. Burbank—His Experiences in Painting Indian Life." *Fine Arts Journal* 24, no. 1 (January 1911): 34–47.

Plummer, E. H. Letter to the Commissioner of Indian Affairs in Washington, dated December 20, 1893, Fort Defiance AZ. National Archives and Records Administration Laguna Niguel, Records of the Bureau of Indian Affairs 75, Navajo Agency Fort Defiance, Vol. 20, box 7, 201–203.

Powers, Willow Roberts. *Navajo Trading: The End of an Era*. Albuquerque: University of New Mexico Press, 2001.

Prucha, Paul. "Thomas Jefferson Morgan 1889–93." In *The Commissioners of Indian Affairs, 1824–1977*, edited by Robert M. Kvasnicka and Herman J. Viola, 193–203. Lincoln: University of Nebraska Press, 1979.

Record, Sanford P. "Report of Training-School at Grand Junction, Colo., September 5, 1890." *Annual Report of the Commissioner of Indian Affairs*. Washington DC: Office of Indian Affairs, 1890.

Reichard, Gladys A. *Navajo Religion: A Study of Symbolism*. Bollingen Series 18. Princeton NJ: Princeton University Press, 1950.

———. *Social Life of the Navajo Indians with Some Attention to Minor Ceremonies*. New York: Columbia University Press, 1928.

———. *Spider Woman: A Story of Navajo Weavers and Chanters*. Albuquerque: University of New Mexico Press, 1997. First published 1934 by Macmillan (New York).

———. *Weaving a Navajo Blanket*. New York: Dover, 1974. First published 1936 under the title *Navajo Shepherd and Weaver* by J. J. Augustin (New York).

Reyhner, Jon. "American Indian Boarding Schools: What Went Wrong? What Is Going Right?" *Journal of American Indian Education* 57, no. 1 (Spring 2018): 58–78.

Reyhner, Jon, and Jeanne Eder. *American Indian Education: A History*. Norman: University of Oklahoma Press, 2004.

Riordan, D. M. "Report of the Navajo Agency, Fort Defiance, Ariz., August 14, 1883." *Annual Report of the Commissioner of Indian Affairs*. Washington DC: Office of Indian Affairs, 1883.

Rodee, Marian E. *One Hundred Years of Navajo Rugs*. Albuquerque: University of New Mexico Press, 1995.

Roosevelt, Theodore. *A Book-Lover's Holidays in the Open*. New York: Scribners, 1916.

———. *The Letters of Theodore Roosevelt*. Edited by Elting E. Morison. Cambridge MA: Harvard University Press, 1954.

Rosenak, Chuck, and Jan Rosenak. *Navajo Folk Art: The People Speak*. Flagstaff AZ: Northland, 1994.

Ruland-Thorne, Kate. *Historic Tales of Colorado's Grand Valley*. Charleston SC: History Press, 2016.

Saunders, Charles Francis. *The Indians of the Terraced Houses*. New York: Putnam's Sons, 1912.

Schwarz, Maureen Trudelle. "Unraveling the Anchoring Cord: Navajo Relocation, 1974–1996." *American Anthropologist* 99, no. 1 (March 1997): 43–55.

Secakuku, Alph H. *Following the Sun and Moon: Hopi Kachina Tradition*. Flagstaff AZ: Northland, 1995.

Shipley, David L. "Census, Navajo Indian Agency, June 30, 1890." Washington DC: Office of Indian Affairs, 1891.

———. "Report of Navajo Agency, August 25, 1892." *Annual Report of the Commissioner of Indian Affairs*. Washington DC: Office of Indian Affairs, 1892.

Simonelli, Jeanne M., and Charles D. Winters. *Crossing between Worlds: The Navajos of Canyon de Chelly*. Santa Fe: School of American Research Press, 1997.

Smith, Dama Margaret (Mrs. White Mountain). "Trader at Thunderbird." *Desert Magazine* 1, no. 5 (May 1938): 10–13.

Sotheby Parke Bernet. *The C.G. Wallace Collection of American Indian Art, November 14–16, 1975*. New York: Sotheby Parke Bernet, 1975.

Southwick, Sally J. "Papists, Presbyters, and Primers: A Comparative Study of Catholic and Presbyterian Mission Schools among the Navajo, 1898–1928." Master's thesis, University of Montana, Missoula, 1993.

Stevenson, James. "Ceremonial of Hasjelti Dailjis and Mythical Sand Painting of the Navajo Indians." *Eighth Annual Report of the Bureau of Ethnology, 1886–87*. Washington DC: Government Printing Office, 1891.

Sturt, George. *The Wheelwright's Shop*. Cambridge: Cambridge University Press, 1923.

Tanner, Clara Lee. *Southwest Indian Craft Arts*. Tucson: University of Arizona Press, 1968.

Teiwes, Helga. *Kachina Dolls: The Art of Hopi Carvers*. Tucson: University of Arizona Press, 1991.

Thornton, W. L. "Report of the Governor of New Mexico." *Annual Report of the Commissioner of the General Land Office, 1893*. Washington DC: House of Representatives, 1893.

Tools Machinery Blacksmiths Supplies. Chicago: Sears, Roebuck & Co., 1915. Reprinted 1984 by the Mid-West Tool Collectors Association.

Travelers' Official Guide of the Railway and Steam Navigation Lines in the United States and Canada. New York: National Railway, June 1893.

Troester, Marcellus, OFM. *Navajo Census Cards.* St. Michaels AZ: Franciscan Friars Archives, n.d.

Tso, Kimberly C. "Relearning My Cultural Identity: On My Past Descendants, My Great Paternal Grandfather Clitso Dedman." Paper presented at the 13th Annual Navajo Studies Conference, Northern Arizona University, Flagstaff, Arizona, October 16–20, 2001.

Valette, Jean-Paul, and Rebecca M. Valette. "In Search of Yah-nah-pah: The Early Gallegos 'Yei' Blankets and Their Weavers." *American Indian Art Magazine* 23, no. 1 (Winter 1997): 58–69.

Valette, Rebecca M. "Early Navajo Sandpainting Blankets: A Reassessment." *American Indian Art Magazine* 37, no. 2 (Spring 2012): 54–82.

——. "Yeibichai Weavings Featuring Women Dancers." *Native American Art* 26 (April–May 2020): 50–57.

Valette, Rebecca M., and Jean-Paul Valette. "The Life and Work of Clitso Dedman, Navajo Woodcarver (1879?–1953)." *American Indian Art Magazine* 25, no. 2 (Spring 2000): 54–67.

——. *Navajo Weavings with Ceremonial Themes: A Historical Overview of a Secular Art Form.* Atglen PA: Schiffer, 2017.

——. *Weaving the Dance: Navajo Yeibichai Textiles (1910–1950).* Albuquerque: Adobe Gallery, and Seattle: University of Washington Press, 2000.

Vandever, C. E. "Report of the Navajo Agency, August 9, 1889." *Annual Report of the Commissioner of Indian Affairs.* Washington DC: Office of Indian Affairs, 1889.

——. "Report of the Navajo Agency, August 22, 1890." *Annual Report of the Commissioner of Indian Affairs.* Washington DC: Office of Indian Affairs, 1890.

Vecsey, Christopher. "Navajo Morals and Myths, Ethics and Ethicists." *Journal of Religious Ethics* 43, no. 1 (March 2015): 78–121.

Wagner, Sallie. *Wide Ruins: Memories from a Navajo Trading Post.* Albuquerque: University of New Mexico Press, 1997.

Walsh, Barry. *The Great Tradition of Hopi Katsina Carvers: 1880 to Present.* Tucson AZ: Rio Nuevo, 2019.

Warner, Michael J. "Protestant Missionary Activity among the Navajo, 1890–1912." *New Mexico Historical Review* 45 (1970): 209–32.

Washburn, Dorothy E., ed. *The Elkus Collection.* San Francisco: California Academy of Sciences, 1984.

Waters, Frank. *Masked Gods: Navaho and Pueblo Ceremonialism.* Athens OH: Swallow Press, 1950.

Watson, Aldren A. *The Blacksmith: Ironworker and Farrier.* New York: W. W. Norton, 2000.

Wayne, Flynn. "Distinctive American Art." *The National Magazine* 39 (October 1913–March 1914): 81–82.

Weber, Anselm, OFM. "Congressional Committee Visit." *Franciscan Missions of the Southwest: An Annual* 18 (1920): 40.

Wetherill, Louisa Wade. *Wolfkiller: Wisdom from a Nineteenth-Century Shepherd.* Salt Lake City: Gibbs Smith, 2007.

Wheeler, George. "Report of School at Grand Junction, Colo., September 21, 1889." *Annual Report of the Commissioner of Indian Affairs.* Washington DC: Office of Indian Affairs, 1889.

Wilken, Robert L. *Anselm Weber, O.F.M., Missionary to the Navajo 1898–1921.* Milwaukee WI: Bruce Publishing, 1955.

Wilkins, Teresa J. *Patterns of Exchange: Navajo Weavers and Traders.* Norman: University of Oklahoma Press, 2008.

Williams, Lester L. *C. N. Cotton and His Navajo Blankets.* Gallup NM: Avanyu, 1989.

Witherspoon, Gary. "Navajo Social Organization." In *Handbook of North American Indians, Vol. 10: Southwest,* edited by Alfonso Ortiz. Washington DC: Smithsonian Institution, 1983).

Wolfe, M. Melissa. *American Indian Portraits: Elbridge Ayer Burbank in the West (1897–1910).* Youngstown OH: Butler Institute of American Art, 2000.

Wright, Barton. *Hopi Kachinas: The Complete Guide to Collecting Kachina Dolls.* Flagstaff AZ: Northland, 1977.

Wyatt, Charles D. "A New Navajo Art." *Arizona Highways* 20, no. 4 (April 1944): 34–35.

Wyman, Leland C. *Southwest Indian Drypainting.* Santa Fe NM: School of American Research, 1983.

Young, Robert. *The Navajo Yearbook 1951–1960: A Decade of Progress.* Window Rock AZ: Navajo Agency, 1961.

Young, Robert, and William Morgan. *The Navajo Language: A Grammar and Colloquial Dictionary.* Albuquerque: University of New Mexico Press, 1980.

Youngdahl, Jay. *Working on the Railroad Walking in Beauty: Navajos, Hózhó, and Track Work.* Logan: Utah State University Press, 2011.

Yurth, Cindy. "Tsélani/Cottonwood Went After What It Needed and Still Does." *Navajo Times,* August 21, 2014.

Zahn, Curtis. "The Automobile Is Here to Stay." *Arizona Highways* 22, no. 6 (June 1946): 14–15.

INDEX

Page numbers in italics indicate illustrations